FALCO AND BEYOND

Studies in Popular Music

Series Editors: Alyn Shipton, lecturer in jazz history at the Royal Academy of Music, London, and at City University, London; and Christopher Partridge, Professor of Religious Studies, Lancaster University

From jazz to reggae, bhangra to heavy metal, electronica to qawwali, and from production to consumption, *Studies in Popular Music* is a multi-disciplinary series which aims to contribute to a comprehensive understanding of popular music. It will provide analyses of theoretical perspectives, a broad range of case studies, and discussion of key issues.

Published

Open Up the Doors: Music in the Modern Church
Mark Evans

Technomad: Global Raving Countercultures
Graham St John

Dub in Babylon: Understanding the Evolution and Significance of Dub Reggae in Jamaica and Britain from King Tubby to Post-Punk
Christopher Partridge

Send in the Clones: A Cultural Study of Tribute Bands
Georgina Gregory

The Lost Women of Rock Music: Female Musicians of the Punk Era
(second edition)
Helen Reddington

Global Tribe: Technology, Spirituality and Psytrance
Graham St John

Nick Cave: A Study of Love, Death and Apocalypse
Roland Boer

*Heavy Metal
Controversies and Countercultures*
Edited by Titus Hjelm, Keith Kahn-Harris and Mark LeVine

FALCO AND BEYOND

NEO NOTHING POST OF ALL

EWA MAZIERSKA

equinox

SHEFFIELD UK   BRISTOL CT

Published by Equinox Publishing Ltd.

UK: Kelham House, 3 Lancaster Street, Sheffield, S3 8AF
USA: ISD, 70 Enterprise Drive, Bristol, CT 06010

www.equinoxpub.com

First published 2013

British Library Cataloguing-in-Publication Data
A catalogue record for this book is available from the British Library.

Library of Congress Cataloging-in-Publication Data
Mazierska, Ewa.
 Falco and beyond : neo nothing post of all / Ewa Mazierska.
   pages cm. -- (Studies in popular music)
 Includes bibliographical references, discography, and index.
 Summary: "Falco and Beyond is devoted to the most popular Austrian song-writer, singer
and rapper of the twentieth century and one of the most successful European singers of
all time. Falco was born in 1957, reached the peak of his popularity in the 1980s with
songs such as Der Kommissar, Rock Me Amadeus and Jeanny, with mixed luck attempted
to revive his career in the 1990s and died in a car crash in 1998. He sold over 30 million
records worldwide and remains a successful posthumous artist. The book attempts to
identify the most salient and contradictory features of Falco's art, such as linguistic inven-
tiveness and dexterity, rapping and adopting a posture of a romantic artist. It argues that
Falco's songs betray an apocalyptic imagination, picturing the image of an exhausted and
unhappy world. It looks at Falco's career and his phenomenon in the context of international and Austrian music business and politics, and investigates how his popularity has
been maintained after his death, by means such as records released posthumously, cover
versions of his songs, mashup songs and videos, biographies and Falco fandom."
 ISBN 978-1-84553-238-3 (hb) -- ISBN 978-1-84553-235-2 (pb)
 1. Falco. 2. Rock musicians--Austria--Biography. 3. Neoliberalism--Austria. I. Title.
 ML420.F225M39 2014
 782.42166092--dc23
 [B]
                                    2013008585

ISBN: 978 1 84553 238 3 (hardback)
ISBN: 978 1 84553 235 2 (paperback)

Typeset by CA Typesetting Ltd, www.publisherservices.co.uk
Printed and bound in the UK by Lightning Source UK Ltd., Milton Keynes and
Lightning Source Inc., La Vergne, TN

Let's deca-dance in jedem Fall

P.S.Y.C.H.O.S. – they gotta say yes to another excess

Just follow the light there's no time to share
We're cuttin' through the night
City on fire, angel with the flute
Cuttin' through the night

Cyberspace has got to be anarchy

Tricks
That's the only reason my heart still ticks

They all knew I'm a gambler, corresponding with death
They know life is white light, slightly out of focus

Moderne Menschen leben allein
Das neue Leben fängt sie ein
Liebe macht Herztod, Sprechverbot

(Falco)

Contents

List of Illustrations

Acknowledgements

This book would not be possible without the help of many people, to whom I wish to express my gratitude. First, I am grateful to Falco collaborators, Thomas Rabitsch, Peter Paul Skrepek, Raoul Herget and Hannes Rossacher, for granting me time to inform myself about Falco and Austrian music from their first-hand experience. My work colleagues, Georgina Gregory and Lars Kristensen, convinced me that I was able to write a book on Falco despite my lack of relevant experience. Peter Paul Skrepek, Raul Herget, Rainer Hosch, Georgina Gregory, Lars Kristensen, Żaneta Jamrozik, Paweł Miech and Elżbieta Ostrowska read the whole or parts of this manuscript and provided valuable comments. Falco fans and detractors helped me to understand why I like him so much despite his numerous imperfections. Kevin Dooley kept me company on my first Falco pilgrimage and showed me places linked to Falco which otherwise I would not have found in Vienna. Members of my family, Gifford, Kamila and Magda, proved supportive of my work and assisted me with solving numerous linguistic problems. I am also grateful to all institutions and individuals who allowed me to use the stills in the book, most importantly the Falco Foundation, as well as Peter Paul Skrepek, Helmut Riedl, Rainer Hosch and Niki Witoszynskyj. I am grateful to Christopher Partridge for his interest in this project.

I am especially indebted to Michael Rager for sharing with me his insights on Falco, many of which are reflected in the final version of this study, providing me with much of the secondary material and correcting my mistakes. Michael also compiled the Falco discography, used in the book.

I dedicate this book to my son, Daniel, whose love of *The Simpsons* and, subsequently, his enchantment with Falco proved a decisive factor in writing this book.

Introduction

This book is devoted to Falco, the Austrian song-writer, singer and rapper of international fame. Falco was born in 1957, reached the peak of his popularity in the 1980s with songs such as 'Der Kommissar', 'Rock Me Amadeus' and 'Jeanny', with mixed fortunes attempted to revive his career in the 1990s, and died in a car crash in 1998, becoming a cult figure, at least in the German-speaking world.

I embarked on this project in multiple guises, including as a cultural historian, who until this point specialized in film history, a person interested in rap, and a Falco fan. In this sense I bear some similarity to my protagonist, whose multiplicity is reflected in his many names: Falco, as he was known in his professional life and Johann, Hans or Hansi Hölzel privately. In common with Falco, who refused to separate his roles and even regarded questions about how much there was of Falco and Hans Hölzel in his real self as pointless, I see no problem in approaching Falco professionally and emotionally. After all, love does need to be blind and work should be an extension of love, not toil.[1]

I was exposed to Falco's music twice in different periods of my life, and in different countries. The first time was in 1980s Poland, at the peak of his career, when it was difficult to avoid his hits, which attacked one from every corner. Back then I found his music irritating due to its enveloping presence and some of its qualities which I identified as pertaining to low art. The second was in January 2012, in circumstances which will be presented in the last part of this study. This time, however, I became "Falconised". My growing enchantment with Falco led me to search for more information about his work and its cultural context, ideally in English. When I realized that such a study does not exist, and even that the numerous books on Falco in German, with one exception, focus on his private life rather than other facets of "Falco", I decided to write such a book myself. The moment to embark on such a study seemed right, as the time distance allowed me to see many aspects of Falco's work in a new way. His mixing of German with English and other languages, which in the 1980s might have looked like a sign of him not being able to master any language, today renders him as the most transnational *auteur* of songs of all time – the Jean-Luc Godard of pop music. Falco also turned out to be the perfect material to investigate what is of special interest to me as a scholar and privately – a political and cultural system, known as neoliberalism. I would like to understand neoliberal politics, neoliberal work, neoliberal war, etc. Falco is a perfect lens to research neoliberal popular art, because his career began when this system was coming into existence. He showed an awareness of this shift and attempted to adjust to it, tailor his image to the new times, in a way which set him apart from his peers in Austria. I also see his art as a means of making sense of this system, its "heroic" period or "imperial" phase, coinciding with the 1980s, and its crisis stage, which began in the 1990s.

But to say that Falco is a neoliberal pop singer neither does justice to his oeuvre nor exhausts my interest in him. I find Falco also fascinating because of his position in relation to different types of music and strands of culture. He can be seen as belonging to the low end of pop music and postmodern high art. Paradoxically, because of the extremity with which he embraced certain strategies of postmodern art, such as stylistic and linguistic hybridity, and repetition, largely for commercial reasons, he is viewed as reaching the low end of pop music, becoming the godfather of Eurotrash. Or conversely, his commercial bias renders him original. In this study I will follow in the footsteps of those who argue that Falco deserves a place on the pantheon of high art, most importantly the authors of the essays, included in the collection devoted to Falco's poetry, *Falco's Many Languages* (Hintze 2010), but at the same time I insist that this high-art aspect of his work cannot be divorced from its overtly commercial character. Falco thus can be compared to Andy Warhol, whose artistic originality stemmed from being openly, even cynically, commercial in his style and attitude.

I see Falco as a unique artist and man, and as a text, existing in relation with other texts (artworks, personalities and ideologies). My work is meant to be a love letter and a study in intertextuality, where – to use the terminology of Gérard Genette (Stam 2000: 65–66) – a specific aspect of Falco's life and art is considered a "hypertext" which transforms, modifies, elaborates or extends an anterior text, the "hypotext", and is itself a hypotext affecting subsequent texts – "hypertexts". I intend to unravel some elements of this intertextual web, although with awareness that such unravelling is always contingent. I shall also add that in this study "Falco" will function most of the time as a shorthand to describe the input of many people, such as music and video producers, fellow performers, photographers, managers, journalists, as well as fans, in creating this complex text. On other occasions, however, I will try to pinpoint the effect of some of these people in creating "Falco-text" and to highlight the match or conflict between Falco and his collaborators.

To account for Falco's connection with neoliberalism and his links with other texts, I will look at him synchronically and diachronically. This will allow me to analyse constant motifs in his work and life and account for their transformations. "Falco Synchronic" will fill Part II of this monograph. I will discuss there Falco's self-representation as a Romantic artist, his specific uses of words and music and recurrent themes of his songs. In this part I will argue that Falco was a rapper, both in a narrow sense, because his style of performance was rap, and in a wider sense, due to ostentatiously rejecting the modernist ideals of originality, purity and unity, and offering us work which was by design intertextual, fragmented and heterogeneous. In Part III, entitled "Falco Diachronic", I will look at his career chronologically, paying particular attention to the changes in his records, videos and his live performances. This part will "shadow" Falco's biography, written by his manager, Horst Bork (2009), but I will offer there different readings of many facts Bork recalls. I will also draw on other biographies of Falco, written by Rudi Dolezal and Hannes Rossacher (1998), Peter Lanz (2007) and Beatrice Castaldi (2012) and my interviews with Falco collaborators: Thomas Rabitsch, Raoul Herget, Peter Paul Skrepek and Hannes Rossacher. One function of this part is to provide a short biography of Falco for those interested in his life with no access to biographies written in German. Part IV will be devoted to Falco's afterlife, as reflected in his records, released posthumously, monuments, biographies, biopics, cover versions of his songs, mashup videos, as well as the role of his collaborators, family and fans in preserving and expanding his heritage. I will also reflect there on how this afterlife is affected by development of digital technologies and discuss my own fandom.

My book will also contain Part I, which will be theoretical. I will present there my principal framework – the idea of the culture industry, as elaborated by Theodor Adorno and its application to the neoliberal condition, as conceptualized by David Harvey, the relationship between neoliberalism and postmodern art, and the basis of my aesthetic judgements. I decided to include such a theoretical part, despite remembering what the film critic, Pauline Kael, said about the famous film theoretician, Siegfried Kracauer: "Siegfried Kracauer is the sort of man who can't say 'It's a lovely day' without first establishing that it is day, that the term 'day' is meaningless without the dialectical concept of 'night', that both these terms have no meaning unless there is a world in which day and night alternate, and so forth. By the time he has established an epistemological system to support his right to observe that it's a lovely day, our day has been spoiled" (Kael 1965: 269). To paraphrase Kael, my hope is that the readers, who manage to get through Part I, will not feel that I have completely spoilt Falco for them before I even started. But for those who do not want to take this risk, I advise beginning with Part II, and only return to Part I if they find my statements unclear or their basis shaky.

I shall emphasize that I have no ambition to discover here the "real Falco" and not only because I never met him in person and never lived in his country, but also because the "real Falco" is unattainable – we can only create discourses on him. In my investigation I will avoid a "disembodied voice of authority" (Cook 1995–96: 29), believing that behind every "disembodied voice of authority" there is an embodied voice, betraying a specific class, level of education, gender, race, taste and personal history. One of the tasks of this study is to examine such voices, which with authority elevated or, more often, denigrated Falco, and reflect on how my own voice reflects my position and how it changed as a result of my intellectual and real travels. My writing thus by design comes close to what the feminist theatre theorist Peggy Phelan describes as "performative writing" (Phelan 1993). That said, I hope that due to being a "non-authoritative" study, it will encourage other readers to return to Falco in his numerous incarnations, "mash him up" and from doing so draw as much joy as I had writing this book.

Part I

Falco and the Logic of the Neoliberal Culture Industry

1 The concept of the culture industry

The concept of the "culture industry" is the brainchild of Theodor Adorno and Max Horkheimer, the leading representatives of the Frankfurt School. In a rudimentary form it appeared in Adorno's essay from 1938, "On the Fetish-Character in Music and the Regression of Listening" (1978), was presented in a developed form in Adorno and Max Horkheimer's *Dialectic of Enlighten-ment*, written by them during the Second World War (2002), which includes an essay "The Culture Industry: Enlightenment as Mass Deception" and revis-ited in Adorno's article "Culture Industry Reconsidered", published in 1963 (1975). I will treat the latter as my departure point, mainly because it was published at a time which lends itself to comparison with the 1980s, when Falco began his solo career. In this essay Adorno presents himself as an ardent opponent of the "culture industry", a model of popular culture whose sole purpose is generating profit, which, as he believes, dominated in his time. In creating this concept Adorno borrowed from Marx, who argued that the capitalist market transformed art into a commodity to an extent it had never been before.

Adorno's criticism has two components: aesthetic and moral, and by the same token, political. He argues that the products of the culture industry, such as Hollywood genre films and popular music, are mass-produced and stand-ardized, therefore of low artistic value, although they try to conceal their char-acter by inserting various pseudo-innovations. By expecting artists to comply with rules which are meant to increase the profit of the industry, the culture industry denies them the chance to fulfil their artistic potential, as only art free from commercial pressures is worthy of its name. The culture industry also denies autonomy to its consumers because, as he puts it, it

> intentionally integrates its consumers from above... Although the culture industry undeniably speculates on the conscious and uncon-scious state of the millions towards which it is directed, the masses are not primary, but secondary, they are an object of calculation; an appendage of the machinery. The customer is not king, as the cul-ture industry would like to have us believe, not its subject but its object (Adorno 1975: 12).

Adorno further argues that the culture industry locks the artists and the spectators into a reality which is ultimately bad for them in a political sense, due to denying them emancipation from the shackles of capitalism: "The advice to be gained from manifestations of the culture industry is vacuous, banal or worse, and the behaviour patterns are shamelessly conformist" (1975: 16).

Adorno's fierce attack on the culture industry betrays his enormous faith in the emancipatory potential of art, presented in the fullest (albeit unfinished) form in his *Aesthetic Theory*, published in 1970, where he elaborates the idea of an autonomous art, not reducible to the requirements of the capitalist system. Autonomous art, in his view, had preserved the utopia that evaporated from religion; artists could thus provide an alternative to existing (capitalist) society, till it reaches the communist stage. However, Adorno did not advocate art that would fiercely and openly criticize capitalist conditions, far from it – such art, encapsulated by Bertolt Brecht's works, was for him not very different to that produced by the culture industry. Autonomous art should attack society and culture subtly, perhaps even unconsciously, by employing language which challenges the dominant code(s). One example he gives is that of Kafka:

> Nowhere in his work did he address monopoly capitalism directly. Yet by zeroing in on the dregs of the administered world, he laid bare the inhumanity of a repressive social totality, and he did so more powerfully and uncompromisingly than if he had written novels about corruption in multinational corporations. That form is the key to understanding social content can be shown concretely in Kafka's language, the Kleistian matter-of-factness of which has often be noticed. Sensitive readers will invariably recognize the contrast that exists in Kafka between stylistic sobriety and highly imaginary happenings (Adorno 2004: 301).

Adorno was not the only author thinking along these lines. A similar approach, although based on researching plastic arts, is offered by Clement Greenberg, who in his famous essay "Avant-Garde and Kitsch", published for the first time in 1939, edified avant-garde as the highest form of art and denounced popular art as kitsch. Kitsch for Greenberg is a product of the industrial revolution which urbanized the masses of Western Europe and America and established what is called universal literacy:

> The peasants who settled in the cities as proletariat and petty bourgeois learned to read and write for the sake of efficiency, but they did not win the leisure and comfort necessary for the enjoyment of the city's traditional culture. Losing, nevertheless, their taste for the

folk culture whose background was the countryside, and discovering a new capacity for boredom at the same time, the new urban masses set up a pressure on society to provide them with a kind of culture fit for their own consumption. To fill the demand of the new market, a new commodity was devised: ersatz culture, kitsch, destined for those who, insensible to the values of genuine culture, are hungry nevertheless for the diversion that only culture of some sort can provide.

Kitsch, using for raw material the debased and academicized simulacra of genuine culture, welcomes and cultivates this insensibility. It is the source of its profits. Kitsch is mechanical and operates by formulas. Kitsch is vicarious experience and faked sensations. Kitsch changes according to style, but remains always the same. Kitsch is the epitome of all that is spurious in the life of our times. Kitsch pretends to demand nothing of its customers except their money -- not even their time (Greenberg 1973: 10).

Although the similarity between Greenberg and Adorno's arguments is striking, I will use the latter as my main point of reference because, unlike Greenberg, who is only interested in the textual characteristics of what he described as the avant-garde and kitsch, Adorno evokes an idea of the culture industry as a system of production, the dissemination and consumption of "kitsch". However, he fails to explain how these aspects are interconnected and what does it mean in practice to be integrated into the culture industry. Is the very fact of working for a large film studio, or making records for a large record company, sufficient to be regarded in this way? If Kafka signed a deal for an equivalent of a million dollars, would he lose his special place in Adorno's hierarchy of art?[2] While Greenberg and Adorno condemned popular and mechanical art as kitsch, other authors, such as the Futurists, Constructivists and, according to some interpretations, Walter Benjamin (1992), heralded the triumphs of democratic, mechanical art (encapsulated in their times by cinema) and wanted to have done with all traces of "high culture".

Adorno's theory can be criticized for aesthetic and political reasons. On the aesthetic side is his elitism and essentialism. The author assigns himself a position of one who knows what constitutes high quality, autonomous art and is immune to cultural fashions. However, it can easily be demonstrated that Adorno's aesthetic views were culturally constructed, for example, reflecting an influence of the work of Viennese composer Alban Berg, whom he met in the 1920s. Had he lived in different places and times, he would have had different taste and aesthetic standards. Secondly, Adorno puts all products of the culture industry, including "the perennial fashion – jazz" (nowadays epitomising elitist rather than low culture), into one bag: "kitsch". In this way he disagrees with the majority of its consumers (hence practically everybody, as it is difficult to find people not using them), who divide the products of popular culture according to their quality. A reflection of this approach is the placement of some genres of popular art higher than others, such as rock over pop. Nicholas Cook notes that the common perception is that:

> Rock musicians perform live, create their own music, and forge their own identities; in short, they control their own destinies. Pop musicians, by contrast, are the puppets of the music business, cynically or naively pandering to popular tastes, and performing music composed and arranged by others; they lack authenticity, and as such they come at the bottom of the hierarchy of musicianship (Cook 1998a: 11).

However, Cook himself, as well as other authors, criticize such a simple division, pointing to the fact that the standards of quality and authenticity in pop and rock constantly change and depend not only on the music itself but also on factors such as the listener's knowledge about the history of a specific artist or expectations of his work (Frith 1981: 11; Frith 2001; Keightley 2001; Auslander 2008: 88). There are special cases on both the pop and rock sides of popular music, such as pop stars who write their own music and rock stars who do not. Equally, it is not easy to differentiate between those who cynically pander to popular taste and those who create new tastes, which happen to have a wide appeal.[3] Falco's case, I will argue, illuminates the problems of differentiating between pop and rock and non-pop popular music in a wide sense, partly because he oscillated between pop and non-pop and because as a pop artist he offered new, postmodern standards of authenticity.

In his bland rejection of all art produced for profit Adorno parted ways with Marx, who was a great admirer of such art, as documented in this famous passage in *The Communist Manifesto*: "The bourgeoisie...has accomplished wonders far surpassing Egyptian pyramids, Roman aqueducts, and Gothic cathedrals" (Marx and Engels 2008: 37). In Marx's view the achievements of capitalist art are of this high value precisely because a capitalist condition enforces such a high standard. I shall add that in socialist Poland, where I used to live, this view was widely shared. The condition of capitalist bondage was regarded as a sufficient guarantee of quality. Conversely, Polish and socialist art at large, and especially popular art (as well as everyday commodities), was regarded as sub-standard precisely because it was not produced under the capitalist whip.

I disagree with the aesthetic part of Adorno's theory, as I am not an essentialist but a relativist. My own theory is a fusion of the views of two authors:

Nelson Goodman and Michel Foucault. In common with Goodman, aesthetics for me is a branch of epistemology. I see no sharp division between art and other forms of human knowledge. The aim of art is to understand (and help others to understand), where understanding is a broader concept than knowledge, one that is not bound by literal truth. Artistic symbols, as symbols in general, are to be judged for the classifications they bring about, for how novel and insightful those categorizations are, for how they change our perception of the world and ourselves (Goodman 1968: 258–65). "A work may be successively offensive, fascinating, comfortable, and boring. There are the vicissitudes of the vehicles and instruments of knowledge" (1968: 259). Therefore the question "What is art?" should be replaced with the question "When is art?" This also means that certain objects are discarded as art, when they travel in time and space. Similarly, some objects become art when they are placed in the context of art – Marcel Duchamp demonstrated this in a simple and persuasive way. Like Goodman, I also believe that "excessive concentration on the question of excellence has been responsible for constriction and distortion of aesthetic inquiry" (1968: 261). Thus, instead of judging Falco's excellence or lack thereof, I will try to share my understanding of his work.

From Foucault I borrow the idea that knowledge (and art as being a form of it) is a function of power, which is manifested by the type of discourse in which a specific artefact is located. In a most basic sense, it is manifested by the places where art is displayed. We tend to believe that if a specific piece of music is performed by a symphonic orchestra, it is more artistic than the same piece played on the computer or in a strip club, and a series of music videos packaged as a luxurious DVD is more precious than when it is scattered on the internet. Similarly, song lyrics become more high art by virtue of being published in the form of a book. I am not choosing these examples at random, but drawing on Falco's career, to illustrate that he is more arty in 2012 than he was in 1998 and in expectation that my own research will add to his elevated status.[4] At the same time, knowledge and art can be powerful too: they can affect what we think and do, our identities and life choices. It should be added that such a fusion of Goodman and Foucault is increasingly used in pop and rock theory and criticism, even if the authors of specific concepts do not evoke their names (see, for example, Frith 1987).

Let's turn now to the second aspect of Adorno's argument: popular culture, due to being made for profit, is integrated into the capitalist system and therefore cannot liberate those slaving in factories, or to update this image, in call centres. There is no point in denying that profit is a crucial goal of film studios and record companies, as it is, increasingly, of the British academia. But does it ultimately make filmmakers and musicians (and academics) working for such institutions lacking in autonomy, thwarted, enslaved to it? Richard Shusterman, a leading proponent of pragmatist aesthetics, asks: "Do we need to be fully outside something in order to criticize it effectively?" (Shusterman 1992: 214). Shusterman implies that even if being entirely outside the capitalist system, entirely autonomous, would be possible, it might not be conducive to launching its effective critique. Only those familiar with its logic and tainted by its power understand it well enough to be able to challenge its "ungodly reality". This might happen in different ways: conveying subversive messages in proposed texts, creating alternative institutions, producing and distributing art and embracing life strategies which undermine the capitalist system. Audiences play a part in this process as they have the power of interpreting the messages sent by the artists. In practice, the majority of authors researching popular music and popular culture at large claim that it is neither fully integrated nor autonomous; neither it affirms entirely the system nor subverts it. But in my opinion this is not a reason to reject Adorno's categories, only to use them with care. As some authors notice, the ideal situation for a pop star is to project an image of somebody who resists capitalism, yet get financial benefits from working for it. The culture industry does not mind such a schizophrenic or hypocritical attitude to capitalism. As Simon Frith observes in his by now classical study, *Sound Effects: Youth, Leisure, and the Politics of Rock'n'Roll*, "If pornography, drugs, weapons, or revolution will sell, then they will be sold" (Frith 1981: 253–54).

The 1960s, when Adorno wrote his essay, and the 1970s, brought into sharp relief some of the problems highlighted above. During this period there was an upsurge of popular art, as part of a counter-cultural movement, which challenged Adorno's view that popular art under capitalism was both politically conformist and of low standard. Examples of such art, in part inspired by the literature and culture of the Beat Generation of the 1950s, were the songs of Bob Dylan, Janis Joplin or Jimi Hendrix; in cinema it became epitomised by the films of Jean-Luc Godard, Rainer Werner Fassbinder and Alexander Kluge. This movement, culminating in the events of the late 1960s, such as May 1968 in France, attracted great attention from left-wing sociologists and philosophers, who saw in it an antidote to the passivity of the proletariat, which, as Herbert Marcuse pronounced in *One-Dimensional Man* (1964), became integrated into the capitalist project and lost its revolutionary potential. There was hope that young people, enthused by their cultural leaders, would change the world that the working class failed to transform.

However, this very movement testified to the difficulties in differentiating between autonomous and integrated art. This is because while there is little controversy in stating that they were (and some still are) great artists in their period, their relationship to the capitalist order is ambiguous. Some openly admitted that they frequently bowed to the pressures of capitalism. Godard, for example, confessed that he included more nudity in *Le Mépris* (1963) than he initially intended because the producers demanded it of him. Fassbinder wrote different endings to his *Mutter Küsters fahrt zum Himmel* (*Mother Küsters Goes to Heaven*, 1975) to cater for different tastes of American and German audiences, hence to increase his profit. These artists admitted that one can fight with capitalism only on capitalism's own terms; rejecting them entirely would mean sentencing themselves to muteness. Equally, few rockers turned down the opportunity to work for such capitalist institutions as large record companies or television. But there were also moments when not only the message was anti-capitalist, but profit did not rule. For example, Artie Kornfeld, one of the creators of the famous Woodstock Festival of 1969, attended by an estimated half a million people, in the film by Michael Wadleigh dedicated to this event, confessed with pride that financially the festival was a disaster because the audience got in for free. But most likely he would have been happier had they paid. A similar situation happened at the 1970 Isle of Wight Festival. As John Street claims, this event, starring the Doors, Jimi Hendrix, the Who and Joni Mitchell,

> was a microcosm of pop's politics. The stars played along with radical rhetoric, but haggled over their fees backstage. Activists from France to Britain pulled down fences, while the organisers pleaded with them to stop and for the fans to pay, all in the name of a utopian communal goal. The entrepreneurs, like the musicians, were caught between political idealism and commercial reality, between belief and the bottom line (Street 2001: 244).

Drawing a boundary between autonomous and integrated art is further complicated by the fact that the 1960s showed that pro-capitalist, conformist art can be used by its consumers for non-conformist purposes. The best known example of such strategy was a détournement: a technique developed by the Situationists, which consisted of turning expressions of the capitalist system against itself by, for example, adding new subtitles to genre, commercial films which subverted their original message. But the success of the Situationists also showed the possibility of the opposite route – using intentionally anti-capitalist art in the service of capitalism. A well-known example is the last song recorded by Janis Joplin, 'Mercedes Benz' (1970). The song ridiculed people who equate happiness with cars, colour television and partying, but was later used in Mercedes adverts to convey the idea that a Mercedes will make its owner happy, as in the scheme described by Frith.[5] It is also a widely known fact that modern television advertising owes its techniques more to Jean-Luc Godard, who is the greatest living symbol of autonomous, anti-capitalist cinema than any overtly, pro-capitalist, integrated director, such as Steven Spielberg. Equally, as I will argue in due course, many music videos that Rudi Dolezal and Hannes Rossacher made for Falco can be viewed as pocket-size precursors of Godard's *Histoire(s) du cinéma* (1988–98). Ultimately, these examples show that assessing art's autonomy and integration is a complex procedure, involving researching texts, institutions and audiences and is always ideology-driven.

2 The culture industry under neoliberal regime

Despite my reservations, I regard Adorno's thesis about the growing commodification and integration of art into capitalist structures, and artists' growing compliance with the capitalist ideology, as an important hypothesis to account for the specificity of the period described as "late capitalism" or "neoliberalism" (the second term being favoured by me), which coincides with Falco's career. This period began in the West in the late 1970s/early 1980s, following a period termed "embedded liberalism" or "Keynesianism", during which Adorno wrote his "Culture Industry Reconsidered". If Adorno's diagnosis is sound, even if crude, then it should be more visible in the 1980s and the subsequent decades than it was in the 1960s. This is because there is more capitalism (as described by Marx) in neoliberalism than there was in embedded liberalism. As David Harvey observes, a neoliberal regime is marked by privatization and commodification of public assets and, hence, total financialization, in which any kind of good can be turned into an instrument of economic speculation (Harvey 2005: 160–62). This contrasts with Keynesianism, which excluded certain spheres of human activity from the regime of profit generation or at least subjugated them to this regime to a lesser extent than nowadays. Education, health, as well as a large chunk of culture, were allowed to realize different values than what Marx terms "surplus value".

In spite of many failures, most importantly a failure to create a just and prosperous world for everybody, neoliberal order comes across as less contentious than embedded liberalism. It seems as if under this system things simply happen, as if of their own internal logic: some people get rich, others get impoverished or killed. The only value clearly advocated by neoliberalism is economic freedom, presented as a basis of all other freedoms and, indeed, of all other values, and of course, it is difficult to be against freedom. This ideological success of neoliberalism to present itself as non-ideological and silence critical voices was captured by Fredric Jameson (2003), who famously said that it is easier to imagine the end of the world than the end of capitalism. This is also a reason why neoliberalism does not enthuse anybody, even its most committed supporters. Apathy is the most common reaction to it. Not surprisingly, neoliberalism is a fertile ground for theories pronouncing the end of politics or an advent of a new, minimalistic, ideology-free politics. Slavoj Žižek conflated such ideas and, drawing on the concepts of Jacques Rancière and Giorgio Agamben, coins the term "post-political bio-politics" (Žižek 2009: 34).

The power of neoliberal ideology to spill into many other aspects of human activity does not go unopposed by some cultural historians and philosophers. They observe that what concurs with neoliberal ideology is presented as rational and just, and what opposes it as deranged and morally wrong. Jean-François Lyotard claimed that "The games of the scientific language become the games of the rich, in which whoever is the wealthiest has the best chance of being right. An equation between wealth, efficiency, and truth is thus established" (Lyotard 1984: 45). Terry Eagleton, commenting on this statement, added that

> It is not difficult, then, to see a relation between the philosophy of J. L. Austen and IBM, or between the various neo-Nietzscheanisms of a post-structuralist epoch and Standard Oil. It is not surprising that classical models of truth and cognition are increasingly out of favour in a society where what matters is whether you deliver the commercial or rhetorical goods. Whether among discourse theorists or the Institute of Directors, the goal is no longer truth but performativity, not reason but power (Eagleton 1992: 93).

Eagleton's argument, when applied to art, can be seen as a version of Marx's famous claim that under capitalism there is no difference between the most beautiful painting and a certain amount of manure.

The turn towards neoliberalism has had profound consequences for both high art and the culture industry/low art in Adorno's sense. They have been integrated into a regime of profit generation to a much larger extent than under Keynesian rules: in both cases material success became the main measure of artistic accomplishment. This led to many changes, in comparison with the previous periods, most importantly the closing of the stylistic gap between high and low art. Under neoliberalism the styles of high and low art blend or, to use Greenberg's terms, kitsch invades the avant-garde and vice versa to an extent unknown before. Serious novelists utilize pornography, serious painters make references to cartoons, vernacular forms penetrate metropolitan art salons and vice versa. The question of autonomy, central for Adorno, almost disappeared from the discussions about art, following the assumption that if there is freedom of trade, there must be also autonomy of art. In the material sense, the successful representatives of high art and the culture industry never had it so good. Since the 1980s, more authors of popular books, film directors, actors, singers, models, sportsmen, became multi-millionaires than

ever before and the new rich artists tend to be more wealthier than their predecessors. Their success is both reflected in and facilitates professionalization
of all types of art. A successful neoliberal writer is not somebody like Goethe
or Kafka, who has a day job and writes books in his spare time, but a full-time
professional. Consequently, unlike Kafka, s/he cannot stand aloof from the
operations of the market, because his/her livelihood depends on it. Many of
the successful representatives of art, media and sport under neoliberal conditions became successful entrepreneurs, investing their profit in new ventures.
Belonging to this strata chains them even more to a neoliberal regime than if
they were merely writers, musicians and painters.

It seems that Falco accepted that during his lifetime artistic quality equals
commercial performance. "I am good, because I sell" or "I failed because I lost
in the charts" is a conclusion of many of his interviews. At the same time,
one can detect in his behaviour an opposition to such logic by adopting the
posture of a Romantic artist (see Part II), his discomfort when in order to
make money he had to abandon his standards of good work (see Part III) and
later his disappointment with the fleeting character of his career and his life
as an ex-star. His conviction that the production of pop music should be more
than a money-making machine is also demonstrated by his near-worshipping
of some stars and attributing to certain songs the power to reveal a deeper
meaning about his own life.

The art and culture created under conditions of neoliberalism is typically
described as "postmodern". Authors such as David Harvey (1990) and Fredric
Jameson (1991) point to the connections between neoliberal economy and
art in the neoliberal age, for example accumulation of the capital and time-
space compression and the playing down of the importance of class divisions.
However, it will be a mistake to equate such culture with one which merely
replicates institutional circumstances and the ideology of neoliberalism. Hans
Bertens, for example, identifies two strands of postmodern art: postmodernism of resistance and postmodernism of reaction (Bertens 1995). The former
retains or even develops some of the radical moments of modernism (or what
Adorno would label as "autonomous art"), while the latter reacts against this
feature of modernism, embracing commercialization of art.

Postmodern art also reflects certain aspects of everyday life, which do not
need to be linked to the development of neoliberal capitalism, but rather due
to a left-wing critique of some aspects of modernism, such as the loss of historicity, hence its embracing such forms as pastiche, parody and irony in a
wider sense, and moving away from grand to mini-narratives, which leads
to bringing into visibility art which was previously marginalized, that created
by women, minorities and those who are lacking resources to create high

art, and therefore in the opinion of Greenberg, is sentenced to kitsch. Wayne Bowman, enchanted by postmodern ethos, claims that postmodern musical aesthetic reflects shifts

> from text to image, from linearity to simultaneity, from coherence to rupture, from argument to story, from the universal to the particular, from the "voice of authority" to populist heteroglossia. It embraces incongruous juxtapositions, fragmentation, and splicing – pastiche and collage – instead of organically unfolding unity... It is largely indifferent towards authenticity and stylistic integrity (Bowman 1998: 401–2).

Bowman seems to believe that postmodern art is liberating and in a sense it is, as it liberates the artists and art consumers from the rigidity of the standards of high modernism but not, as I believe, from the shackles of capitalism.

Bowman, in common with some other authors, such as the previously quoted Richard Shusterman (1992) and Russell A. Potter (1995), identifies rap as a postmodern music par excellence because it embraces technology, the popular, the recycled, juxtaposes incongruous styles, idioms and contexts and rejects the modernist concept of originality. Rap thus did to music (all music, not only its popular variety) what Robert Rauschenberg and pop art did to modernist art. Moreover, being originally music of the black urban ghetto, rap is precisely the type of art which was marginalized or even rendered as non-art under modernism. Russell A. Potter maintains that "Given the cultural and material realities of white colonialism and slavery, black sensibilities were 'postmodern' long before academics and intellectuals named that territory and began exploring it" (Potter, quoted in Bowman 1998: 402). This, however, does not mean that rap is immune to capitalist exploitation, even if it gives voice to the victims of capitalism. The fact that it expresses anger of the poor and dispossessed is even regarded as its main selling point (Krims 2002), confirming the point Firth made earlier and an important reason why performers of "non-hip-hop roots", such as Madonna or the Spice Girls, adopted rap idiom as a badge of their progressiveness.[6]

Operations of the culture industry frequently provide a subject for the culture industry. There are numerous songs and films devoted to the position of those at its top, the stars, and the closer we approach contemporary times, the more we find them; self-reflectiveness being an important feature of postmodern art. I would like to ponder on one such example, the film *Privilege* (1967) by Peter Watkins, because, like Adorno's theory, it provides a useful model with which to compare Falco's life and work. Watkins, like the previously mentioned Godard and Kluge, all his life worked on the margins of the culture industry, in search of work, switching between film and television and travelling to different countries. He is the director and screenwriter of one of the most original films about the artist of the type edified by Greenberg and Adorno, *Edvard Munch* (1974). In both *Privilege* and *Edvard Munch* the central issue is of the influence of cultural and economic circumstances on the artist's work and his/her life. In *Privilege* the director takes issue with the position of a music star in what can be described as "Adorno hell": a music industry totally integrated into the capitalist system. In reality total integration had never taken place and Watkins was aware of that, therefore he set his film in what, from a 1960s perspective, was the near apocalyptic future, namely the 1990s, no doubt regarding his film as a warning to the artists, audiences and producers of art.

The main character in *Privilege* is Steven Shorter, a reformed criminal (in line with the stereotype of a pop star as a rowdy teenager) and the most popular British pop artist, on his way to conquering the rest of the world with his performances. Shorter is played by Paul Jones, at the time a member of the popular 1960s group, Manfred Mann. Steven reached the peak of the pop Parnassus not by his own will and effort but thanks to being carefully managed by the "system", which subsequently used his popularity for its own goals. We first see Steven performing handcuffed and locked in a cage, surrounded by policemen wielding truncheons, which is presented by the narrator (Watkins himself) as recreating Steven's situation from the time he was a troublemaker. Such a violent performance allows the audience to release their negative energy, as opposed to directing it towards the political establishment. Politicians even approach music agencies to stage violent performances to keep the youth off the streets. Such use of the dark side of Steven points to the concept of the culture industry's ability to integrate the subversive elements into its project, as mentioned previously. Joseph Heath and Andrew Potter summarize such strategy in relation to neoliberalism, writing that "Cultural rebellion is not a threat to the system – it *is* the system" (Heath and Potter 2006: 3).

Later Steven is playing in an advert, sponsored by the Ministry of Agriculture and Fisheries and producers of fruit, which encourages people to eat more apples, to help to manage their unusually large crop. Finally, his power over the audience is meant to increase the popularity of the Church. These three circles of power (politics, economy, religion), in a way recollecting Marxist critique of capitalism, are represented as united and reinforcing each other. All this happens when Britain is governed by a coalition government, and the programmes of the main political parties are indistinguishable. Watkins's film thus foretells the advent of neoliberalism, when political differences between left and right collapsed and the main task of the state became to create the best possible conditions for business.

Steven Shorter is depicted as a total victim of this system. Although he exerts great power over the crowds of his followers, this power originates not in him, but his masters; he is merely its transmitter. In the process of becoming a star, Shorter is deprived of his subjectivity – he becomes the property of his managers, the political establishment and his audience, having no control over his time or space. He performs practically all the time and everywhere his masters send him. Thus Watkins suggests that the greater value of the artist as a commodity and the deeper his integration into the capitalist system, the deeper is his alienation. It is worth mentioning that Paul Jones partly confirms this assessment, confessing that in real life he endured a similarly gruelling schedule as Shorter, performing practically non-stop: at live concerts, on television and for charity events (Pratt 2010: 18). Unable to sustain his life, Steven eventually rebels, having a mental breakdown and pronouncing meekly that "he is a person", as opposed to being a wheel in a machine of power. This leads to the establishment withdrawing its support from Steven. He was banned from public appearances and "within about a year, all that remained of Steven Shorter were a few old records and a piece of archive film with the sound, of course, removed". The audience, we can deduce, could not affect Steven's fate, because it was as passive and manipulated by the establishment as Steven himself.

Steven's position as the darling of the crowds is contrasted with that of Vanessa Ritchie, a successful painter commissioned to paint his portrait. Unlike Steven, Vanessa enjoys artistic autonomy and personal freedom, reflecting the gap between low and high art, as it was still perceived in the 1960s, and Watkins's idealistic views on high art. Fans do not follow her; she does not have a manager who controls her private life and she paints what and how she wants. Unlike Steven, who is only talked about by others, she is also shown as having control over the film's narrative. In a voice-over she presents her assessment of Steven, confessing that she found a strange emptiness about Steven and therefore decided to paint him, perhaps in order to fill this void in him. Vanessa also possesses her own space – an artist's studio – and this is the only space where Steven enjoys some privacy. Ironically, Vanessa is played by Jean Shrimpton, one of the most popular models of the 1960s and, no less than Jones, somebody perceived at the time as "public property".

Watkins's representation of the culture industry, marked by a disempowered and tormented pop star, passive audience and authoritarian establishment, should be treated as an ideal type, with which to compare a specific reality, rather than reality itself. In the subsequent chapters I will attempt to do so, by looking at Falco's case. In this way, however, I hope to account for some possible mistakes and "blind spots" in Watkins's representation, in particular his unwillingness to deal with the question of why every year millions of young people attempt to enter the "Adorno hell" and become pop stars, whatever it takes.

Part II

Falco Synchronic: Romanticism and Intertextuality

3 Ganz allein und so romantisch: beyond classes and masses

Falco's artistic output and image are remarkably versatile, reflecting in the fact that he was active as a pop artist for over twenty years and his desire to stay "in the game" of show business by constantly reinventing himself. However, there are also common traits in his work and persona, which played a similar function of "chaining" his fans to his music. The chapters in this Part are devoted to presenting these traits.

Falco was born in 1957 in Vienna as Johann (Hans) Hölzel into a working- to lower-middle-class family. His mother ran a small grocery shop and his father was a factory worker, who later set up his own business. His father left Falco's mother for another woman when Hans was eleven. As a result of the break-up of his parents' marriage and his grandmother's death in 1971, Falco described his mother's life as full of sacrifices. Yet it was not a life of poverty or misery, as indicated by his receiving private music lessons from the age of five. Postwar Austria, as a result of adopting Keynesian principles, was quite a prosperous country. This was especially the case in the 1970s, under the chancellorship of socialist Bruno Kreisky, which coincided with Falco's formative years. Kreisky's ethos was distinctly egalitarian (see Part III), which affected what people thought or thought they needed to think at the time. In the 1970s, and to some extent the 1980s, it was a sign of backwardness to praise capitalist values or show wealth in an ostentatious way. In his interviews in the 1980s Falco usually refers to this ethos negatively, mentioning the moral pressure to make a pretence of being an "ordinary guy" who drives a small car, irrespective of one's real status, unlike in the United States, where it is acceptable to be rich and show it. Yet, no doubt, the singer benefited from this attitude at least twice. Early in life it gave him confidence that he could "climb the mountains", as he put it, despite his modest background, and in the 1990s it helped him to sustain his high status in Austria, be recognized as a poet, a man of letters, a *Kunstfigur*,[7] despite increasingly failing according to American standards of success.

The career his parents envisaged for Hans was that of a civil servant or a clerk in an insurance office. The civil service used to be the typical dream of working- and middle-class families in the Habsburg empire, who achieved a degree of material comfort against the odds and hoped for their children to continue on a similar path. Such a family situation brings to mind, for example, Kafka and Hitler, whose authoritarian fathers wished for their sons to become clerks.[8] For a short period of time the future Falco worked in an insurance office. However, Vienna at the time was, as Falco himself admits, a porous space, where people of different backgrounds could easily meet. Accordingly, since his teenage years he mingled with people of different classes and social positions, and embarked on a career of a musician. On the rare occasions when the singer says something good about Austria of the 1970s, he mentions that this opening up was possible thanks to Kreisky's socialist policies and the atmosphere of inclusiveness and freedom they created (quoted in Weissbrod 1988).

The "Kreiskyian" upbringing might be one reason why Falco, unlike American rappers, did not want to present himself as a boy from a broken family living on a run-down housing estate, who made it to the top. Such stories would not sound convincing in postwar Austria. Yet, perhaps a more important reason was his unwillingness to be seen as following a specific career path. Falco avoided broaching in interviews or, indeed, in his songs, the issue of his class allegiance. The only time I know it happened was during the filming of the music video of 'Mutter, der Mann mit dem Koks ist da', recorded on a documentary, included in the film *Hoch wie nie*, when he talks about his class in negative terms, as not belonging to the lower middle class, as suggested by a scene of shooting at garden gnomes, or upper class, as shown by having golf clubs on the set, although the image of the singer shooting gnomes can be seen as a metaphor of rejecting his low-class background.

Conversely, Falco presented himself as having an individual identity, being one of a kind and an heir to the Romantic tradition with its cult of lonely geniuses. He peppered his interviews with quotations from Goethe and Heine and ordered a portrait of Oskar Werner, an Austrian actor and *Kunstfigur*, renowned for his knowledge of Romantic poetry and somewhat tragic life, no doubt as a reflection or projection of his own fate. Replacing his common Christian name, almost a byword for "everyman" in German, and a surname, which can be translated as "that who lisps" (from hölzeln – to lisp), with "Falco" – a name which did not exist, hence has to denote somebody unique (although, as I will argue in due course, there is more to "Falco" than being one of a kind) – can be seen as part of this project. "Ich bin nicht jeder" (I am not everyone) is what Falco used to tell journalists, when they performed their Fordist operation of asking different celebrities the same questions. He also invested much of his verbal dexterity in describing various dimensions of his solitude. In one of his interviews we can hear that he is "Einzelgänger, Egoist,

Eigenbrötler, Einsiedler, Partisan, Einzelkämpfer" (lonely wolf, egoist, maverick, hermit, nonconformist). In his allegedly last interview, when quizzed by the popular Austrian journalist Claudia Stöckl why he was not married, he explained that he lived like a monk and that did not suit women. Falco's motto, according to Horst Bork, was "Ich bin ein Unangepasster in einem angepassten Geschäft" (I am a nonconformist in a conformist business) (Bork 2009: 317). Such declarations confirmed Falco's concurrence with Adorno's reading of show business as a branch of capitalist industry, but also emphasized his ability to transgress it.

When Falco talked about his work, he described it as if it was the creation of a single man. He rarely gave credit to his manager, music producers, image-makers, publicists, video makers or members of his band in the creation of the Falco phenomenon. Horst Bork confirms this self-perception, saying that Falco wanted to be seen as a "lonely rider". Equally, he did not want to be seen as a member of a specific music phenomenon, such as Austropop or Neue Deutsche Welle, with which critics compared him, but strove for his music to be regarded as a genre in its own right. Such self-projection could be seen as a defence mechanism against being regarded as merely a pop star, a marionette in the clutches of the culture industry, whose music comes from above: music producers and managers, rather than from below – from his own head and heart.

The lyrics of his songs are also peppered with declarations of being untypical, as in 'America': "Des tüpische an mir, i bin untüpisch, gonz und gor" (The typical for me is being entirely untypical). Uniqueness ultimately involves a degree of solitude, as a unique person has to possess something that cannot be shared or communicated. Falco cultivated this image, as much on- as off-screen. His debut album was named *Einzelhaft* (Solitary Confinement), a title evoking Romantic mythology of an artist as a suffering individual, misunderstood by the masses, locked up in his genius, or a character in a western. Much later, on 'Falco Rides Again', this idea is presented without any ambiguity:

> This is the story of a lonely man
> He saw the heat, the cold weather of the prairie
> Say hey – Ho
> The guitars speak about Germany
> They talk about the lawless Desperado

In this fragment Falco evokes the romantic mythology of falling and rising, death and resurrection. One might think of the famous painting by Caspar David Friedrich, *Wanderer Above the Sea of Fog* (1818). However, we can guess that Falco refers here to a somewhat thwarted, postmodern version of this scenario, understood as the wanderer's personal "relapse and recovery", to quote the titles of Eminem's records, rather than his travels to save some oppressed group.

Another example where Falco deals with solitude is 'Tricks':

> If I feel for driving crazy in the middle of the night
> I smash the party, denn ich zahle bar...
> Ihr wißt ich bin alleine, leine ohne meine
> Tricks
> Tricks, yeah, all right
> That's the only reason my heart still ticks

Here Falco both recalls the Romantic mythology and undermines it, by suggesting that in contemporary times the Romantic effect can be manufactured and purchased by money.

A desire to transcend classes and distance oneself from the masses is also articulated by the artist's aligning himself with equally classless artists and personalities, in a postmodern fashion gleaned from different cultures and periods. The best known example is Mozart, from Falco's greatest hit, 'Rock Me Amadeus'. Falco's Mozart, like the Mozart in Miloš Forman's almost concurrent *Amadeus* (1984), is a spoilt child with no political or moral concerns, narcissistically preoccupied with his own music and pleasure, whom everyone forgives his sins because he is talented and charismatic:

> Because er hatte Flair
> Er war ein Virtuose
> War ein Rockidol
> Und alles rief:
> Come on and rock me Amadeus

Another example is Greta Garbo, thematized in the song 'Garbo'. Falco's Garbo is upper class, but not on the account of her family background, but due to her appearance, style, taste and attitude. She has "supernatural grace", is exceptionally talented and aloof:

> She didn't talk to the press
> Cause she couldn't care less
> She didn't even answer the phone
> She said on one occasion, without persuasion:
> "I want to be left alone"

Reading these verses I think of Roland Barthes musing on the face of Greta Garbo in similar terms, mentioning her "snowy solitary face" and claiming that

"Garbo still belongs to that moment in cinema when capturing the human face still plunged audiences into the deepest ecstasy, when one literally lost oneself in a human image as one would in a philtre" (Barthes 1992: 628). By exhorting Garbo, Falco at the same time reveals his artistic programme, granting himself the right to be aloof and arrogant and expecting to be loved for his/her exceptionality. Paradoxically, choosing such a programme did not make my protagonist especially original: pop music is awash with songs about unique personalities.

When Falco sings about Charles Darwin in 'Genie und Partisan (A Fascinating Man)' (this being his contribution to the Bollands' 'Darwin – The Evolution', 1992), it is even more difficult not to ascertain that the song concerns Falco:

> Er war der Mann – he was a man
> Genie und Partisan – a fascinating man
> Sie sah ihn an – he was a man
> Sie wußte, daß er – kann
> A fascinating man

Romanticism is the perfect tradition for pop artists to pick up because Romanticism was based on a proto-pop ideology and, thanks to being regarded as high art, could be used to dignify pop. It exhorted poetry and music (as opposed to more content-based forms of art), as a means to represent the unrepresentable and allow their creators and readers to reach a higher form of existence, typically through dreams and visions (Rodway 1963: 7; McGann 1983). The highest form of both poetry and music, according to the Romantics, was their synthesis: song, which was also the most accessible form of both music and poetry (Einstein 1947: 35–36). This is especially the case in German Romanticism, which was Falco's main reference point. Goethe and Heine themselves wrote poetry to music; Schubert and Schumann wrote music for poetry and created smaller musical forms inspired by poetry, which gained tremendous popularity. Walter Benjamin describes Heine's *Buch der Lieder* as the last work of poetry which gained mass popularity (Benjamin 2007: 156). Many of their works were inspired by folk art: popular songs and dances. Clement Greenberg claims that unlike other European countries, in Germany (where "Germany" means the entire German speaking world), even in modern times, folk poetry and song on the one hand and high literature on the other cannot be contrasted. Bertolt Brecht, in Greenberg's opinion, perfectly illustrates this trend. This also accounts for the higher status of German poets writing in regional dialects than elsewhere (Greenberg 1973: 252–65).

Falco was aware of this discourse, even if only in a diluted form and used it, refusing to explain what he says in his songs and insisting that pop should have no "nutritional value": contain no factual information, convey no message, refrain from proselytising (quoted in Hertl 1996), while simultaneously expecting to be treated as a national poet. By being, as I will argue in due course, a poet of the "vernacular", Falco could present himself plausibly as a descendant of the Romantics.

Romanticism is also marked by the cult of musical virtuosos, examples being Chopin and Liszt, with their "miraculous fingers". Falco also perceived himself as a musical virtuoso, with bass guitar being his chosen instrument. In various documentaries we can see him building something like a Rubik's cube with his fingers – a sign of having almost super-human dexterity, achieved by many years of playing instruments.

The idea that Falco is a Romantic is also conveyed visually. In the documentary *Hoch wie nie* (1998) made by Rudi Dolezal and Hannes Rossacher, we see a lonely man, writing in his large notebook, with his feet on his desk, shot in profile, not very different from the way Chopin or Schiller (both composers possessing distinctive aquiline or Falco(n)-like noses) were portrayed.

Figure 3.1: The Romantic

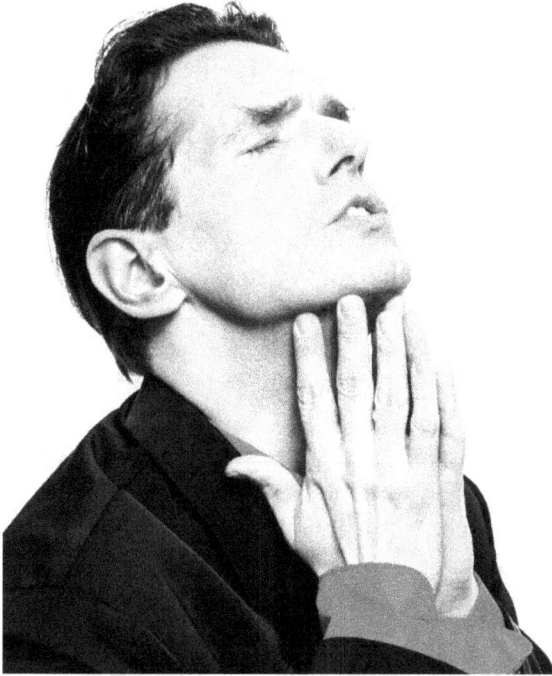

Figure 3.2: Romantic or dandy?

In many music videos, such as 'Rock Me Amadeus' and 'Junge Roemer', Falco is positioned above other characters and on occasion they look up at him, as if he was a god (Stalin also tended to be represented this way in socialist realistic films). Shooting him frequently from a low angle adds to this impression of aloofness. Such a way of presenting a singer is typical for music videos, but in Falco's case the distance between him and other characters is especially accentuated.

Many Romantics also suffered from *Weltschmerz*, loved tragically, lost children and left no heirs. Falco attempted to follow in their footsteps by undertaking a "discursive" and in some cases also real cleansing of those whose presence undermined his belonging to the exclusive society of suffering geniuses. Although he had a father, a mother to whom he was close, a half-sister, uncles, aunts and cousins, in his last recorded television interview he says "I have no family". His break with his daughter Katharina Bianca (to which I will return in due course) I see as a means to present his life as marked by irreparable loss and suffering. He also said "I have no friends". The idea behind such pronouncement was not that he had no pals (he had many who talked with pride about their bond) or lovers (he appeared to be a record-breaker in this field), but that nobody met his standards of friendship and love: nobody could understand him and participate in his suffering. Such self-representation had the double advantage of rendering him both as autonomous and a common property – he gave others what he could not receive in return, like the reverse of a capitalist who gives something only in order to multiply his investment.

But there was a side to the Romantics which Falco was unable or unwilling to emulate – their political commitment, proved by their actions, such as in the case of Byron fighting for the liberation of Greece, Pushkin opposing the Tzar's rule or Heine befriending Marx and supporting the communist cause. Such political commitment could even be attributed to some rock stars of an earlier generation, such as Bob Dylan from the 1960s, when he sang 'Only a Pawn in their Game' or 'The Lonesome Death of Hattie Carroll' about the deaths of poor black people caused by rich white people. Falco himself was aware that his Romanticism was form without content, and on occasions attempted to justify his position or joke about it, typically blaming the apolitical times in which he lived, as in one of his last songs, 'No Time for Revolution'.

The peak of Falco's career in the mid-1980s coincided with the flourishing in Britain of the musical style known as New Romanticism. New Romantics were "empty shell" Romantics – Romantics who took from Romantic poets merely "poet's shirts", but had the cheek to claim that this was enough to collect the whole inheritance. Falco can be compared to this movement, yet due to his awareness that he is not up to the job of being a true Romantic, that he can only quote the Romantics rather than live romantically, he came closer to Romanticism than his British "cousins".

4 Falco's many languages: local, national and transnational

Falco is a rare example of a European pop singer who conquered the American music market. The pinnacle of his triumph was 'Rock Me Amadeus', which topped the American and British charts in 1986. His achievement is the more remarkable, as he reached worldwide fame singing in German.

Such a description, however, simplifies a complex linguistic phenomenon, as Falco mixed German and English lyrics, typically combining an English chorus with a German main text which he rapped. The messages transmitted in the main body of the text tend to be more complex than those conveyed in the choruses and there is often a certain gulf between the two parts of his songs, with choruses sounding cheerful, innocuous and banal and the rest of the songs transmitting darker messages, concerning loneliness, drug addiction and death, as if reflecting the difference between a cheerful low American culture and a dark, Romantic, German high culture. The use of two languages can be seen in the context of splitting languages into "restricted codes" (understood by those who share the language and cultural background with the artist) and "elaborated codes" which are universal, as proposed by Basil Bernstein (1975). It also reflects Walter Benjamin's division of the experience of art by two types of consumers: the "art lover", who contemplates art and "the masses" who merely seek entertainment and whose experience is limited and distracted (Benjamin 1992: 304–305). Falco's mixing of languages might be regarded as a way to ensure that both native German speakers and international audiences, masses and art lovers would enjoy his songs, according to a postmodern strategy of overcoming the division between high and low art and national and international audiences.[9] In his songs we can hear traces of other European languages, such as Italian, Spanish and French. They do not transmit crucial meanings, only adding to the cosmopolitan flair, evoking a mood or creating a specific sound effect, such as "Un ballo nuovo porta ritmo nei fianchi della cittá Ci vediamo, troviamo, cerchiamo che cosa si fa" in 'Junge Roemer' and "Mon amour" in 'Naked'.

Hybridization of German with other languages, leading to what Christian Ide Hintze described as "Manhattan-Schönbrunner-Deutsch" or "Austro-Denglish" (Hintze 2009: 9; Hintze 2010), could outrage German purists and a wider constituency of defenders of European culture against an invasion of American culture.[10] However, in Austria such a practice was more acceptable than in Germany, because of its being the heir of a multicultural Habsburg state. Falco himself defended this manner by claiming that mixing German with English serves German rather than butchering it, because it allows German to work in a song by softening the difficult to pronounce German collections of consonants by the English words, which are richer in vowels. He also added that his mixing of German and English reflected the real German spoken by inhabitants of Austria forced to assimilate English and American influences. His defence of a hybrid language thus evoked the discourse of an Empire which ensured the dominance of German culture only by allowing other elements to contaminate it.

However, saying that Falco privileged German, again, simplifies a complex phenomenon, because he appropriated dialect and slang expressions along with high German (Ernst 2010), and created neologisms, as noted by almost all authors of the essays included in *Falco's Many Languages* (especially Zimmermann 2010; Kastberger 2010). The prime example of this practice is Falco's approach to Schmäh. This term refers to the way (some) Austrians use the German language. It is a witty manner of talking, imbued with irony, inversion of meaning and naughtiness, a means which does not allow one's opponent to show his/her superiority. An example is this fragment from 'Mutter, der Mann mit dem Kos ist da', where Falco plays with the triple meaning of "Koks" as "coal", "cocaine" and "money".

> Man nehme eine einfache Rezeptur
> Und aus Koks wird wieder Kohle
> Wärme, Behaglichkeit, Energie

In the nineteenth-century Habsburg Empire, Schmäh was the way the lower classes attempted to come to terms with their exclusion from positions of power in the hierarchical state, which used high and bureaucratic German as a weapon to maintain the status quo. However, following Austria's loss of its empire, Schmäh lost its working-class inflection and became an idiom of the intelligent, the young, the forward-looking, the subcultural, irrespective of their class origin. The transformation of the use of Schmäh reflects the replacement of the old class hierarchies by the new hierarchy of the "cool". Falco used Schmäh as a restricted code, a language in which he communicated with his Austrian fans, but also as an elaborated code, improvising with words, playing with double meaning and even nonchalantly neglecting the rules of grammar, to achieve a specific sound effect or ambiguity of meaning (Ernst 2010).

Such strategies also pertain to a certain strand of (high) poetry. Not surprisingly, much attention was devoted to the similarity between Falco's approach to language and that of Ernst Jandl, a leading representative of the Vienna school (of poetry). Jandl described himself as a "sound poet" (of *Lautgedichte*). This means that his poetry, not unlike song lyrics, comes alive only when presented aloud, due to being based on repetitions, whose function is to create a specific sound effect, rhythm or even trance (Zimmermann 2010: 21). When seen on paper, much of Jandl's writing appears superfluous. This is also the case with large chunks of Falco's texts. Jandl's public recitations were "marked by deliberate distortions of familiar words and other similar manoeuvres" (Holton and Kuhner 1985: 149). For such distortions Falco was also renowned, most importantly as an author of the lyrics for his record *Data de Groove*. Compare from this perspective Jandl's 'Lenin im Winter' with Falco's 'Expocityvisions':

> *Lenin im winter*
> die revolution
> die schneevolution
> die teevolution
> der schnee
> der tee
> der rehe
>
> (the revolution
> the rearvolution
> the bearvolution
> the rear
> the bear
> the deer)

(quoted in Holton and Kuhner 1985: 148–49)

> *Expocityvisions*
> Expo – niert,
> Explo – diert,
> MA-RA-THON
> King – size,
> Expo – size,
> Expo – beat
> City – heat – new prize

To both Jandl and Falco applies a rule which Elizabeth Klosty Beaujour identified in relation to the works of Vladimir Nabokov: "Bilingualism confers advantages for cognitive tasks involving metalinguistic awareness, separating word sound and meaning, and generating synonyms and original uses. Sensitivity to the pleasures of redundancy and play is fostered by bilinguals' awareness of the inherent separability of sign and referent" (Beaujour 1995: 37). Bilinguals, more than those working in one language, are aware of the potential for defamiliarization provided by even slight variations in vocabulary and levels of language. Bilinguals are less inclined to rely on rigid and unvarying processing strategies and are particularly good at seeking out patterns. They see the words and their collections not as representations of reality, but as representations of representations. They also demonstrate a heightened sense of the "relativity of things" and greater than usual tolerance for certain kinds of ambiguity (ibid.). Bilingualism can be, of course, used poetically. Take Jandl's 'The Flag':

> a fleck
> on the flag
> let's putzen
> a riss
> in the flag
> let's nähen
> where's the nadel
> now
> that's getan
> let's throw it
> werfen
> into a dreck
> that's
> a zweck

In 'The Flag' German is mixed with English to convey the protagonist's rejection of nationalism and militarism. In this sense, it points to the "selective nostalgia" for the social tenets of the pre-1918 world (Dassanowsky 1996: 2), which informed Austria's post-war politics and culture, manifested in its "attempts to play a strong neutralist and internationalist role" (1996: 5). Falco also showed awareness of Austria's role as a bridge between East and West and even as a "neutralizer" of their differences, presenting it as a specific predicament, which made him tense (for example he mentioned the proximity of the Berlin Wall), as well as a creative opportunity. Falco's hybridizing of European languages in a single song can be seen as a re-enactment of what is described as the "Habsburg myth" understood as a golden age of "unity in diversity" and as an experiment in forging a new common European identity, based on embracing the "Tower of Babel" of different languages and, as I will argue in due course, different musical styles. His linguistic play also has a different political dimension, consisting of criticizing rich people who in their real and cultural travels disregard anything which does not suit their sanitized vision of the world, as in 'Sand am Himalaya':

> We drive, drive, overdrive
> That's the rhythm of our life, oversized
> Doch eins und zwei und drei im Wiegeschritt
> Läuft die Zeit dem Geist davon, wer läuft mit?
> Wir suchen Sand am Himalaya,
> Suchen Schnee am Playa
> Das neue Salz des Lebens,
> Die Politik des Schwebens

The content of this song chimes with much criticism of tourism as exploitative, trite and ultimately imprisoning the traveller in his narrow world rather than widening his horizons (Urry and Larsen 2011). Yet, while in Jandl's poem we can identify a clear ideological position: rejection of nationalism, Falco's ideological stance is ambiguous. In a postmodern fashion, he presents himself as both mocking and being complicit with the consumerist culture of oriental travel, drugs and alcohol. He comes across as somebody who more or less knows that it is morally reprehensible and aesthetically unsatisfactory to ramble through the world to feed one's hedonism, but carries on nonetheless, because pleasure matters to him most.

Another Austrian poet to whom Falco bears resemblance is Peter Paul Wiplinger. Wiplinger is known best for his political verses, referring to European war history, which includes the tragedy of the ethnic cleansing of Jews by building ghettos and concentration camps. However, many of his poems are less explicit and they share Falco's linguistic minimalism and mournful and apocalyptic, yet ironic, tone. Both Wiplinger and Falco can be described as poets of the post-apocalypse or lived apocalypse, a tragedy which does not lead to a new state of affairs, but goes on for ever. This is conveyed by the very titles of Wiplinger's poems, which describe the world as being "post": 'Wir haben verloren' (We have lost), 'Ende' (End) and 'Legende' (Legend). Let's have a look at the last of these poems:

> *Legende*
> wir sind
> legende
> totes bild
>
> wir sind
> ein leuchten
> spät und mild

wir sind
nur abbild
einer welt
die mit uns selbst
zusammenfällt

wir sind verloren

(legend
we are
legend
dead image

we are
a weak
and fading light

we are
only a reflection
of a world
that crumbles
with us)

(quoted in Holton and Kuhner 1985: 226–29)

Compare it with Falco's 'That Scene', the English version of 'Ganz Wien':

The rats already leave
See all the zombie boys
Dressed in white
And everyone's his own thief

Falco's use of German language, both in its slang and high versions, as many comments of his foreign fans, posted on YouTube, attest, demonstrated that German can be simple, musical, sexy and infinitely plastic; the opposite of the stereotype of German, associated with "Nazi speak", preserved and caricatured in war films. Perhaps the best example of Falco's talent for rendering German as a simple, almost childish, speech is this chorus from 'Kann es Liebe sein?', again bringing to mind the deceptive simplicity of Jandl's poetry:

Dann und wann,
Kann,
Kann es auch mal Liebe sein
Dann und wann,
Kann,
Kann es auch mal Liebe,
Kann es auch mal Liebe sein

Falco also succeeded in rendering German as urbane in his interviews, in which he came across as assured and in control of the situation. Listening to them one senses that the interviewee chooses words not only for their meanings, but also for their sound effect, making some words last longer than necessary; this perhaps being the sign of an influence of the previously mentioned Oskar Werner, renowned for exquisite interpretation of German poetry.

Falco not only made German his own, but "Falconised" English. One aspect of this is the special care with which he sang and rapped in English. Although German is so difficult to sing fast, it feels as if for singing and rapping in English he needed proportionately more time. The second is incorrect pronunciation of English words, typical for German speakers. For example, he sang "veird" rather than "weird", "Varhol" rather than "Warhol", although on this occasion he resurrected the original pronunciation of the Slovak name. He also made grammatical mistakes or pronounced English words in such a way that it was not obvious what he was singing. A fragment from 'Out of the Dark' provoked fans to such an exchange on YouTube:

> I give up and confessed your tears to the night is not proper grammar.

> It's "I give up and you rest your tears through the night"

> Maybe it's because he says "I give up and you waste your tears to the night". And even if it was wrong grammar, who cares?

The last comment is indicative of the way his incorrect English was received by his fans – either as irrelevant to the overall value of his performance (because poetry in songs acts differently than in normal verse), or as something which enriched it, made it more original. It is worth mentioning that actors with foreign accents are of special value for contemporary postdramatic theatre, precisely because of their uniqueness. The Polish theatre director of international renown, Krzysztof Warlikowski, is a case in point because he employs foreign actors or requires Polish actors to speak in foreign languages.

Although in the most successful period of his career, on the records *Falco 3* and *Emotional*, English thwarted German, Falco always rejected the possibility of switching to English entirely. We can hear him saying "English does not work for me" or words to such effect, which can be interpreted simply as an admission that he lacked the required linguistic fluency to create poetry in English or of being an heir to German culture, which can be expressed adequately only in one's native language. In his insistence that abandoning one's language equals losing one's culture and all privileges attached to it, Falco fol-

lowed Wilhelm von Humboldt's idea (1999) that there resides in every language a characteristic worldview. Each language reflects and creates the world
of a specific community, most importantly a specific ethnic group; hence
using a language, either in poetry or everyday parlance, is a means to com-
mune with this group, wake up a specific *Volksgeist*.

Falco's decision to remain faithful to German invites comparison to the
position taken by those Austrians who either by necessity or choice switched
from German to English. The best known example is Fritz Lang, who left Germany for Hollywood (via Paris), following the Nazi ascent to power. Lang's
success in America lasted much longer than Falco's, but it was not on the artist's own terms and was a source of the director's continued frustration. Near
the end of his career Lang returned to Germany, to direct his lavish Indian
epic (1959–60), as if to confirm that if he had the choice, he would remain
"at home". In *Le Mépris* (1963), a film which still stands as a symbol of the
uneasy relationship between American and European cinema and their different approaches to art and commerce, Godard cast Lang in the role of a poly-
glot, forced to negotiate between different cultures and people, including a
bullying American film producer, for the sake of finishing his film. Although
Godard's Lang preserves his sanity and dignity in a world which loses its way
and heads towards disaster, the message is that it is advisable not to emulate
his act, even by his cosmopolitan countrymen.

Pronouncing his attachment to his native language and culture was a marketing strategy to maximize Falco's standing in the German-speaking world
and Austria especially. That such a strategy worked is proved by Falco's career
in the 1990s (and beyond his grave, so to speak), where his hopes of sustain-
ing American and global interest were thwarted, but he preserved his status
in Austria as its greatest pop star. This was also a strategy to attract American
and transnational audiences by presenting Falco as a special case – the only
Austrian or German-speaking guy who "understands pop". Part of his American audience fell for Falco because of his mild exoticism, although most likely
for the sake of his American career it would have been better to jettison the
German language entirely. Success in the American charts also helped Falco's
position in Austria, according to the rule that nothing makes a small nation
more proud than when world powers recognize its achievements.

Falco defined his position towards German language and Austrian culture
by contrasting himself with another Austrian who achieved worldwide success, Arnold Schwarzenegger, saying that Schwarzenegger is an American of
Austrian origin, while he is a (true) Austrian. He also claimed, hardly being
controversial, that Schwarzenegger owes his success to his physical presence
– his incredible muscles.[11] For those Austrians whose gifts are of a more subtle

nature, it is advisable to remain at home. That Falco came to such a conclusion, we can derive from his biographies and interviews about his travels through America. These scattered observations about this country bear close similarity to what Adorno wrote about America in *Minima Moralia* (1974). Both men were put off by the omnipresent kitsch, as well as the ignorance, superficiality and mundane insincerity of Americans, their talk filled with "have a nice day" etc., which rendered a deeper human contact impossible.[12]

It is difficult to ignore another of Falco's famous countrymen, when talking about his use of language(s): Ludwig Wittgenstein. Wittgenstein's thesis: "The limits of my language mean the limits of my world", perhaps the best known words of a philosopher after Descartes' "Cogito ergo sum", affected in a major way postmodernist philosophy, including that of Foucault and Lyotard, mentioned in the previous part. Wittgenstein's claim also spilled into popular culture. In pop music one example is Bob Dylan, mentioned by Hintze in his discussion of the place of Falco's poetry within a wider culture (Hintze 2009: 10). There is a connection between Dylan's and Falco's attitude to language, but also a difference, reflecting them belonging to different generations and cultural formations. Falco, like Dylan, agreed that language creates reality, rather than merely mirroring it, as demonstrated most conspicuously in his album *Data de Groove* (see Part III). Dylan, however, underscored the language's potential of distortion and political manipulation. For Dylan, one can guess, there is, ultimately, a "true language", which can be reached by denouncing the manipulators. Falco, in my view, rejected such a view and in a postmodern passion celebrated the very freedom of *Sprachspiel*.

As a multi-language singer and song-writer Falco also occupies a narrow space between European national pop stars, singing in their own languages, native-English singers and those like Abba or the Austrian group Opus, which sacrificed their native language for an international career, and who are typically labelled as "Europop": music made in Europe for general European consumption (Guilbault 2001: 198). He has something in common with all these artists, yet he is like none of them. Falco's act of using many languages proved impossible to follow, demonstrating that while in theory it is easy to be a national and transnational pop star, in practice it is very difficult. Here it is also worth mentioning that Falco's greatest musical idol was David Bowie. Rather unusually for pop artists, whose native language is English, Bowie showed interest in the European tradition of chanson and German cabaret (ibid.). He lived in Berlin (where Falco hoped to meet him) and covered songs by Brecht/ Weill and Jacques Brel. Initially Falco showed little appreciation of this tradition, himself being a cosmopolitan artist enchanted by "proper", Anglo-American pop. That said, his song from the early 1990s, 'Dance Mephisto', suggests that he was moving in this direction. Another sign is his long-lasting fascination with Hans Albers, a popular German actor and singer, also during the Hitler times. As early as in 1986, in an interview published in *Bravo*, Falco revealed a desire to make a record consisting of cover versions of Albers's songs (Falco 1986) and revisited this idea near the end of his life (Bork 2009: 314).

What is the overall effect of Falco's use of many languages? Is it his one language or many? Hintze's terms "falconisch" and "kreolische Poesie" suggest that it is one, but giving the book he edited the title *Falco's Many Languages* points to the plurality of Falco's languages. Ultimately, there are as many "Falco languages" as his listeners or even as many acts of listening to him. However, I believe that most listeners experience Falco's language as layered and fragmented, not Esperanto, but a Tower of Babel, where various codes fight for hegemony, rather than coalesce and create a coherent whole. This also seems to be the position taken, if not by Falco personally, then by the producers of his records, expressing anxiety about alienating a specific category of audiences by pandering too much to the needs of another category. The proof is him recording multiple versions of his songs, most importantly 'Rock Me Amadeus', for different national audiences: European, American and Canadian. Such practice on the one hand recognized Falco as a "falconisch" artist, but on the other attempted to circumvent this aspect of his work and sell him as an "ordinary" singer, addressing the audience in the language it knows.

5 Falco's many clothes and friends

Leonard Cohen once admitted that he tried wearing blue jeans but did not feel comfortable in them, being the son of a tailor. Falco did not feel similar limitations; clothes were meant to project his intended identity rather than reflect his essential self. In this sense he was a descendant of decadents (whom we can regard as heirs of the Romantics), with their programme of transforming life into art, where clothes are an important means to this goal (Anderson 1992, especially 1–18; Loos 1998), and a typical postmodernist, rejecting the idea of a "natural" look or style. The term "man of many languages" also refers to Falco's choice of clothes. We can divide them into two overlapping groups: costumes, in which he performed and "normal", everyday clothes, although the latter he also chose with care, expecting to be photographed.

The first distinct costume, which he adopted even before he became famous, was a red mock military jacket with golden epaulettes, buttons and fake medals, a reference to the clothes sported by the Beatles on the record cover for *Sgt. Pepper's Lonely Hearts Club Band* (1967) and an ironic, yet tender, nod to a Habsburg tradition. This costume communicated that Falco is musically eclectic, whimsical, psychedelic and prone to camp. The singer eventually allowed it to be eaten by moths or abandoned it, realizing that it better suits a younger than a mature man.

The most persistent and best remembered of Falco's costumes is a black tuxedo, with a bow tie and a white shirt. This is the costume of a timeless gentleman or a dandy, who knows how to behave in metropolitan salons. He can be compared to a flâneur, an urban and urbane character, who is in the crowd, but not of the crowd (Benjamin 1983: 128–29). A man dressed this way respects tradition; most likely he enjoys the ball season in Vienna, if he comes from this city. Yet he is not like everybody, because he is upper class and such a costume at the end of the twentieth century is practically an anachronism. This costume also links Falco to British "new romantics", mentioned earlier, and those whom Iain Chambers labels "electro-dandies" (Chambers 1985: 176). How attached Falco was to this costume is best illustrated by an anecdote told by Hannes Rossacher, according to which, during the shooting of the video for 'Jeanny', the singer said that he would appear in the outfit of a of a psychiatric hospital patient only if it was designed by Armani. In the mid-1990s the black tuxedo and white shirt metamorphosed into colourful shirts made of soft materials, that one does not find in an ordinary department store. This change pointed to the fact that Falco's dandy taste refined: he stopped being a "generic" dandy and became one of a kind. Adding bright colour to his costume suggests embracing or returning to his psychedelic roots. In my opinion, Falco's attachment to the dandy costume and its mutations reflects his emotional distance from his working-class roots and his desire to be seen as upper class: a "male Garbo".

Falco was also a man of many leather jackets (on occasion he even called himself a "man in a leather jacket"), costumes evoking American "hells angels" and "rebels without a cause", immortalized by Marlon Brando and James Dean. Leather jackets were also one of the favourite costumes of his favourite male performer: David Bowie. Like Bowie, Falco experimented with jackets of different shapes and colours. Near the end of Falco's life this costume metamorphosed into a long leather coat, the necessary accessory of a male Nazi in American films. This transformation can be, again, related to Bowie, who at one point became fascinated by all things Nazi, following his meeting with Christopher Isherwood and who even, apparently, revealed pro-Nazi sympathies (Trynka 2011: 249). In my opinion, however, Falco's "Nazi outfit" does not tell us anything specific about Falco's attitude to Nazism; it merely betrays his lack of awareness of the way Austrians are contextualized abroad (if they are not taken for Australians). Finally, the private clothes of late Falco, consisting of a polo shirt, a track suit, trainers and a baseball cap, can be seen as a European version of rap attire. Falco dressed this way strikes me as even more sincerely, even naïvely, rap than American rappers, because he wears such clothes merely for comfort, rather than with a consciousness of specific rap fashions.

A unifying element of Falco's image was a pair of sunglasses. Since the 1960s sunglasses are very common among celebrities; one of the first artists who wore them regularly was Andy Warhol. Sunglasses signified Falco's dandyism, because sunglasses can be very expensive. They also acted as a wall dividing him from the audience; they connoted his fame fatigue and search for privacy. We see less of them in Falco's later performances. He does not wear them during his Donauinsel or in Wiener Neustadt concerts, in 1993 and 1994 respectively, as on these occasions the singer wanted to be seen as a "man of the people", embracing the crowds rather than running away from them, and a serious musician, who does not need any gimmicks to prove his value.

Figure 5.1: Man of leather

Figure 5.2: The Hell's Angel

The strategy of embracing diversity, but privileging a German element, applies to Falco's choice of lovers and friends. His long-time girlfriend and later wife, Isabella Vitkovic, was Austrian, but with a Yugoslav surname. The surname of his best friend, Billy Filanowski, sounds Polish and his manager, Horst Bork, was German. The man who put Bork and Falco in contact with the Bolland brothers, the music producers from Holland, was Jewish. Such a list, which can be easily extended, reflects the diversity of post-war Austria, which in part replicates the diversity of the Habsburg monarchy and the transnational, yet mostly European, character of Falco's work.

6 Der weiße Schwarze: the uses and meanings of Falco's rap

The drive towards hybridization applies not only to Falco's texts, but also his music. It is difficult to find an artist who in his/her career explored so many musical styles: funk, punk, rock, disco, techno, symphonic music, opera, reggae, tango, bossa nova, Indian sounds and rap. Not only did he navigate between different musical traditions as he matured as a musician, but he mingled many musical languages in one piece. The privileged site of this remarkable hybridization was a standard three- to four-minute song. It felt like he gave himself a lot of freedom to experiment, but within a prescribed format. His song might begin like a waltz, change into a dynamic rock piece and finish in a jazzy way or yodelling.

In the same way that German became the master code of his linguistic expression, rap became the privileged idiom of his music. Falco is even recognized as the first European rapper, or at least the first of national and international renown,[13] and one who did not merely imitate American musicians but independently created a similar style. Why rap and was it really rap? This question can be answered in different ways. According to Thomas Rabitsch and Peter Paul Skrepek, Falco's long-time collaborators, the origin of Falco's rapping lies in his beginnings as a jazz and bass player, and being influenced by the Motown legends and the American soul and funk scene, especially musicians such as Jaco Pastorius, Paul Jackson and Stanley Clarke. Falco's trajectory from jazz to rap thus mimics the history of American rap, which Russell A. Potter summarizes as "soul into hip hop" (Potter 2001). Even the names of Falco's favourite jazz musicians, such as James Brown, coincide with those mentioned in the histories of hip hop.

Falco's musician friends also claim that there is a certain affinity between playing bass and rapping. This is because one needs much talent and practice to play the bass and sing at the same time. But once one is able to play a "James Brown bass-line" (a term used by Skrepek, which I am repeating without trying to understand), one can use the same rhythm concept in connection with words: syncopated and always an eyelid flick later than the beat, in order to sound relaxed. Rabitsch links Falco's rapping specifically to his slapping style of playing bass guitar, which he borrowed from Stanley Clarke. In slapping, the string is plucked so hard that when released it bounces off the finger board, making a distinctive percussive sound. Such a sound, claims Rabitsch, lends itself to rap more than to singing. Robert Ponger, the composer of Falco's first hit, 'Der Kommissar', claims that he wrote the song in rap style; Falco's rapping was thus the consequence of the material at hand.

Figure 6.1: Man of guitars

Falco was also following developments on the American hip hop scene and, on his first trip to the States, he met Afrika Bambaataa, a DJ from New York, who was an important figure in the 1970s and 1980s hip hop scene. Bambaataa, in contrast to the stereotype of American rappers as somewhat ghettoized and inward-looking, proved to be very receptive to European influences, most importantly Kraftwerk, creating "electro funk" (Perkins 1996: 1–13). Bambaataa was very interested in Falco's work and he played a crucial role in popularizing 'Der Kommissar' in New York, by playing it on his programme. There was talk about the two artists making a record together. However, these plans did not materialize. According to Hannes Rossacher, Falco was unwilling to appreciate Bambaataa's input into his career nor go the "American way"; he felt his style had little in common with what Bambaataa and others in his circle were doing. To put it paradoxically, at the time he was too much of a rapper (in a sense of being a local artist), to be a hip hop artist.

Moreover, Bambaataa's politics was distinctly emancipatory; it harked back to the civil rights movement, as suggested by his adopted name. This differentiated him from the new generation of American rappers, who promoted a much more individualistic and even neoliberal ethos (and who were typically more image-conscious than him), as exemplified by the appropriately named 50 Cent (b. 1975), whose debut album was entitled *Get Rich or Die Tryin'*. Falco, with his romanticization of the yuppie condition and frequent broaching of the subject of money, had ideologically more in common with those younger rappers, whom, however, he had no chance of meeting.

Rapping was for Falco one means to distinguish himself from the dominant styles of popular music in Austria. On the one hand, this was the "crooner" style of Peter Alexander and Udo Jürgens, which for him was the music of the old for the old. On the other hand, there were "anarchists" such as Stefan "Wickerl" Adam, with whom Falco collaborated at the beginning of his career and whom he regarded as posthumous children of the hippie generation. Both these styles, although so different from each other, signified for him the provinciality and outmodedness of Austrian pop.

Falco's rapping style comes across as highly idiosyncratic. One reason is the timbre of his voice, which is different from that of black musicians, a factor which was particularly important in the 1980s, when there were fewer white rappers than now. Secondly, while the majority of "traditional" rappers do not sing, Falco felt equally comfortable in both types of performance and he often switched from rapping to singing within a short period of time. Thirdly, he was a versatile rapper – his rap in 'Der Kommissar' sounds very different to that in 'Rock Me Amadeus'; and is different still to that in 'Naked'. On some occasions he does not rap but recites poetry to music, as in 'The Kiss of Kathleen Turner'. However, I list these particularities of Falco's style not to undermine his status as a rapper but, on the contrary, to present him as somebody who stretched and innovated this style, therefore is especially deserving of praise.

Rap has the status of the ultimate postmodern musical style (Potter 1995), not unlike bricolage, which is the privileged postmodern style in plastic arts. As Richard Shusterman notices, "artistic appropriation is the historical source of hip hop... The music is composed by selecting and combining parts of prerecorded songs to produce a 'new' soundtrack" (Shusterman 1992: 204). Not only did

Falco rap, but he revealed a "rap mindset" by quoting, fusing, cutting and pasting. He also made cover versions of old songs of other artists and offered new versions of his own songs, sometimes even several versions of the same song; the record in this respect belonging to 'Der Kommissar' and 'Rock Me Amadeus'.

By constantly re-presenting others' and his own work, he posed a question about their originality and artistry. Should we regard the various versions of 'Der Kommissar' or 'Metamorphic Rocks' and 'From the North to the South' as different versions of the same song or different songs? Does the multiplicity of 'Der Kommissar' add to or diminish its artistic value? The answer to these questions depends not only on one's attitude to specific songs, but on one's overall aesthetics. Adorno, who worshipped modernist art, would dismiss them, claiming that the different versions offer "pseudo-innovations", which were meant to fool the audience. Indeed, Falco's "rap mindset" reflects the commercial character of his art (and Falco's overall integration into the neoliberal culture industry) because an important reason for the proliferation of the versions of a specific "original" was an assumption that they would be bought as "new songs".

My position, in common with that of Falco, is that they are all original, because each new version involves a new performance, not mentioning a new reception, hence cultural translation. Their multiplication does not undermine their artistry, similarly as making many versions of a portrait of Marilyn Monroe or Mick Jagger by Warhol does not deprive each individual portrait of its value. On the contrary, making multiple versions was an important sign of Warhol's uniqueness, almost his "logo". By rejecting the old standards of modernist originality and authenticity in so ostentatious a way, he did not merely deprive his works of an aura of original work, as defined by Walter Benjamin (1992), but gave them a new aura and a new type of uniqueness, which can be described as postmodern. People wanted to buy and display his works because they were, in a sense, all copies without an original. By analogy, the periodical reworking of 'Der Kommissar' furnishes the different versions with a specific, "Warholian" or "rap" aura. Rather than having them scattered on different records, I would prefer to have all these versions assembled together, to find out whether their effect would be similar to having Marilyn Monroe in different colours. Falco's approach to 'Der Kommissar' provided a standard for the behaviour of the next generation of stars. For example, when writing this chapter, I found out that Gotye, the author of a mega-hit from 2011, 'Somebody That I Used To Know', announced that he would release a digital compilation of its ten official remixes (Gotye 2012).

As a co-creator, together with composers, fellow performers and most importantly video makers of rich "hypertext", constructed by juxtaposing numerous anterior texts, Falco can also be compared to Jean-Luc Godard, the ultimate "rapper" of European cinema. There is even a temporary match between Falco's incessant mixing, which reached its apogee in 1985–87, with videos for 'Rock Me Amadeus', 'Jeanny' and 'The Sound of Musik', and Godard's starting his "mega-rap" (or mega-bricolage) project of *Histoire(s) du cinéma* (finished in 1998), which consists of cutting, mixing and rearranging fragments of films, as well as paintings, accompanied by a very complex soundtrack and a typical "rap" scratching sound. Godard's work, which took him ten years to produce, was instantly recognized as a masterpiece. The status of Falco's work, however, was distinctly lower, both due to its popular and commercial character and its miniature size, contrasting with the epic dimension of Godard's project.

Rap "highlights the artwork's temporality and likely impermanence ... by explicitly thematizing its own temporality in its lyrics" (Shusterman 1992: 204). In line with this rule, Falco devoted his texts to popular actresses and models (Kathleen Turner, Cindy Crawford, Tatjana Patitz in 'The Kiss of Kathleen Turner' and 'Tanja P nicht Cindy C'), who some years later became less popular, somewhat infecting his songs with their obsolescence. He mentioned politicians (Gorbachev and Reagan in 'Cowboyz and Indianz'), with the same effect. The sense of temporality was also effected by such means as interrupting the song with a news flash in 'Jeanny', an announcement by an airline attendant in 'Que pasa hombre' and informing the listener when a specific song was recorded in the American version of 'Rock Me Amadeus'. However, such themes were balanced by enduring and eternal motifs, as Falco also sang about Greta Garbo and the never-changing character of monarchy.

Rap is a style of the vernacular due to rappers using local record companies, radio stations and performance venues, as well as due to communicating in their lyrics a sense of space with cartographic details and referring to specific local problems and rivalries (Forman 2000). Falco also started his career as a local, Viennese artist (although in the case of Austria, which is a small country, the difference between local and national is much smaller than in the U.S.), using local music producers (Robert Ponger and his friend, Thomas Rabitsch), sang about places of importance for the local population, such as the club U4 in 'Ganz Wien' and 'U.4.2.P.1' and referred to the local music, for example Udo Jürgens's song in 'Siebzehn Jahr'.

Rap is also a style of the marginalized, the nonconformist, the angry. Although on- and off- screen Falco mostly "flirted with the establishment" as opposed to fighting with it, at the beginning of his career he presented himself as a spokesman for the disadvantaged: the young without prospects, those harassed by the police, those who burn out in the pursuit of excitement. He broached subjects such as drug addiction and prostitution, which older stars such as Peter Alexander and Udo Jürgens rather avoided.

One can list "high art" arguments for Falco's uses of rap. Rap allows for the integrity of the spoken word, rather than subordinating it to the demands of music, as happens in a "normal" song. It is worth evoking the ideas of the poet and essayist Paul Valéry, who defined prose, poetry and song as the three distinct states of language, which he graded in relation to signification and musicality. Prose and everyday speech are not without musicality, but their musicality is subordinated to their function of communication and signification. Song functions inversely: signification almost disappears; words tend to lose their meaning and function simply as sounds without a corresponding reality. Poetry is for Valéry a privileged form because it "holds an admirable and very delicate balance between the sensual and intellectual forces of language" (Valéry 1958: 164).

As if to confirm that poetry is preserved in rap rather than drowned in music, Shusterman adds that all qualities of the rapper are "presented as secondary to and derivative of his verbal power, reflecting the fact – surprising or even unacceptable to some whites – that verbal virtuosity is greatly appreciated in the black urban ghetto" (Shusterman 1992: 205). "Rap English" is a descendent of the language of the Negro slaves who were compelled to create a semi-clandestine vernacular to defend themselves from their white masters. As G. S. Holt maintains,

> The slaves turned the language as it was presented to them to their own purposes, and in fact to the precise purposes which their owners sought to prevent ... Blacks clearly recognized that to master the language of whites was in effect to consent to be mastered by it through the white definitions of caste built into the semantic/social system. Inversion therefore becomes the defensive mechanism which enables blacks to fight linguistic, and therefore psychological entrapment ... Whites, denied access to the semantic extensions of duality, connotations, and denotations that developed within black usage, could only interpret the same material according to its original singular meaning. White interpretation of the communication event was quite different from that made by the other person in the interaction, enabling blacks to deceive and manipulate whites without penalty. This protective process, understood and shared by blacks, became a contest of matching wits and a form of linguistic guerrilla warfare which protected the subordinated, permitted the masking and disguising of true feelings, allowed the subtle assertion of the self and promoted group solidarity. The purpose of the game was *to appear to but not to* (Holt 1972: 153–54; original emphasis).

In this sense rap can be compared to Schmäh (see Chapter 2), as both types of speech were initially used by the lower classes as a means to assert their discursive power in situations of lack of real political power.

Falco was not only *ein weißer Schwarzer*, as he described himself, evoking Jimi Hendrix's description as a black man who borrowed from whites (Murray 2005: 7), but also a white man performing against the background of black artists. This is the case in the videos of 'Brillantin' Brutal', 'Emotional' and 'The Sound of Musik'. Such a mise-en-scène, on the one hand, recognizes Falco's debt to black music, but also his inability to embrace it entirely and a latently colonial attitude to black culture. In his videos black musicians are represented in line with their archaic role – merely as a background to the action of a white man. In 'Brillantin' Brutal' they belong to a jazz band accompanying players in a casino. In 'Emotional' one black man hands Falco a microphone, as if he was his humble assistant. Interaction of this type contrasts with Eminem's performances, which are often duets with black rappers, who either rap with him or conduct the show, introducing the songs and telling the audience how to react. Yet, as one of the few (continental) European pop artists who referred to black music in his work, Falco had hardly any examples to follow and should be appreciated for "blackening" his music and performance rather than criticized for not doing it sufficiently.

7 "And then I waste it...": scandalizing in the age of neoliberalism

In a fragment of an interview, included in the *Hoch wie nie* documentary, the young Falco says with a theatrical air: "Scandal, scandal", adding that "That is good, that is show business". Such words, on the one hand, render show business as a natural site of scandal, but on the other hand normalize this state. If show business is a part of the culture, where one can scandalize with impunity, then the truly scandalous state of show business will be one that fails to scandalize, not unlike a carnival where nobody violates the norms of decency.

Was Falco a scandalist? In order to answer this question, one needs to establish a standard of scandal. The one I am using here is borrowed from Alain Badiou's book, *The Century*, in which the author ponders that the spirit of rebellion (which I will equate here with "scandal") evaporated from the twentieth century's ideologies:

> In the real present of the century, the new man primarily stood –
> if one was progressive – for the escape from family, property and
> state despotism. Today, it seems that "modernization", as our mas-
> ters like to call it, amounts to being a good little dad, a good little
> mum, a good little son, to becoming an efficient employee, enrich-
> ing oneself as much as possible, at playing at the responsible citizen.
> This is the new motto: "Money, Family, Elections" (Badiou 2007: 66).

What Badiou describes as "today" can be identified as a period of neoliberalism, while "the real present of the century", the progressive period, finished in the 1960s. But Badiou identifies here only the main cultural trends. Individual people can endorse or resist the dominant values of their times. How does Falco score in "Badiou's test" as a man and as an artist?

Let's begin with money. Falco, as I already indicated, came from a family of modest material resources. Consequently, for him money was one of the main perks of being famous and off-screen he identified with the capitalist idea of rewarding success with money. He typically assessed the value of his work by the number of records sold. When he talked about the changes in his music style, he presented them in terms of tapping into a specific market;

in this way he explained, for instance, his move to techno in the mid-1990s. Practically all pop and rock musicians follow such an agenda, yet in his frankness Falco revealed the neoliberal mindset, as in this ideology profit is the ultimate value and there is no need to obscure this fact.

Falco was quoting Johann Wolfgang von Goethe rather than Friedrich von Hayek, saying that "Ein gesunder Mensch ohne Geld ist halb krank" (A healthy man without money is half-sick),[14] but this was to argue that it is cool to be rich, rather than that rich people should share their wealth with the poor so that nobody remains half-sick from poverty. His excessive, yuppie lifestyle was also frequently a subject of criticism, not unlike Abba a decade before in Sweden, where the pressure to live like everybody else was even stronger than in socialist Austria.[15] That said, in his supposedly last interview, he confessed to being corrupted by money. Although he did not elaborate on this statement, one can guess that he meant that wealth changed his perception of the world and made him seek pleasures obtainable with money, such as alcohol, drugs, and sex with prostitutes.

A sign of Falco's subscribing to the neoliberal agenda was also his public association with two rich Austrian men. One is the billionaire ex-racing driver and aviation entrepreneur, Niki Lauda, a living advert of the neoliberal project, being an exceptional individual from a middle-class family, who risked his health and life to be rich and successful. Lauda is captured on camera during Falco's birthday celebrations and is prominent during Falco's televised funeral. Lauda also named one of his planes after Falco, in this way for decades linking the singer with a symbol of "yuppismo", i.e. the privatization of natural resources and human disrespect for nature. The second of Falco's friends is Ronnie Seunig, a "duty free" millionaire and creator of Excalibur City, a gigantic shopping mall, encapsulating the neoliberal concept of changing cities into profit-generating machines.

Unlike Lauda or Seunig, Falco, however, was not an instinctive businessman; on the contrary. Bork claims that he had no interest in the intricacies of his contracts and he behaved as if he always wanted to blow his money on the spot rather than invest it or save it for later. As a "cash-burner", he was extremely successful. His other biographer, Peter Lanz, claims that during his career the singer earned the equivalent of €50,000,000, but near the end of his life almost nothing of this money was left; on the contrary, there were debts. This nonchalant attitude to money suggests that Falco did not value money the way Badiou describes. Rather he fits the idea of a Romantic artist, for whom money was a passport to instant pleasure, easily used and disposed of, or at best a means of acquiring "cool" style (an idea one can find most famously in Francis Fitzgerald's writings). Judging by his interviews, he was also suspicious that people, and women especially, might use him for money. An example is his complaint that his wife's family treated him like a winning lottery ticket. But his suspiciousness betrayed the fact that he himself gave a lot of thought to the value of money.

Money, together with drugs and the decline of Western civilization, is the most enduring motif of Falco's songs, examples being 'Les nouveaux riches', 'Psychos' and 'Geld'. All these songs refer to money as the most desired good. Such an idea might today be regarded as obvious but this was not the case in the 1960s and 1970s, when love and themes of emancipation were more common in rock texts. In this sense Falco's songs bear close similarity with the work of such pop stars like Abba, most importantly 'Money, Money, Money' (1976) and Madonna's 'Material Girl' (1984), with Madonna being regarded as a truly "material(istic) girl". But there are also differences. Abba and Madonna sang about people or, more precisely, women, who have little money, but want to get more and are prepared to sell themselves for money. In Abba's song we find such words:

> In my dreams I have a plan
> If I got me a wealthy man
> I wouldn't have to work at all
> I'd fool around and have a ball...

In 'Material Girl', "there is an initial couplet that says what the boys do, while the following couplet is a commentary saying that what counts is their money: this is in each case focused around the last word in line 3 – credit, cash, interest, pennies, rich. (There is a persistent punning relationship between human and monetary values, most obviously seen in the words 'credit' and 'interest')" (Cook 1998b: 152).

The world, created by Abba and Madonna, is thus populated by the "to-be-rich", who might never achieve their goal; the protagonist of Abba's song even reveals a Cinderella-like naïveté about money. These characters are not in a position to question the value of money, lest to be disillusioned about it. It is different with Falco. He writes from the perspective of someone who understands that money is a language and religion: an idea which was first put forward by Marx and reappeared with amazing force under neoliberalism. Money, we learn from Falco's songs, breaks all barriers, allows those who have nothing in common to communicate effectively, travel in space and time, not just "fool around and have a ball". There is also a sense that the world ruled by money is cruel, sad and "flat", as money destroys cultural differences. This is also a Marxist concept, as well as conveyed by the critics of neoliberalism, such as Marc Augé (1995), who point to the homogenization of neoliberal space.

Furthermore, in 'Les nouveaux riches' Falco asks:

> Where do you go when the money's gone?
> Where do you go when you're all alone?

In 'Geld' we read

> D'rum, wenn ich das große Los zieh und es geht nicht alles d'rauf
> Mach in der nächsten Stadt ich mir doch glatt ein Spielcasino auf
> Und man kann bekanntlich alles – auch die Liebe – dafür kaufen,
> Doch der beste Weg von allen, na, ist es einfach zu versaufen

> (That's why, if I pull the winning ticket and don't waste everything,
> I'll open a Casino in the next city.
> You can buy everything with it – even love –
> But the best way to spend it is to simply drink it away)

The elegiac tone of the second fragment brings to mind the lines of Bertolt Brecht:

> Every day, to earn my daily bread
> I go to the market where lies are bought
> Hopefully
> I take up my place among the sellers

Brecht is the more suitable to evoke in this context, as 'Geld' is Falco's cover version of a piece written by Rio Reiser, who can be labelled the Bertolt Brecht of German pop music. Reiser was a singer politically active on the side of the German radical left, who, in common with many left-wing pop artists who managed to break into the mainstream and enjoy affluence, was accused of "selling out" to the capitalist machine. By recycling Rio Reiser's song Falco inevitably confronted his own position as a "compulsive seller" to the monster of capitalism, but also pointed to the fact that those arguably more principled artists, such as Reiser or even Brecht, were not very different from him.

Falco's assessment of money can be summarized in this way: Money is not good, but you cannot do without, all alternatives are hopelessly utopian, so maybe it is not so bad after all. Ultimately, he reveals the attitude of a "knave", as described by Slavoj Žižek (Žižek 1997: 45–47): somebody who looks with derision at the surrounding world, yet without advocating any alternative or even hinting that an alternative might be worse than what is now.

As for his attitude to family, the private Falco did not conform to the neoliberal ideal of a "good little dad and husband", which Badiou treats with derision, but neither, as I will argue in Part IV, did he adhere to Badiou's maximalistic concept of love. Falco's unwillingness or inability to fulfil bourgeois ideals of family already transpired at the moment when he tried to fit it – during his marriage to Isabella Vitkovic. Their wedding took place in Las Vegas, the perennial temple of fake weddings and speedy divorces of spoilt celebrities. With the couple clad in garishly adorned denim outfits and no close family in sight, the wedding was an offence to the traditional Catholic concept of a wedding. Even in its somewhat caricatured form, in Falco's own words, the wedding was merely a nod to convention, to save his daughter the stigma of a bastard child and a prelude to a divorce, which took place less than a year later. Falco also confessed that bourgeois family life did not suit him either as a market strategy, as his fans did not like the fact that he settled down, or as a means to achieve happiness. Following his divorce, Falco remained unmarried, although practically never single, with a new woman replacing the old one almost immediately after the previous one had left him, and the story of him buying wedding rings being recounted by a number of his girlfriends. We can deduce that the singer secretly yearned to become a jeweller, but we will need the "Viennese quack" to find out why he took such a roundabout route to fulfil this dream.

Falco was rather candid about his private life in interviews and, again, what is striking, is his unromantic attitude to his erotic life, mirroring that to his music. He depicted it in terms of needs (his needs and those of his girlfriends) and a specific person (himself or his girlfriend) tapping into these needs, not unlike a market product responding to the needs of a customer. He presented the break-ups with his girlfriends like they were a specific product expiring and in need of replacement. Again, one can describe it as a neoliberal approach, where any good, even as lofty as love, can be reduced to a market value.

There are two distinct approaches to love in Falco's songs. One is conventionally romantic or sentimental and it is revealed primarily in the record *Wiener Blut*, in tracks such as 'Solid Booze' and 'Read a Book' and the title song from his earlier record, *Emotional*. In these songs we hear about lovers holding hands and giving each other warmth and support. However, such love is usually presented as belonging to the future or a dream and contrasted with the present reality. In 'Emotional' the singer pronounces that his beloved woman is not yet born. It is also worth noting that the standard of lyrics and typically of music in Falco's "romantic songs" is much below Falco's usual fare, as epitomised by the awkward title 'Solid Booze'.

In Falco's other love songs the protagonist's actions diverge from the accepted standards of erotic behaviour. 'Jeanny', the first song in what would become Falco's "Jeanny Trilogy" (where a number of songs compete for the position of the third part) is the best known case. Accompanied by an elaborate music video, which comes across as a mini-encyclopaedia of cult cinema, with references to *American Graffiti* (1973) by George Lucas, *M* (1931) by Fritz Lang, *The Third Man* (1949) by Carol Reed and several films by Alfred Hitchcock, it tells the story of a man who possibly killed the object of his love to preserve her beauty, like the protagonist of the famous story by Edgar Allan Poe, *The Oval Portrait*. The connection with Poe is at its strongest in the most dramatic part of the video, when Jeanny lies on a catafalque, in corset and jewellery, surrounded by candles and stuffed animals, while her lover plays on a grand piano, looking ahead rather than sideways, where he put his beloved. Like the painter in Poe's story, the pianist is more interested in his art than its subject; Jeanny, most likely an under-age prostitute, is merely a trigger for his creativity. But on a more mundane level, the video is also about a rapist and murderer, masquerading as a romantic lover. The fact that the song and the video glamorizes him was regarded as unacceptable and led to censoring of the song, which – as is often the case – only added to its popularity and, subsequently, cult status, as would be later the case with Eminem's (much more explicit) songs about raping and murdering women. At the same time, even the most ardent critics of the song, such as the priest and sociologist Horst Albrecht, conceded that the song awoke a quasi-religious elevation among its listeners, including youngsters preparing for their confirmation (Albrecht 1993: 10). This is in part due to the authors skilfully drawing on Christian imagery, such as the gospels and stories of Don Juan and Hansel and Gretel (Albrecht 1993: 14).

The second part of 'Jeanny', 'Coming Home', does not add much to the narrative. We learn that the lover/pervert was locked up in a psychiatric asylum and either is "coming home", searching for a new Jeanny or merely fantasizes about it. By the time Falco embarked on the third part of 'Jeanny', probably his fans split into those who wanted its protagonist to reform and marry Jeanny and those who expected him to be beaten to death by anti-paedophile activists, with both solutions fitting the neoliberal scenario. In the meantime the satirical magazine *Mad*, in a humorous sequel to 'Jeanny', portrayed Falco as a man, who for the sake of the next hit, remains unhappily married to Jeanny for ten years (Vielmeister n.d.). It feels like in 'Bar Minor 7/11 (Jeanny Dry)' Falco took a cue from this story. This song not only fails to offer us any new love story, but suggests that the romance from the earlier albums was a sham – it was invented by the culture industry, personified, as in the story run in *Mad*, by "der Chef meiner Plattenfirma" and the only 'Jeanny' which ever existed was dry gin(nie), consumed by the singer in smoky bars. The shift from a high-pitched romance to a tribute to a single man's "best friend" is conveyed by the change in music. 'Bar Minor 7/11 (Jeanny Dry)' is made in a

Antônio Carlos Jobim bossa nova style, as a perfect background to sipping gin in a bar in an exotic place, such as the Dominican Republic, where Falco would set up his new home several years later.

'Jeanny' also sparked a discussion in the East German press, illuminating the perennial problem of those analysing cultural artefacts: how to assess their ideological stance. A journalist from *Junge Welt*, Wolfgang Khort, condemned the song for revealing the utter depth of depravity of these men from the capitalist world, who do not stop raping and murdering young girls for pleasure, thus implying that in the socialist East such things do not happen. But his view was criticized by one sophisticated reader, perhaps familiar with Adorno's work, for being too simplistic. He claimed that art, even popular art, is not about ideals but ideas – its purpose is to give food for thought, not ready-made recipes for life. Inevitably this argument did not convince Mr Khort, who demanded that *Jeanny* be banned from the socialist radio, ironically in this way suggesting that even citizens of East Germany are vulnerable to dangerous seduction (Khort 1986).

Another of Falco's attempts to project a different type of erotic relation than that mentioned by Badiou is 'Naked'. In the artist's own words, the song and the video are a tribute to the fashion industry, which dresses women, and to his own desire, which accompanied him from adolescence, to undress them. Indeed, the video shows the fashion industry's extraordinary achievement of dressing women (beautiful women, one should add) in a way which makes men willing to undress them. But this is not the full story. While showing dressed and almost undressed women, the video glorifies sexual violence. The singer/protagonist confesses that he wants to "take it, shake it, taste it, waste it" and we see him first with a knife in his hand and then breaking a glass cupboard, containing photographs of women. This reference to male violence harks back to 'Jeanny' and one can guess that the makers of this song, Falco included, might have planned it as a new, more daring version of this song. There are further differences. While 'Jeanny' showed a man as vulnerable to his murderous instincts and ultimately defeated by being locked in a psychiatric ward and haunted by the memory of a woman for whom he lusted, 'Naked' conveys a sense of unpunished and unchallenged male mastery over women. The man, played by Falco, is individualized; there are no other men in this narrative other than him, unlike women, who are rendered as interchangeable and disposable, like a mass of flesh on display for male delectation. This impression is strengthened by placing the actresses on a round, rotating stage and using fast motion in the later part of the video, as in a peepshow.

While all the women playing in this short film are semi-naked, Falco remains dressed in a traditional black suit over a white T-shirt, a variant of his dandy attire. The somewhat mature, yet very attractive face of the singer (as confirmed by numerous comments of forlorn female fans on YouTube), adds to the impression that the film's protagonist knows all too well how to handle women. The video also points to women's acquiescence to such treatment, testified by the inscription "Waste Me" on a sash decorating one of the actresses in this short film, stylized on a beauty queen in beauty pageants and an episode of two women fighting with each other, as if for a chance to be wasted by this charismatic brute, whose animal nature is underscored by replacing him in some shots with an ape. Among the actresses of the film we see two blond girls with guns, an image which brings to my memory Godard's *Ici et ailleurs* (*Here and Elsewhere*, 1976), where he showed Palestinians of both sexes preparing to fight to regain their country. While in Godard's film, however, the image of children was used politically, here, so to speak, the political image is used aesthetically or erotically. Guns make the girls look kinky. 'Naked' can thus be regarded as a form of postmodern détournement, which serves neoliberal capitalism by disarming political images.

The authors of 'Naked' committed all possible sins not only against the conservative "moral right", but also feminism, confirming the common view of Falco as an unreconstructed, regressive macho. That said, looking at this video in 2012, I was surprised how much it has in common with the music videos of some of the most successful contemporary female performers, such as Lady Gaga and Nicki Minaj, which epitomise female power. The video to Minaj's 'Beez in the Trap' (2012) looks almost like a reworking of 'Naked', with the themes of nudity, sex, bondage and money, except that 'Beez in the Trap' comes across as more explicit.

Due to its peepshow aesthetics, perversion and humour, 'Naked' also awakes association with fin-de-siècle naughtiness, in which the writers and artists of the Habsburg times excelled, one example being Leopold von Sacher-Masoch, the author of *Venus in Furs* (1870). I also see a special affinity between 'Naked' and a short essay entitled "Ladies' Fashion" (1998 [1902]), written by modernist architect and critic, as well as famous paedophile Adolf Loos (no doubt a figure familiar to the Austrian producers of this video), whose beginning perfectly introduces 'Naked's atmosphere:

> Ladies' fashion! What a horrible chapter in our cultural history, laying bare mankind's secret lusts. Reading its pages, one shudders to one's very soul at dreadful perversions and unbelievable vices; one can hear the whimpering of abused children, the shrieks of maltreated women, the ear-splitting screams of tortured people, the wailing of victims burning at the stake. Whips crack, and the air is filled with the smell of roasting human flesh. La bete humaine ... (Loos 1998: 106).

Loos offers us an explanation for why the style of male and female dresses in the video are so different and why women keep changing their clothes, while Falco remains in the same attire:

> [The man] is filled with a longing to belong to the upper classes, which he also expresses in his dress ... The leaders of fashion in men's clothing are those who hold the highest social position, while the leaders in ladies' fashion will be those women who have to show the greatest skill in arousing men's sensuality, namely the cocottes (Loos 1998: 107 and 109).

Loos also argues that the power of a man, as conveyed by fashion, lies in his avoiding ornament – "the lower the cultural level, the greater the degree of ornamentation", which is, besides, an idea at the centre of the modernist project (1998: 109).

The lack of autobiographism in Falco's song and his focus on non-marital love sets him apart from the previously mentioned Eminem, whose dysfunctional family, including a working-class single mother and a bickering wife who misunderstands him, became an important part of his performing persona. Paradoxically, in this way Eminem elevates family to the most important institution in a person's life (as described by Badiou) and absolves other institutions (the state, the army, the capitalist class) from having any effect on one's successes or failures, which is a concept which neoliberal ideologues cherish and promote.

Finally, let's move to "elections", which for Badiou is shorthand for the ideal of being a good, obedient citizen. As for elections in the literal sense, I was not able to find out whether Falco supported any party or, indeed, whether he voted at all. According to Peter Paul Skrepek, he tried to stay away from politics, adhering to the rule, identified by Stuart Hall, that post-1968, the "cool" political position meant being against any parties and political programmes and observing political games from a distance (Hall 1988: 181). Such an attitude is transmitted in 'Monarchy Now' and 'No Time for Revolution', which render all political personalities and programmes equally untrustworthy. Yet, staying away from politics equals voting for the winners and this captures Falco's political and existential position well.

At the same time, being an obedient citizen was not Falco's objective and at least in one distinct way he was in collision with the social norms – he abused alcohol and took drugs, with cocaine and whisky being his favourite mixture. This put him in conflict with the law – he caused traffic accidents and mayhem in hotels. Drugs also feature prominently in his lyrics. Superficially, the drive towards drugs connects him with the hippie culture. For the hippie guru, the poet Timothy Leary, drugs, most importantly LSD, were a tool of a fundamental personal and social transformation, a vehicle of a political revolution and the revolution of everyday life (Leary *et al.* 2008). If we are to believe Horst Bork, drugs did not play the same role in Falco's life – they were not a means to transport the artist to a more spiritual reality, but a fast track to success in the material reality and a means to survive its pressures. The singer even jokingly asked his manager whether success in show business was worth his investment in drugs: "Ich hoffe, dieser ganze Scheiss ist es wert, was ich hier an Substanz investiere" (Bork 2009: 39).

The artist stuffed himself with illegal substances to be able to work longer hours and then to relax, to take his mind away from the constant worry that his record would not sell and the fans desert him. Very often his days, including the last day of his life, were divided between working, drug-taking, a session at the gym or a long run. His favourite drug was a Viennese drug: cocaine. One of its first researchers and ardent users was Sigmund Freud. In the letters to his fiancée, Martha Bernays, he praised cocaine for making people capable of enduring the most strenuous tasks and curing them from nervous exhaustion (Markel 2011). For the reason outlined by Freud, cocaine is also a neoliberal drug, part of yuppie culture, being fast, clean and relatively safe, unlike heroin; its upper-class connotations are underscored by its lower-class version of "dirty" crack-cocaine. John Barker confirms such a reading in an article entitled "Intensities of Labour: From Amphetamine to Cocaine":

> Audiovisual production, advertising, fashion, the production of software, photography, cultural activities, etc. ... activities which tend to define and fix cultural artistic norms, fashions, tastes, consumer standards and, more strategically, public opinion. Descriptions of this work in the "immaterial labour" canon, however, do not look at the intensities of labour involved. The widespread use of cocaine in this sector is not accidental. Its availability in the UK obviously has to do with a range of factors – the nature of some Latin American economies and their staggering inequalities, sophisticated criminal organisation, the increasing rise in the worldwide transportation of material goods and so on – but it is also because the demand is there. It has been the perfect drug for this relatively privileged sector; not creative in any real sense, but perfect for generating an indiscriminate intensity of enthusiasm for the projects provided in this sector, and for believing in the great importance of what one is doing at any given time (Barker 2006).

The matter-of-fact attitude to drugs dominates Falco's lyrics. They are not about the beauty of psychedelic experience: ecstasy, liberation, illumination, but about the mundane business of drug taking, which is like an exaggerated version of any other business: buying, selling, making profit or being cheated. Drug culture does not undermine capitalism, but confirms its hegemonic status. In 'Der Kommissar' Falco sings "Jede Nacht hat ihren Preis" and "Hey, wanna buy some stuff, man, ha?" Something like a quarter-century later Eminem became even more precise in describing the capitalist character of a "drug scene", rapping in 'Going Through the Changes':

> Fuckin' drug dealers hang around me like "yes men",
> And they gon' do whatever I says when, I says it,
> It's in their best interest to protect their investment.
> And I just lost my fuckin' best friend, so fuck it, I guess then...

A similar attitude to drugs can be found in most rap songs tackling this subject; a famous example is 'Smoke Weed Everyday' by Snoop Dogg.

There is a similarity between the unromantic approach to drugs, revealed by Falco in his songs and that in one of the most popular 1980s/1990s books (set in the 1980s, published in the 1990s) on drugs, *Trainspotting* by Irvine Welsh. In both, the recurring motif is listing the names of drugs, as in 'Ganz Wien', where Falco sings about "Kokain und Kodein, Heroin und Mozambin". The whole of Falco's Vienna, like the whole of Welsh's Edinburgh, is on drugs so one does not stand out from the crowd by taking them. Drugs act as a social leveller and are a new tradition, enriching the old "imperial" ones, such as the winter ball season in Vienna, as stated in 'Ganz Wien':

> Ganz Wien greift auch zu Kokain
> Überhaupt in der Ballsaison
> Man sieht ganz Wien, Wien, Wien
> Ist so herrlich (h)in, (h)in, (h)in

The last line of this song is based on a word play, as "hin" means dead and "in" means being in fashion. The idea that drugs are a common denominator of society is put forward in the video to 'Mutter, der Mann mit dem Koks is da'. Its story is set in the period of the economic crisis of the 1930s and ostensibly concerns the working-class milieu of a poor mother with many children, who has no money to pay for coal needed to heat her house. However, by word play and visual means, Falco makes clear that what the poor mother is missing is not really coal but cocaine. The proletarian for Falco thus becomes a metaphor of a junkie, who can belong to any class. Unlike the reader of Leary, who gets a sense of the unique quality of drugs, the listener of Falco, like the reader of Welsh, sees drugs in their quantity, their mass, their ordinariness, their exchange value. This impression is encouraged in the video to 'Mutter, der Mann mit dem Koks is da', where the dealer brings a whole sack of "koks" – cocaine. Falco pictures a closed circuit where "koks" (cocaine) and "kohle" (money) are interchangeable, bringing all the goods one needs for living: "warmth, comfort and energy". These are basic goods, for which strive either those who are so down-trodden that they have no capacity left to seek more idealistic goals or those who believe that "warmth, comfort and energy" (all quite easy to obtain with money) are everything worth striving for.

As if to confirm that drugs are for him a matter of the mundane not the exceptional, in relation to 'Mutter, der Mann mit dem Koks is da' Falco confessed that he never experimented with drugs – he simply took them (Falco 1996). Ultimately, what is scandalous in Falco's take on drugs is that he sees nothing scandalous about them.

Falco as an auteur

In conclusion, I want to refer to a question which I addressed, albeit indirectly in this part, and which perplexes Falco's fans, even if they do not pose it this way: is Falco an *auteur* of his songs? To answer it, I will refer to two ideas of authorship, known in film studies. According to an earlier one, linked to the writings in *Cahiers du cinéma*, an *auteur* is somebody who preserves a unique style despite working in a highly regulated and commercial Hollywood film industry. S/he does so chiefly by innovating from within, perfecting and subtly changing inherited patterns, mostly by using mise-en-scène. The model *auteur*, according to this approach, is Alfred Hitchcock, as demonstrated by the classic book, written by François Truffaut (1986), which practically elevated Hitchcock to this high status. According to the second approach, prevailing today, an *auteur* is a creator of artistic cinema, who turns his back on the commercial industry and innovates without paying attention to whether s/he has any following. The model *auteur* understood in such terms is Jean-Luc Godard. My view of Falco is that we should judge him according to the criteria applied to Hitchcock rather than to Godard. If he ever was an *auteur*, and I believe he was, he was one in the straitjacket of a standard song, and always feeling great pressure, as much external as internal, to produce music that would sell. That said, among Falco's records we also find *Data de Groove*, a favourite of Falco's "hard core fans" (including myself), a work suggesting that there was a fair dose of Godard in him too.

Part III

Falco Diachronic: From Grace to Gravity

8 The 1970s: leaving the Hallucination Company behind

As with most music stars, Falco's career began early. According to his mother, he was the loudest crying baby on the maternity ward, which was a premonition of his singing career. As a toddler he was able to repeat any music he heard on the radio, thus foretelling his postmodern talent for mimicry. When he was five, a professor at the Vienna Music Academy, impressed by his perfect pitch, pronounced him a "new Amadeus", a prophecy fulfilled in the mid-1980s, where in his song, 'Rock Me Amadeus', it is suggested that by recording this song Falco metaphorically takes the baton from Mozart. Whether these early successes were decisive in Falco's choice of music as his profession is difficult to say; most likely they belong to a mythology of becoming an artist, created post factum. What is, however, almost certain, is that as a teenager he firmly set his eye on the possibility of making his living from music.

Before moving to Falco's beginnings in the 1970s, let's look at what happened in politics and music during this decade. From the first perspective the 1970s in the West constitute a watershed. During this period Keynesian order, introduced as a means to prevent a new world war, underwent a deep crisis and eventually crumbled, giving way to a new system – neoliberalism. The best known symbol of this shift is Margaret Thatcher's becoming British Prime Minister in 1979. There is, however, another, more subtle symbol of the new epoch and it pertains to Austria – awarding of the Nobel Prize in economics to one of the leading figures in neoliberal thought, Austrian Friedrich von Hayek, in 1974. Hayek was also widely known for his unwavering support of Pinochet, another important political figure in the 1970s. By and large, in the 1970s, unlike now, free-market capitalism was not so much associated with freedom as with supporting neo-fascist regimes, which in geographically distant areas (distant from Europe, at least) resurrected Nazi practices by building concentration camps and digging mass graves for political enemies.

The 1970s were also a period of greater fragmentation of the left, with the radical wing, especially in Germany and Italy, engaging in terrorist attacks. With the widening of spectrum of political voices came the loss of hierarchy of political agents and causes; they had all drowned in the cacophony of "postmodern politics". Alain Badiou, echoing Jean-François Lyotard's idea of the end of "grand narratives" (1984), describes the 1970s as a watershed, which divides "the final years of revolutionary fervour" from "the triumph of minuscule ideas" (Badiou 2007: 3). After the 1970s everything could be political, including personal choices concerning one's appearance, but nothing is just simply, unequivocally political any more. The old labels of left and right fail to capture the new reality, while the new ones still wait to be invented.

However, in Austria the political turmoil was less visible than in Germany or Britain. The 1970s was a period of stability and prosperity, symbolized by the long chancellorship of the socialist Bruno Kreisky. This Jewish good old man, old even at the beginning of his term in office, remembered the Anschluss and the Second World War, and drew from these years the same conclusions as the leaders of the West post-1945: if you don't want to have a new economic crisis, a new Hitler and a war, give people a welfare state, meaning tame the capitalist beast by not allowing the rich to be obscenely wealthy. Kreisky thus curbed capitalist excess by high taxes, expanded employee benefits, cut the working week to 40 hours, and introduced legislation providing for equality for women and language rights for Austrian Slovene and Croatian minorities. The last aspect can be seen as an attempt to revitalize the noble (from the current perspective) aspect of the Habsburg empire: multiculturalism.

A sense that in Austria time passed slower than in other European countries also concerns its popular music and youth culture, as confirmed by Falco's colleague from his band, the guitarist Peter Paul Skrepek, whom I asked to describe his country's music scene:

> Rock'n'roll or pop music hardly could be heard in Austrian radio programmes until 1967. At that time the so-called Austropop emerged and took Austria by storm. Compared to the existing music-scene (classical music, operetta, Wienerlied, traditional jazz, deutscher Schlager) it was a rough rock-oriented style, which was promoted by a new programme of Austrian public radio. The Worried Men Skiffle Group appeared in a popular TV-show [more than 15 years after the skiffle-wave had reached England]. Artists like jazz singer Marianne Mendt, The Madcaps and working-class hero Wolfgang Ambros sang in the language of the common people – and sold records. Much to the surprise of the [music] establishment the new style became very popular immediately. Although Austropop mainly was straight, simple handmade music, the studio musicians who recorded the basic tracks had a jazz background, and quite a few of them were addicted to the upcoming fusion of blues, jazz and rock. When Miles Davis served his *Bitches Brew* in Vienna's biggest concert hall, it changed almost everything: finally Black Music had found its way to central Europe.

A similar diagnosis of the Austrian music scene is offered by Michael Huber (2012), who emphasizes both international influences and the local character of Austropop. It modelled itself on Anglo-American beat and rock music, but also drew on the more local tradition of Austrian cabaret music and German *Schlagers*.

It is also worth mentioning here achievements of Austrian musicians on the international scene, most importantly those of Josef "Joe" Zawinul, who in the 1970s combined jazz with rock and world music; hence he lends himself to comparison with Falco. However, from the late 1950s Zawinul lived in the States and his impact on the Austrian pop and rock scene was minimal. If at all, Zawinul's music and career might have been for Falco a source of inspiration, rather than a direct influence.

By and large, Austria's pop and rock of the 1970s comes across as backward, and not only in relation to the English speaking world, but also West Germany, which by the time Falco started his career had Can, Tangerine Dream and Kraftwerk, labelled krautrock (Stubbs *et al.* 2009) or even Eastern European countries such as Hungary with Omega and Poland with Breakout. It is a measure of how far Hans Hölzel had to go to reach a place his contemporaries elsewhere took for granted. The sense of Austria's lagging behind in music and youth culture was the reason that Falco sought his inspiration mostly in Anglo-American music rather than the local or regional scene. It is also logical that his idol became David Bowie. This is not only because Bowie was a major pop act at the time, but also because, as Nick Stevenson observes, he instinctively understood the change in politics between the 1960s and the 1970s, from class and counter-cultural politics to postmodern identity politics.

> If the counter-culture sought to find the 'real me' that was submerged beneath the 'false needs' imposed by mainstream society, such ideas at the turn of the decade [the 1970s] were coming to look more like restriction than liberation. What, many were beginning to ask, if there were no 'real me' waiting to be discovered? (Stevenson 2006: 39).

Bowie's answer to this question was: "one can create one's self", by using a costume, make-up or even playing with one's body and changing one's gender characteristics. Such an answer was especially attractive to those who were too young to have a developed sense of the "real me" or wanted to escape it, regarding it as unattractive due to, for example, belonging to a "wrong" class or nationality, which was the case of Falco in the 1970s.

As in the case of many other stars, Falco (or rather the future Falco) spent several years waiting for the breakthrough, while polishing his skills in various jazz, rock and punk bands, most importantly Spinning Wheel, the Hallucination Company and Drahdiwaberl. With Spinning Wheel he played in fashionable Zürs and Seefeld "Tenne" during the winter season and spent the summer holidays in the number one club of Porec on the Yugoslav coast. In 1976 he travelled from Vienna to West Berlin in search of success. In Berlin he adopted his stage name Falco, inspired by the performance of East German ski jumper Falko Weißpflog. The shedding of his original name Johann Hölzel, which Falco described as too ordinary for a pop star, brings association with David Bowie, who was David Jones before he became Bowie or, in Falco's times, Madonna, who shortened her foreign-sounding name to her first name to appear more international and provocative. The change of name demonstrates that Falco, like Bowie and Madonna, did not wait passively to be manufactured by the culture industry – he was willing to manufacture himself to become "somebody" and increase his market value.

Figure 8.1: Falco with the Hallucination Company

Thanks to the fragments of amateur films from concerts, photographs and interviews of Falco's collaborators included in the documentary *Hoch wie nie*, it is possible to reconstruct an ideology of Falco's first bands and his place in them. The Hallucination Company and Drahdiwaberl were performance troupes rather than ordinary music bands and the Hallucination Company performed in small theatres. Edward Larkey describes them as "theatre rock groups" (Larkey 1993: 237–56). On film, the members of the Hallucination Company come across as a group of sleep-walkers, with painted faces and bodies, singing and playing Hindu-inspired music. Such an image evokes the hippie project of finding one's "inner child" and in this way transform the world, and pertains to fin-de-siècle Vienna, with Freud, Arthur Schnitzler, Klimt in one way or another artists of dreams. Falco is at the periphery of this project, due to merely playing guitar, rather than "hallucinating" and singing. As Simon Frith argues, voice is central to rock and pop stardom (Frith 1987: 145–46); the one who does not sing has little chance of being loved by the crowds.

While the Hallucination Company harked back to the 1960s, as conveyed by its English name, Drahdiwaberl, a band set up in 1969 by an art teacher, Stefan Weber, which Falco joined in 1978, comes across as a child of the more radical 1970s, symbolized by throwing food at the audience, a sign of the impossibility to reconcile bourgeois values (private comfort, status and family) with being on the left, as professed by, among others, Ulrike Meinhof. A difficult to pronounce "Drahdiwaberl" does not exist in official German dictionaries. It is an old Viennese slang word referring to a spinning top with a woman's face on it, literally meaning "Dreh das Weib" (spin the woman). Such a name suggests that Drahdiwaberl aimed at the local (Viennese) and niche, subcultural audience. Falco was, again, metaphorically and literally on the fringe of Weber's project. Horst Bork suggests that not only Drahdiwaberl's music was somewhat different from what Falco wanted to play, but also that Weber's antics did not suit Falco's natural sense of order. Falco's discoverer, Markus Spiegel, goes even further by saying that Falco in Drahdiwaberl looked like Alain Delon among the loony sociopaths (quoted in Mießgang 2008). It is difficult to consider these two groups as "youth", "pop" or "rock" music, or at least they are rather different from what was then considered its mainstream, confirming Skrepek's opinion about Austria's backwardness.

By contrast, Spinning Wheel made a connection with the prevailing musical trends by virtue of covering popular songs of the time, such as those by Rod Stewart, Blood, Sweat & Tears and Santana. The name Spinning Wheel, taken from a song by Blood, Sweat & Tears, was obviously English, but did not have any distinct connotation – it was bland and inoffensive, the right name to play in tourist resorts. And the band looked the part. On the photo of the group, included in Bork's biography, the members of Spinning Wheel come across as an ensemble of Falco clones: seven young men in identical neat white costumes, well-combed hair (with Falco having the slickest hair of all) and smiling enthusiastically at the camera, as if they just read Dale Carnegie's *How to Win Friends and Influence People*. All smiles and no sign of rebellion might be one reason that Spinning Wheel did not spin beyond the more luxurious end of the provincial scene. Nevertheless, in this group Falco learnt to sing, becoming the focus of the audience's attention. As Skrepek told me, quoting band member Bernhard Rabitsch, that was when Falco was chosen the guy to sing Rod Stewart's 'Do Ya Think I'm Sexy'. Touring discos made the future star very sensitive to the audience's reaction – if the audience did not dance, the tune had to be changed. Falco followed this basic rule and its versions (if the record does not sell, the next one has to be different) all his life.

Playing live in a band is a necessary condition for the rock artist to gain a certain type of cultural capital, by being recognized as an "authentic" musician, who has paid his dues and whose subsequent visibility is a result of earlier popularity with a local following (Auslander 2008: 88). Falco in this sense followed a typical career, being chosen to record by industry scouts on the basis of live performance. No doubt this capital as an "authentic musician" mattered for him most when it was questioned. It is not an accident, in my opinion, that on the sleeve of *Wiener Blut*, often described as his most manufactured, inauthentic record, we see a guitar – a symbol of both his skill and his contact with a live audience.

Although these three bands were merely stop-gaps on Falco's way to stardom, they left a trace on his performance. For example, in many of his concerts we see him not only taking to a bass, but playing with another guitarist, as if he was willing to shed his role as front man, and be one of many. As I will argue later, there is also something pitiable about Falco singing without the band. Falco's collaborators also admit that there was always a danger during concerts that Falco would do something unpredictable or offend his audience. This could be viewed as his personal trait or something he got from Weber.

For Drahdiwaberl Falco wrote his first hit, 'Ganz Wien', which led to meeting his future manager, Horst Bork, and Markus Spiegel, the chairman of the record company which signed Falco, GiG Records, two men with whom Falco would be connected for many years. If playing live was for Falco a sign of "authenticity", writing, playing and singing 'Ganz Wien' confirmed this status. Not surprisingly, this is a song which can be heard during all his concerts, as if he carried it as his badge of authenticity. 'Ganz Wien' has all the markers of an "authentic" song. As I wrote in the previous part, it is a "local" song (in the same way "rap" is local), as it references places, traditions and problems known to the performer first-hand, and it is written in German (although Falco also made an English version) and has a prolonged guitar solo, in the tradition of 1960s and 1970s rock. Musically, it is very simple, which is both a proof of the musician's talent and him being genuine – writing and singing from "his heart", as opposed to experimenting with synthetic sounds. Ironically, it is also an untypical song in Falco's career as later he would be associated with artificial sounds and staged performances.

Falco's political views from this period can hardly be reconstructed from his professional choices, as most likely he played where there was a chance to play and be paid, rather than because his political outlook coincided with that of the other players. A better source are his interviews, where he assesses these bands and his place in them. In an interview given in 1988, Falco reveals some sympathy to these bands' ideology and correctly links such projects as Drahdiwaberl to the socialist policies of Kreisky. Yet, he also describes them as political, social and cultural anachronisms and locates himself ideologically outside this formation, claiming that it was a product of a doomed generation, not least due to its death wish, which manifested itself in heroin abuse (quoted in Weissbrod 1988). Such words resonate in a wider context of the fate of the 1970s left, most importantly the deaths of the members of the Baader-Meinhof Gang. Falco, by contrast, wanted to live and be successful and there was no other way than to join the winners. The change of his image – from an egalitarian hippie with long hair, who is keen to embrace the whole world, to an elitist dandy, demanding special treatment on account of being special, is symptomatic in this context. It reflects Falco's attitude to the competing ideologies of this time and his belief, mirroring Bowie, that one can invent oneself – identity is not given. As a result of his work on self, however, as Skrepek and Martin Huber (2012) confirm, Falco became an isolated figure on the Austrian music scene.

When thinking about those who underwent a similar transformation of image in the 1970s, Tony Blair (b. 1953) comes to my mind. He also played in a rock band (albeit with less success) and sported long hair, but is best known for inventing "New Labour", a neoliberal political project, which successfully usurped the place of the mainstream left on the British political scene. This was also a route taken in the late 1970s and 1980s by some who were on the fringe of the RAF or sympathized with this organization.

In the same interview, in which he discusses the politics of Drahdiwaberl, Falco mentions that the atmosphere in which he began his career remained an important point of reference for his work and life. He might not be a pop star "with values", where "values" mean "emancipatory values", traditionally associated with the left, but at least he retained their memory. But, as I already argued, the standards of pop music idealism, as standards of authenticity, are constantly shifting. The change of Abba's status is symptomatic in this respect, from being a byword for kitsch and crude materialism, to epitomising the most genuine pop and "living for the music" rather than money. Equally, while for many people in the 1980s Falco epitomised the lack of authenticity, nowadays many people on YouTube contrast him with Justin Bieber; for them Falco stands for being natural, Bieber for a manufactured star.

9 The 1980s: the stories of Brill(i)ant(in) Brutal

While Falco's beginnings coincide with the swan song of Keynesianism, the early 1980s, when he achieved his early successes, mark the beginning of neo-liberalism. As this book is not a treaty in economic history, I will only sketch what caused this (as it turned out) profound change. An important factor was the world economic crisis of the 1970s, marked by the oil embargo following the Arab-Israeli war, property crashes worldwide and the simultaneous collapse of several financial institutions (Hobsbawm 1995: 403; Harvey 2005: 5–24; Harvey 2006: x). This crisis ultimately served the right, in many places re-labelled the New Right, to underscore its new vitality. According to the French sociologists, Luc Boltanski and Eve Chiapello in their influential book *The New Spirit of Capitalism*, the right did so by regaining some of the oppositional themes articulated by the left during the 1960s, which can be regarded as "the decade of the left". It addressed its critics, such as students complaining of alienation, by changing its structures and mode of operation, becoming open to creativity and flexibility. At the same time, the demand for greater equality and prosperity for all was thwarted by capitalist corporations and states, which withdrew from responsibility for the workers' wellbeing, in a new fashion arguing that the natural laws of economics and workers' own skills should ensure their prosperity (Boltanski and Chiapello 2005: 184) – a dogma which we are fed till now. With the new organization of the economy came a new mindset: individualistic, competitive and non-egalitarian. It is not an accident that Foucault's concept of "technologies of the self" became so widely used in the last thirty years or so. Neoliberalism is about "managing one's self" – managing stress, anger, time; it is about learning self-empowerment and self-respect. As the subtle ideologues of this order teach us, if we lose, this is not because the world became too competitive, but because some people have not learnt yet to compete effectively; some are not sufficiently "empowered".

I call the 1980s a period of "heroic neoliberalism", as at the time the system was associated with dynamism and youth. Then many young entrepreneurs and managers became millionaires almost overnight, in part due to privatization of public assets. The dogma was that everybody could be rich – if only s/he tries. Such perception was reflected in the discourse on popular music of the time. For example, the period of the greatest commercial successes of the

Pet Shop Boys, leading chronicles of 1980s mores, circa 1986–88, is described as its "imperial phase".

Optimism started to evaporate in the 1990s and disappeared in the 2000s, when there was less state property to divide and the young had to carry the brunt of perpetual crisis by suffering debt, unemployment and casual employment.

The neoliberal tide swept the whole of Europe, including the socialist East, but not with the same speed. Austria, in this respect, lagged behind Britain. When Thatcher was finishing her first term in office, Austria was still governed by Bruno Kreisky. However, by the early 1980s Kreisky came across as an anachronism, on account of his age and being in office for over ten years. Time was ripe for new, neoliberal leaders and new citizens with a new outlook and image. Falco, as I argued, fit the bill, as he decided that people like Stefan Weber were losers, and he wanted to be in with the winners. As a talented working-class child he was particularly receptive to the neoliberal ideology with its promise to "reward the best", as the prospect of spending his life on a working-class estate was not very appealing. Of course, for those talented and handsome it seems easier to escape one's class on one's own, rather than – as Marx advised – do it with the whole class.

In terms of pop and rock music, the 1980s was a period of the "new wave", "new pop", "new pop mainstream", all terms signifying an advent of postmodernism in pop music. Heterogeneity was at the core of this phenomenon, as reflected in the mixing of such styles as punk and disco, use of new electronic instruments and drawing on more diverse cultural influences, such as South American rhythms. Progressive rock, which defined the standards of taste in the 1970s, declined (Straw 1993; Covach 1997).

These stylistic changes were accompanied by structural transformations. Will Straw, discussing the American rock scene, mentions an increase in the rate of turnover of acts and records, and general intensification of the velocity of rock music and rock culture; the resurgence of the 45-rpm single and the individual song as the basic units within the marketing of rock music; and changes in the function of celebrity and performer identity within rock culture (Straw 1993: 7). The last factor is linked especially to the launch of MTV in 1981 and the fact that music video became a significant factor in selling music. Straw identifies an interesting paradox of popular music in the 1980s: while the institutions of celebrity and glamour seemed so crucial to it, the individual performer's identity was much less important as a guarantee of successful records than in earlier periods (1993: 10).

It is not difficult to locate these changes to a wider framework of neoliberalism, as they boil down to submitting pop music to the rules of capitalism to a larger extent than in earlier decades. The modus operandi of the pop music business in the 1980s coincided with or even pioneered the employment practices which became the norm in other areas of neoliberal economy. I refer here especially to the privileging of younger workers who could be paid less than older, more experienced employees (the Bowies and Jaggers of specific industries), expecting from them quick turnout of material at hand (hence problems relating to over-saturation of the market and burnout of artists) and discarding them when they stop being "hot".

The factors mentioned by Straw initially benefited Falco's international career, but also contributed to his prompt demise on the global market. His career pattern, when looked at from a global perspective, is not different from those of Culture Club, the Human League and ABC, mentioned by Straw, as in each case the successful records were followed by clear failures (1993: 10). In the case of Falco, the commercial successes of *Falco 3* and *Emotional* were followed by the flops of *Wiener Blut* and *Data de Groove*. What is different, however, is that Falco, to a greater extent than British and American stars, was a national and regional star. His expulsion from the global hall of fame meant a setback, but not the end of his career.

Let's look at the three factors listed by Straw one by one. The first element, the increased velocity of pop music, was important for Falco because it opened up a space for incomers and outsiders, even those whose principal language was not English. German artists had an extra advantage because they had a tradition of new wave before this term was coined, thanks to groups such as Can and Kraftwerk, which pioneered the use of synthesizers. Falco also benefited from the second factor, the resurgence of the 45-rpm single, because he became known to an international audience thanks to a number of catchy songs from singles. His most successful album, *Falco 3*, comes across as a collection of singles and was made according to the 1980s recipe, by following a string of successful singles. Thirdly, as I already mentioned in the previous part, Falco was physically attractive. He had a "chiselled" face, perfect, white teeth, slim body and graceful movements. Moreover, he projected a distinct screen persona, a 1980s incarnation of a dandy, wearing a tuxedo with a bow tie, sunglasses and short, gelled hair. He had the right look for the music video. In addition, from his second album he worked with Rudi Dolezal and Hannes Rossacher, the founders of DoRo Productions, regarded as the best music video makers in the German speaking countries, and some of the best in the world. He would collaborate with them till the end of his life and even, so to speak, beyond his grave. Dolezal and Rossacher invested much of their creative energy in the "Falco project"; he appeared to be their favourite child, even if in private their relationship was less rosy, because they were all both global and local artists, living in the same town and sharing the same language.

The role of the music video and MTV in shaping the music culture of the 1980s is a subject of controversy. Jack Banks argues that

> music video revitalised a troubled record industry by prompting renewed consumer interest in pop music and successfully developing several new recording acts such as Madonna, Boy George, Cyndi Lauper, and Duran Duran, who adeptly showcased their provocative visual images in this new media form. Music video has since become an indispensable means of promotion for recording artists, who are expected to have accompanying videos for their songs in order to become commercially successful (Banks 1996: 1).

For Straw the main impact of MTV was the increase in the velocity of innovation, and by the same token giving a chance to records which were unable to make the playlists of album-rock radio stations (Straw 1993: 8).

Music video initially attracted mainly bad press, because the integration of music and image was seen as a sign of art moving away from the modernist project of "shedding the ornament" and instead becoming impure again. This shift is also regarded as testimony to an increased integration of pop music into the capitalist project. E. Ann Kaplan in 1987 wrote that

> In its overall, 24-hour flow, MTV functions like one continuous ad in that nearly all of its short segments are indeed ads of one kind or another. If it is true that commercials constitute the *real* TV dramas in the case of series programs like soaps then how much true is this of a channel like Music Television that contains little else *but* ads of various kinds... MTV, more than any other television, may be said to be *about* consumption. It evokes a kind of hypnotic trance in which the spectator is suspended in a state of unsatisfied desire but forever under the illusion of *imminent* satisfaction through some kind of purchase. The desire is displaced onto the record that will embody the star's magnetism and fascination.
>
> The rock video idea was originally an advertising idea; in fact, a better name for rock videos is really "rock promos", since they are widely seen as promotional tools for the record companies (Kaplan 1987: 12–13).

Here Kaplan comes close to Adorno, pronouncing MTV as a creator of fake needs and a supplier of fake emotions. Although she does not say it overtly, for her this is not a site of art. But others, taking cue from Susan Sontag, who advocated art which "programmes sensations" and is "something" rather than "about something", argued that music videos fulfilled the Wagnerian ideal of *Gesamtkunstwerk* – a total work of art (Wollen 1986). Experiencing an unin-

terrupted stream of videos would thus be a fast track to becoming homo aes-
theticus, rather than cutting off oneself from "true art".

A sign of Falco's being not only in tune with the new times, when music
was visible again, but ripe for becoming a spokesman for its ideology, was
his behaviour at the first meeting with Horst Bork in his office in Hamburg
in 1981, after he and Markus Spiegel spotted him performing 'Ganz Wien'
with Drahdiwaberl. Bork mentions that the young man arrived in a black suit
and white hat, and brought with him a box of chocolate *Mozartkugeln* for the
ladies working in the office. He wanted to project himself as the right material for a star and a nice young man: somebody worth an investment. But
even more telling is his attitude to the two songs on his demo tape: 'Helden
von heute' and 'Der Kommissar'. Falco, correctly recognizing his place in the
order of things, but misunderstanding the way pop music works, insisted
that 'Helden von heute' would be a world hit. It is not difficult to see why he
had such faith in this song – it was a song about the ascent of a new man –
the neoliberal hero, as suggested by the title, in English "Heroes for today",
dynamic music and the lyrics:

> Wir haben den Fuß am Gas
> Und die Mode fest im Griff
> Uns entgeht kein letzter Schrei
> Unser Outfit hat den letzten Schliff
>
> (We have the foot on the gas
> And everything firmly under control
> We don't miss a single trend
> Our outfits are the newest style)

These verses are about speed, fashion and being the new heroes. Even if
such a description is tinged with a dose of irony, it is drowned in a sea of
enthusiasm and affirmation. Bork, however, was not convinced – he admitted that it was a nice song, which would do for Vienna, but world hit it would
not be and asked Falco to show him his "B" track, which was 'Der Kommissar'.
This he recognized immediately as a potential hit and he was, of course, right.
The second song proved so successful nationally and internationally, selling
over six million copies worldwide, that almost instantaneously it catapulted
Falco to the position of the No. 1 pop star coming from the German-speaking
world. Why was it the case? The reasons for successes and failures of songs
are complex and largely mysterious. Nevertheless it is fair to say 'Der Kommissar' "feels" more melodic and the rapping style comes across as more original
and quirky than the simple singing, offered by Falco in 'Helden von heute', all
things Bork understood all too well, being a professional talent scout. But they

also have to do with ideology. Pop and rock, perhaps because of their black roots, need to convey a sense of loss and yearning: of love wasted, friends gone, or at minimum of the whisky bottle emptied. Think, for example, about Bob Dylan's 'It's All Over Now, Baby Blue', which Falco would "adopt" some years later. This rule obeys even in neoliberal times, when it is particularly shameful to be a loser. But then, perhaps, we need nostalgic songs even more, to make up for what we cannot express openly in everyday life.

That 'Helden von heute' was a mis-start is visible when compared to David Bowie's song '"Heroes"' (1977), which inspired Falco's song. Bowie is one of the most mournful singers, whose big theme is finding a moment of respite from some existential anguish for people who do not fit. He dignified the condition of a freak, heightening his difference from the rest of the world by make-up, hairstyle, clothes, even by living away from England. It is not an accident that he created characters such as Ziggy Stardust and sang Brel's 'Dans le port d'Amsterdam', one of the greatest songs about temporary escape. Bowie's '"Heroes"' fits this paradigm, as he sings about those who are doomed to an eternity of unhappiness, and if they manage to steal some happiness, they are heroes for only one day. His voice sounds like a cry or an accusation. 'Helden von heute', by contrast, is cheerful by the virtue of its lyrics, music and the mode of delivery. A sense that it is too upbeat for its own good affected its video, which is not about the young hero, who has the world at his feet, but a young delinquent, a prisoner escaping from jail in a Cadillac, who most likely will be caught sooner rather than later or maybe is only dreaming about escape. In due course Falco learnt to romanticize the condition of a winner, a yuppie.

'Helden von heute' and 'Der Kommissar', as well as 'Ganz Wien', were incorporated into Falco's first solo album, *Einzelhaft*, released in 1982 and produced by Robert Ponger, who also produced Falco's next album, *Junge Roemer*. There were many advantages of bringing these two men together, as well, as it will turn out, disadvantages. Ponger was technically the most advanced music producer in Austria and – as the case of 'Der Kommissar' demonstrates – able to write hits. Bork also suggests that the two men enjoyed each other's company, as both of them were proficient in Schmäh. In addition, Ponger gave Falco's work a "local product certificate", important in the Austrian context. On the other hand, Ponger was a bit of a geek, more preoccupied with musical experiments and technical perfection than finding the right formula for a global hit.

Although by this point Falco managed to present himself to a wider audience not only through his music, but also visually, the impact of music video on Falco's career was felt only from his second record. For *Einzelhaft* few videos were made. They were of low production value and DoRo did not produce them. The video for 'Der Kommissar', in which Falco runs against a background of police cars which stay the same distance away from him throughout the duration of the song, comes across as amateurish even in the context of the early 1980s. The record gives a different image of Falco than all his later works: natural, boyish and a victim rather than a victor, reflecting the time when Falco still had fresh memories of being a drop-out and an aspiring musician rather than a star. Falco sings about the end of school, being seventeen, taking drugs somewhere in a blind alley and getting into trouble with the law. Although the title of the record is *Einzelhaft* – meaning solitary confinement – the record gives a sense of a fragile community. Songs are written in the first person singular or plural – "we are the heroes of today", "this town has nothing for you and me". The community is fragile, because it is ridden with drug-related problems, which, on the one hand, require collaboration for its members to survive (they warn each other that der "Kommissar" is approaching and too much heat leads to freezing), but on the other hand, undermine the community. Such representation brings to mind "skagboys" from *Trainspotting* by Irvine Welsh, whose main character, Renton, pronounces that "we are not friends, only pals". The difference between a friend and a pal lies in that friendship requires loyalty, while being a pal not. The songs give a sense of urgency, of being on the run. Their protagonists have to run to avoid police and death from overdose. Running, however, does not guarantee successful escape; lust for life brings a risk of death. This is not an especially original insight, but it sounded sincere, especially in Austria, where this type of pop music was undeveloped.

There are a lot of synthesizer and guitar sounds on *Einzelhaft*, and the music is put in a straitjacket of the electric LinnDrum, which at the time was very expensive, as confirmed by the fact that in Austria only Ponger had one. No wonder he used this "toy" as much as possible. The repetitive sound of the LinnDrum gives *Einzelhaft* a certain heaviness and anguish, absent from Falco's later records. Such an impression is added by the lyrics being dominated by German: this is the most German record in Falco's career and for many of his fans his most authentic.

'Der Kommissar' was the most successful song on the album and one of the biggest hits in Falco's career, subsequently covered by other artists, as well as by Falco himself. Its success is owed partly to its paradoxical relation to time. On the one hand, it is about being "here and now", as conveyed by short words, primarily verbs in the form of commands, such as "schau schau". On the other hand, there is a timelessness about it, which is not the case with Falco's later hits, such as 'Rock Me Amadeus'. The titular *Kommissar*, which can be understood as a policeman or any figure of authority, has an archaic inflection, bringing to mind *Kommissare* visiting provinces in the Habsburg times, as described by Jaroslav Hašek's *The Good Soldier Švejk*. If we replaced *Kommissar* with *Polizist* or its English equivalent, the song would lose much of its charm. Joe and Jill are names from English nursery rhymes, who never grow up. "Rappin' to the beat" is an essence of rap. "Funky friends" is an ambiguous term belonging to jazz and rap idiom; it can be translated as "cool friends" or "weird friends", perhaps also signifying drugs. 'Der Kommissar' has no clear beginning or end and thus no progression – it can be put on a loop and effectively it was treated this way in the various remixes which made a trick of adding to it extra seconds while simultaneously speeding it up.

'Auf der Flucht' and the eponymous 'Einzelhaft' also deserve attention because, albeit timidly, they introduce Falco's great theme: a "lived", mundane apocalypse. This is one reason I regard Falco as a great artist, because, although apocalypse is a frequent theme of popular music (Partridge 2012), it is presented as leading to a new state of affairs. Falco, by contrast, renders apocalypse as permanent. This catastrophe might be political or metaphysical and is, inevitably, personal too: individuals have to adjust to it. In 'Auf der Flucht' the singer refers to a riot in 1967 Berlin, which police pacified with tear gas. Such an image brings to mind the beginning of the Red Army Faction where defenceless students were shot by powerful authorities. But after that Falco transports us to 1982 Zurich, where there are no more protests, the city centre is empty and the opera house is undergoing renovation. The opera house stands for a revitalization of the past at the expense of putting effort into shaping the future as a distinctly new area. It is a metaphor for theatrical, fake, postmodern politics. How Falco came to write this song, and why he chose Zurich, remains a mystery. But it is meaningful that he identified a certain political trend, marked by the lack of political activity, deadly peace, neutrality serving the rich (Zurich is one of richest and most saturated cities in terms of museums and theatres in Europe), and linked it with the defeat of the radical left. His song thus summarizes the political and social transformation, as offered by sociologists and philosophers, such as the previously quoted Boltanski and Chiapello, David Harvey and Alain Badiou.

The song 'Einzelhaft', finishing the record, can be read as an elaboration of the sociological situation in the early 1980s: people became selfish, cruel and lonely and dependent on drugs to carry on. There is, however, no encouragement to change the world nor a warning that a Messiah will come and do the "cleaning up" for us; this world will go on forever. Such an impression is amplified by the music, which is heavy and monotonous. It is worth mentioning that in his "afterlife" Falco was adopted by representatives of the very apocalyptic style known as "industrial techno" (on apocalypse in heavy metal see Partridge 2012: x–xii; see also Part IV of this volume). The song 'Einzelhaft' can be seen as a link between Falco and this style.

In his first album Falco comes across as a spokesperson for young misfits, but its cover foretells the coming of the new Falco. The photograph presents the singer sitting in a dark room on a stool, a reference to solitary confinement. However, he does not look like a down-trodden, imprisoned junkie. Rather, in his fancy, shiny jacket and shirt and elaborate pose, and the light coming from the window, partly revealing, partly hiding his body, he comes across as a lounge lizard or a star of film noir – more Brian Ferry than David Bowie. Although many of the songs are about "us": us "the heroes" or "funky friends", the cover does not convey any sense of real or imagined community. This rule would apply to covers of all Falco's subsequent records – they show the singer in his solitary confinement.

Junge Roemer, released in 1984, is a very different record from *Einzelhaft* in terms of Falco's approach to its production, the music and its overall *Weltanschauung*. This is, because, paradoxically, "young Romans" are the more successful children of the restless runners locked in solitary confinement. *Einzelhaft* proved so successful that it emboldened the singer to create something more ambitious than a collection of new songs – his new self. As in a scheme of vulgar Marxism, Falco's economic conditions improved so much that his consciousness changed dramatically. It is worth mentioning that between the release of *Einzelhaft* and *Junge Roemer*, in 1983, the Socialists lost their majority in the Austrian parliament and Bruno Kreisky resigned as Austria's chancellor, after thirteen years in office. Symbolically, 1983 marks the beginning of the end of embedded liberalism in Austria and an advent of neoliberalism. The shift from counter-cultural *Einzelhaft* to *Junge Roemer* captures this symbolism very well.

To fulfil his Bowie-like ambition to change "Falco" into a *Gesamtkunstwerk*, as opposed to merely remain a transmitter of music, Falco turned to the best image-creators in his country, the couturier Helmut Lang and photographer Rudi Molacek. Moreover, *Junge Roemer* was integrated into a videowork, produced by DoRo. There is a video for each song and together they make up a *Falco Show*, produced by Austrian television for the Montreux Festival. Such visualization of the whole record was and remains an unusual practice, testifying to great hope invested in Falco's image as a commodity marketable across Europe.

The persona, which Falco wanted to attain, had to be ultra-cool, unattainable for the ordinary audience by being detached from the normal flow of time. The symbols of this morbid refinement are the extremely thin, hairless "sphinx" cats whom Falco strokes, sitting on the back seat of a car in the video for 'Kann es Liebe sein'; the kind of cats bred for snobs, rather than for people who simply like cats. Other objects of similar connotations used in *Falco Show* include a white Rolls Royce, in which he is driven to a casino, Roman baths, pyramids and attractive women. The cinematic references to the classics of noir, such as *Casablanca* (1942) by Michael Curtiz, *Gilda* (1946) by Charles Vidor and Federico Fellini's *La Dolce Vita* (1960) augment this effect.

Yet, we also learn that this super-cool persona is merely a mask, covering the uneventful life of a young man, a mechanic working on a scrapyard for disused planes, a janitor pretending to be a rich hotel guest or a poor emigrant from Germany, lost in New York. The rule applied by the authors of these short films, as in 'Helden von heute', is to show the luxurious life of the "new Romans", but not alienate the "common man". The overall result, compounded by the use of numerous settings (Vienna, New York, Arizona's desert, Egypt), is somewhat schizophrenic: a bit of Brian Ferry, a bit of Freddie Mercury and a drop of James Dean.

The most accomplished songs and videos are 'Junge Roemer' and 'Brillantin' Brutal'. 'Junge Roemer' successfully romanticizes the condition of a "junge Roemer" (an expression invented by Falco to describe a yuppie), trying to escape their anguish into the pleasures of clubbing and casual sex. The phrase "junge Roemer" also sends us back to the Roman Empire, which degenerated and collapsed, allegedly due to the weight of its excesses. In this sense this song is the first instalment in Falco's narrative of the crumbling empires. The use of Italian in the lyrics points to this link as well as suggesting that such restless and fragile "young Romans" are everywhere in the West. The video shows us a group of young people entering a ballroom in a palace. They look like a cross between the mimes from Michelangelo Antonioni's *Blow-up* (1966) and the characters in the Nazi orgy from Luchino Visconti's *La caduta degli dei* (*The Damned*, 1970) and other works trying to explain Nazism through theatrical performance, such as Hans-Jürgen Syberberg's *Hitler* (1977). One can also see a similarity with the New Romantic band Culture Club, with which Falco shared some ideological and musical connections. If Falco was influenced by the German queer artist, Klaus Nomi, as Markus Spiegel claims (quoted in Mießgang 2008), this is a moment when this influence can be pinpointed. Almost all the men look more like women than men, with make-up, dresses and elaborate hairstyles, conforming to the stereotypical image of decadence. Including in the scene an older obese man, who is treated as an important guest, adds to the association with Visconti's film. The character played by Falco, however, does not partake in the festivities, only observes them from a balcony, and there is nothing androgynous or decadent about his image. In his black suit, white shirt and a bow tie, he epitomizes straight, "healthy" masculinity. The overall connotation of the video is mildly homophobic. It is worth mentioning here that Falco, even if he was influenced by gay or androgynous artists, and included some queer figures in his videos, always comes across as "straight" in his performance. In 'Junge Roemer' this is attested by him leaving the palace to go for a cigarette towards the end of the video, as if in need to leave this scene of decadence and get fresh air.

'Brillantin' Brutal', in common with 'Junge Roemer', pictures a dance scene, but here dancing is no longer an escape from business, but its continuation; in dance people are still talking about "software, hardware". Dancers choose their partners according to their value, therefore every dance has its price and provides a chance to add to one's "human capital". Work and relaxation thus intermingle or rather work invades the sites of rest and pleasure. This is thus a perfect neoliberal world, where business lasts 24 hours a day and people network rather than make friends. The title of the song plays on a similarity between "brilliance" and "brilliantine", a hair-grooming product, making hair look slick and shiny, a useful accessory for a dandy. The message is that "brillantine appearance" makes people brilliant: the outside is the inside, style is content, image is reality. Such an idea is at the core of postmodern worldview and a reason why the postmodern era comes across as shallow and banal. But for apologists of postmodernism, such as Susan Sontag (1994), shallowness should be allowed, even encouraged, because it allows for experiencing the world in aesthetic terms. The figure of a dandy is a perfect incarnation of this aesthetic ideal; a dandy is a shallow man, but so seductive that we cannot resist his charm – his shallowness is better than most people's depth.

The video for the song locates 'Falco-brutal' in the black and white *Casablanca* world of a casino, to make the point that Falco incarnates an eternal type. The singer is provided with a Lauren Bacall-looking partner, with whom he dances, at whom he looks, but with whom he really does not fall in love – brillantin' brutals are too narcissistic for love. The video also includes an introduction and a coda showing that its protagonist is really a fake – he does not have the car, the money and the power he pretends to have. Yet, in this case, Falco reminds me of Rita Hayworth in *Gilda*, for whom Richard Dyer (1988) coined the term "resistance through charisma". This is because although Hayworth plays a loser in the film, she dominates it. A similar effect is achieved by Falco – it does not really matter that he is presented as a loser in the story, as he wins through the power of his performance, remaining true to the song's title.

The story of producing the album *Junge Roemer*, as presented by Horst Bork, reads like a reversal of the relationship between the artist and the culture industry, as imagined by Adorno and as showed by Peter Watkins in *Privilege*, where the industry manufactures the star against his or her deepest wishes to remain genuine. Bork and the record company did not advise Falco to shed his "authenticity". The manager, the proverbial German, from whom one is not afraid to buy a second-hand car, was even hostile to all those "gimmicks" which were meant to enhance Falco's appearance and he believes that they contributed to the record's poor sales.

The importance of style is reflected in the record's cover, which is filled with Falco photographed in medium shot, clad in a dark suit, white shirt and a bow tie and looking sideways. Light and shadow are used to sculpture his face, as if it was a shot from a film. The person on the cover comes across as inaccessible – if we are lucky, we can catch him on his journey, but he will pay no attention to us. One can see a similarity between Falco in this photo and the English actor, Rupert Everett, who also had his heyday in the 1980s, specializing then, not unlike Falco, in the roles of unattainable and cruel young men, as in *Dance with a Stranger* (1985) by Mike Newell, where he played an upper-class racing-car driver, killed by his working-class lover.

Falco was himself a "young Roman" at the time: ambitious and insecure. In Bork's opinion, he even amplified his anguish, claiming that for him only global success was true success; less than that equalled total failure. Against such inflated criteria *Junge Roemer* was a flop, although it reached No. 1 in the Austrian charts and attracted positive reviews. Falco's career might have developed differently if it was measured against more modest commercial expectations: be less spectacular, but last longer. Bork claims that Falco took full responsibility for the commercial underperformance of *Junge Roemer*, which led to a personal crisis or perhaps only deepened that which he suffered permanently until his death. To allow the artist to recuperate his strength, the manager sent him for a holiday in Thailand with his friend Billy Filanowski, while he looked for a way to revive Falco's career. He came to the conclusion that there was no future in further collaboration between Falco and Robert Ponger, whose rigid perfectionism prevented the songs (from Falco's second record) from becoming hits.

Inspired by a box of material sent by his Jewish business colleague, Frits Hirschland (of the banker's family swept away by the Nazi tide), Bork came up with the idea of merging Falco with Rob and Ferdi Bollands, the music producers from Holland, but born in South Africa. The reason was that the Bollands' music was as good as that made in London, New York or Los Angeles, but was made much closer and cheaper than in England or the United States. The Bollands had what Ponger was missing and what Falco needed to become a product marketable beyond Austria. Merging the cosmopolitan Bollands with Falco's Viennese Schmäh was effectively moving Falco to the level of Europop, which, depending on perspective, could be viewed as promotion or demotion. For the commercially oriented Bork, it was a promotion. For Markus Spiegel, the Austrian producer of Falco's first two records, it was a recipe to lose what was unique about the singer without gaining anything of true value. Both men, in a sense, proved right. Bringing together the Bollands with Falco led to the production of his most popular songs and made him a wealthy man, yet also made "Falco" a byword for "Eurotrash", a monstrous commercialism and a measure of the length Europe is prepared to go to catch up with what is worst in American pop music. For the rest of his career, as he later admitted, Falco was unable to shed "this profile, this corporate identity" (Falco 1996), this "cultural capital", to use Bourdieu's term, which he acquired at the time. There was also a personal cost. Both Beatrice Castaldi in her biography of Falco and Peter Paul Skrepek allude to the fact that Falco's success was met with hostility among fellow musicians in Austria. This is only natural: his success undermined their (local) achievements and laid bare their provinciality, even if it encouraged some (very narrow, I believe) section of the global audience to check what else originated in Austria aside from Falco and Mozart. In due course, when Falco became an ex-star, it was also the perfect tool to humiliate him.

Both Bork and Falco himself describe the singer's relation with the Bollands as strained. They never stayed in each other's company for longer than was necessary. This was not because the Bollands lowered Falco's standards. On the contrary, they alienated him because they demonstrated to Falco that one can write hits coming from, as he put it, a "flat country": having no distinct cultural heritage, spending a large chunk of their life travelling from country to a country, having no experience as live musicians, perhaps also being conventionally bourgeois. As a result, their high quality undermined Falco's musical history, of which he was proud and reduced him to a status of merely performer rather than "auteur" of songs. Bork writes with regret that Falco was unwilling to share his limelight with the Bollands and insisted on being credited as the main author of the works they created together, despite the fact that in reality the Bollands' input was larger than his. This might be attributed to Falco's narcissism and arrogance – terms often used to describe him. However, this fact might also testify to the gap between his self-perception as an "authentic artist" and his realization that what he was doing rendered him "inauthentic" or even kitsch or "trash".

The criteria of authenticity are culturally constructed and reflect a specific historical moment. In the 1980s the rootless, transnational Bollands, due to their life stories and musical influences, could still be viewed as "inauthentic", particularly by a "rooted" Austrian. Nowadays it would be less the case, due to a widespread perception of migration as a privileged, "authentic" experience of the (post)modern man (Bauman 1996). In the commercial context of pop music produced for the global audience the lack of roots can be seen as an asset, as it frees its maker from the danger of provincialism: putting too much emphasis on one's own cultural context, as opposed to what matters for the targeted audience. The production of Falco's greatest hit, 'Rock Me Amadeus', is a case in point.

The Bollands not only wrote the music for this song, but came up with an idea to capitalize on the immense popularity of Miloš Forman's film, *Amadeus*

(1984), made about Mozart, one of the best known composers in the world, and on Falco and Mozart sharing the same nationality (broadly speaking). They also gave the song its first title, 'Amadeus'. Had they cared about being perceived as local, "authentic" music makers, they might have given it a title such as 'Van Eyck', from the name of the seventeenth-century Dutch virtuoso of carillon, Jakob van Eyck, barely known outside a small circle of Dutch musicologists. But being commercially orientated cultural travellers, they cared about van Eyek less than about Mozart.

The title 'Rock Me Amadeus' awakens associations with two opposing styles in pop music. One is progressive rock, a style developed in the late 1960s and early 1970s, primarily by British rock musicians. During this period, as John Covach observes,

> groups such as King Crimson, the Moody Blues, Procol Harum, the Nice (and later Emerson, Lake, and Palmer), Gentle Giant, Genesis, Yes, Jethro Tull, Van der Graaf Generator, and Deep Purple attempted to blend late-'60s and early '70s rock and pop with elements drawn from the Western art-music tradition. This attempt to develop a kind of "concert-hall rock" – which was nevertheless still often performed in stadiums and arenas – was the result of a tendency on the part of some rockers and their fans to view rock as "listening music" (as opposed to dance music), an aesthetic trend that Wilfrid Mellers attributes to the influence of the Beatles' *Sgt Pepper's Lonely Hearts Club Band* of 1967 (Covach 1997: 3).

An ambition of this movement was to show that pop music can be placed on the same level of cultural respectability as classical music. Progressive rock attempted to achieve this goal by transporting certain features of classical music into its composing and performing style, such as extending the length of a single piece beyond the four-minute standard and using unusual instruments, such as violins and harpsichords. The second style evoked by the title is contemporary dance music, conveyed by the words "rock me" (importantly added by Falco himself), with its connotation of sex (made explicit in the video).

Although 'Rock Me Amadeus' is about Wolfgang Amadeus Mozart, it is as far from a rock symphony as a song can be, being short, dynamic and quirky, and rather than striving for musical unity, it is extremely eclectic, by syncretizing a "gothic" choir singing "Amadeus, Amadeus", which is a nod to classical music, rap, rock and a jazzy-like singing near the end of the song. Moreover, it mixes German and English lyrics. Rather than pronouncing that a pop song can be as serious as Mozart's symphony or opera, it suggests that the pieces Mozart wrote were pop music for audiences of the late eighteenth century.

Such an approach chimes with that of Forman in *Amadeus* and the best known filmmaker, specializing in films about composers, Ken Russell. This approach makes more sense to me than suggesting that Mozart's music was "serious" from the beginning, because it points to the fact that "respectability", "quality", "idealism" are granted to pop music retrospectively, through comparing it with today's "trash".

The video version mimics, amplifies and adds cohesion to the disparate musical motifs. It plays on the difference between high and low art, represented respectively by "Mozart" and "Falco". A temporal distance between these two figures is abolished by placing them in one space and associating "Mozart" with the contemporary culture of motorcycles, and "Falco" with an old culture of formal suits and coaches pulled by horses. Their cultural roles are reversed too, with "Mozart" styled as a punk, while "Falco" becomes respectable as a conductor of a choir of people dressed in rococo clothes. Both characters are played by Falco, which further obliterates their distance, suggesting that Falco is a new incarnation of Mozart, thus adding to the high status of the singer or, conversely, rendering his pretences to be regarded Amadeus's peer ridiculous, while making the centuries-old Amadeus look contemporary. Due to fast montage of Falco and Amadeus's faces they merge into "Falco-Amadeus".

The song informs us that Amadeus did not live respectably: he had debts and was a womanizer, yet everybody forgave him and worshipped him, because he had talent, "flair", style. The notion that talent and style merit special social advantages is a capitalist and specifically neoliberal idea with its cult of celebrities. The role of a celebrity is to dignify capitalism, because a celebrity comes across as somebody who became rich through the sheer power of his or her beauty and talent and is loved by those without those qualities, unlike the proverbial fat capitalist from Eisenstein's movies who, by being fat and ugly, makes capitalism look ugly too. Celebrity can be construed as a fetishized commodity, as behind their shiny, attractive surface they hide heavy investment in clothes, cosmetics, etc., hence labour and exploitation.

The song shows the allure of high, "overaccumulated" life: expensive clothes, abundance of food and free love, to which only the rich have access. To that a touch of subversion is added, in the form of a band of rockers with leather jackets and motorcycles, evoking the hippie culture of the 1960s. They carry "Falco-Amadeus" on their "subversive" vehicle, singing with their tattooed arms stretched out "Amadeus Amadeus", as if he was a kind of new Messiah, a connotation strengthened by "Amadeus" meaning the "love of God". The rockers finally join the merry crowd, consisting of ladies in rococo attire, bishops and even one black servant, giving the impression of a democratizing character of both Mozart and Falco's music. However, their images and gestures, with the stretched arms looking a bit like a Hitler salute, bring to mind also what Marx described as "lumpenproletariat" and his view that lumpenproletariat is ultimately a regressive force, easily used and dumped by their leaders (Marx 1978). That said, one probably needs to be trained in Marxist critique, to interpret the video this way.

Most likely the main inspiration of the video to 'Rock Me Amadeus' was *Mulatschag* (1982) by Drahdiwaberl, a short film documenting an eccentric performance by this group, as it juxtaposes punk culture with that of Mozart's times. The video of 'Rock Me Amadeus' also bears similarity to that of 'Junge Roemer'. Both clips were shot in a circular hall, in reality Schloss Belvedere in 'Junge Roemer' and Palais Schwarzenberg in 'Rock Me Amadeus', both in Vienna. In 'Rock Me Amadeus' Falco recycled a tuxedo he wore in 'Junge Roemer'. Both videos also depict the "high life" of those who have money. However, 'Junge Roemer' shows both beauty and ugliness of the lifestyle of the young Romans and Falco's distance towards it. For this reason it comes across as a perfect "yuppie song", as it is in the nature of a yuppie not to see himself as a typical yuppie, but rather one who is, to quote Falco, "outside-inside" this formation. 'Rock Me Amadeus' paints an image of happy decadence of the "Mozart society", with the singer fully integrated into the spectacle of the rich – he is at its very centre, a living advert for the celebrity culture. This is one reason that 'Rock Me Amadeus' feels like a happy song and it appeals to children. This is my son's (aged nine years at the time of writing) favourite Falco song, despite being exposed to almost all of the singer's works, and my attempts to brainwash him into believing that other Falco songs are better.

Many features of 'Rock Me Amadeus', such as its extreme intertextuality, obliteration of the division between high and low art and past and present, are identified as at the core of the music video genre, as argued by authors such as John Fiske (1986), Peter Wollen (1986) and Fredric Jameson (1991), who also regarded it at the time as the ultimate postmodern genre and a premonition of art to come. Its credentials as a postmodern artwork are reinforced by the fact that, according to some websites, it exists in as many as seventeen official versions, thus blurring or rendering unimportant the difference between copy and original. 'Rock Me Amadeus' has much in common with other works of a similar period, such as the film *Caravaggio* (1986) by Derek Jarman, Godard's 1980s and 1990s films and Forman's *Amadeus*. However, while postmodern-ism in the films of Jarman or Godard was seen as testimony to the high art ambitions of their authors, 'Rock Me Amadeus' was seen merely as a "novelty product", where "novelty" stands for a "kitschy avant-garde" or the "avant-garde for the masses". These terms are oxymorons; the avant-garde, as Green-berg pronounced, is the opposite of kitsch, but the need to put them together illuminates the fact that they became inadequate to capture the specificity of postmodern art.

My intention here is not to upgrade 'Rock Me Amadeus' to the status of high art, but to demonstrate that the division between high and low art is ideological and contextual rather than stylistic and intrinsic, as emphasized by Nelson Goodman. 'Rock Me Amadeus' was regarded as low art because it was perceived as a commercial product; the stylistic innovations employed in it were regarded merely as the means of attracting the most diverse audiences in a minimum amount of time, rather than a way to tell something profound. Moreover, for the majority of audiences outside Austria it was practically an anonymous product because Falco's professional past was not known and music videos functioned as advertisements rather than autonomous artworks, expressing their authors' vision. Not surprisingly, the song was compared unfavourably with other products of popular music and its postmodernism denigrated rather than celebrated, as in an article by Robert Hilburn published in *Los Angeles Times* in 1986, titled, "Here's Falco: From Vienna with Whimsy":

> Be warned: We're not dealing here with a deeply rooted response to the social issues raised by *Born in the U.S.A.* Hans Hoelzel (who took the professional name Falco from the first name of a European skier) is mostly having fun with the British and American pop music traditions that he has long enjoyed. The cartoonish "Rock Me Amadeus" is a lively, junk-food blend of everything you'd find in a week's monitoring of Top 40 radio: disco strings, synth drums, hip-hop, rap, a trace of heavy metal (Hilburn 1986).

Bruce Springsteen here epitomises "authentic rock" by virtue of being "realistic". Steve Frith compares Springsteen's songs and performance to what in cinema studies is described as a "classic realistic text" (Frith 1987: 147). Most people see "social issues" in songs such as *Born in the U.S.A.*, as in comparable products of the film industry, not because they are there (in 'Rock Me Amadeus' they are not), but because they are deployed in a more "readable" way. But in cinema and literature there are alternative versions of realism: surrealism, expressionism, Dadaism, poetic realism, etc. They came into existence due to the artists and audiences' objection to having "social issues" fed to them in too overt a way. The same rule can be identified in pop music, where we find mainstream and alternative realisms. I locate 'Rock Me Amadeus' within the alternative tradition which, as I argued earlier, was edified by Adorno by putting Kafka on the pedestal by virtue of him writing *indirectly* about capitalism or those art critics for whom the abstract paintings of Jackson Pollock or Mark Rothko are unbeatable in capturing the condition of a "modern man".

This is not the same as saying that Falco, the Bollands or Dolezal and Rossacher embarked to create 'Rock Me Amadeus' as a song "with social issues". Indeed, for Falco, as Bork attests, the problem of this song was its being too unrealistic, cosmopolitan and trivial. Rather than anticipate and welcome its global potential, Falco mourned his loss of credibility as an Austrian and Viennese artist by singing about "Amadeus from Vienna", as opposed to "Amadeus from Salzburg". The Bollands perfectly knew about the Mozart–Salzburg connection, but "Salzburg" had to be "edited out" from the story on the grounds of being too obscure for the global audience, which needs stronger signifiers and perhaps sounds too German than the simple "Wien". Salzburg was "inserted" into the extended "Salieri" version of the song, where the voice-over pronounces that "1756, Salzburg, January 27, Wolfgang Amadeus Mozart is born". However, the fact that a longer version was needed to include Salzburg in the song and that it is not part of its main body, but of the additional, "education" material, confirms my theory that the song was meant to be built of major signifiers.

Initially Falco refused to cooperate with the brothers and his manager on its production, bringing everybody involved to the verge of mental breakdown. The same story, although with more drama or comedy, was repeated when the Bollands were asked to prepare the American version of 'Rock Me Amadeus' for American listeners, the "Salieri-Mix". Their idea was for an anonymous synthesized voice to read the stages of Mozart's life, finishing in 1985, when "Austrian rock singer Falco records 'Rock Me Amadeus'". While Horst Bork regarded this idea as genial, Falco described it as a hopelessly cheap trick, suitable only for the retarded Americans, with this opinion driving the emotional Rob Bolland to solitary crying in his car. Both men were, in a sense, right. On the one hand, extending Mozart's life to 1985, when it became represented in a pop song, is an excellent fulfilment of the postmodern programme of blending the past with the present and high with low art. On the other hand, there is something camp and disrespectful in reducing Mozart's life to preparing ground for Falco's performance of 'Rock Me Amadeus'. One can thus understand the singer's outrage at the idea (even if it could massage his ego), which he saw as suitable for "retarded" or rather "immature" Americans, lacking in high culture, as opposed to Austrians, whose cultural memory was more developed. However, Falco had to put up with the Bollands' ideas and even apologize to them. He was thus reduced to the position of Steven Shorter from Watkins's *Privilege*, yet not by the totalitarian power of his superiors, but by his own realization that his commercial interests mattered to him more than his local "authenticity". It is worth mentioning that on the actual record "Salieri" is misspelled as "Solieri", which for me testifies not so much to the philistinism of people producing pop records (many academics are prone to mistakes of this kind too), as to the soundness of the Bollands' idea to omit from 'Rock Me Amadeus' any "minor signifiers", such as local names or minor facts, as they would fail to reach the global audience.[16]

'Rock Me Amadeus' is commercially the most successful German song of all time, as measured by topping the American, British and virtually all other charts in 1986. This no doubt testifies to the considerable talent of Falco, the Bollands and many other people involved in its creation and marketing. But it also points to certain structural features of pop music in the 1980s, most importantly that it was a decade of songs, not singers. A song could come from "nowhere" and climb to the top, without guaranteeing a sustained global career for its performer. 'Rock Me Amadeus's success can also be read as a "glitch in the system" of pop music, where the norm is the dominance of music performed in English. It seems that Falco understood this rule, suspecting that he would have no more global hits. Consequently, the singer never truly warmed to 'Rock Me Amadeus', believing that it overshadowed everything that he did before and after, and "flattened" his image to that of an insolent and commerce-oriented "new Amadeus". For these reasons I also would prefer to know Falco without 'Rock Me Amadeus' but, equally, I doubt I would have ever have come across his name if not for this song.

This song is the centrepiece of Falco's third record, entitled *Falco 3* (1985), released, according to the 1980s recipe, after a series of successful singles. It became the most popular and heterogeneous in Falco's career; both reasons rendering it "unworthy" in the eyes of those who judge it according to high art criteria: elitism and unity. In terms of music, we find here references to disco, rock, country music and jazz. But the songs are subjected to a specific formal discipline – most are within the standard length of 4–5 minutes and conform to the conventions of dance music. Although the record does not have a unifying theme, it is possible to divide its content into certain categories: love and sex ('Jeanny', 'Macho Macho', 'Munich Girls', 'Nothing Sweeter than Arabia'), tourism ('Vienna Calling', 'America') and colonialism and decadence ('Männer des Westens', 'America', 'Nothing Sweeter than Arabia'). The protagonist of many of them is a Western cultural tourist, who can but does not have to travel to experience foreign cultures; the type Zygmunt Bauman identified as a postmodern flâneur (Bauman 1994). He (certainly not a she) visits brothels, samples the local cuisine, reads "exotic" (maybe porno) novels in his free time, ponders on the miracles and madness of the "men of the West", but does not intervene in the world he crosses. The songs themselves are a product of "tourist gaze": they exaggerate, romanticize, idealize, homogenize and decontextualize locations, sounds and experiences (on the tourist gaze see Albers and James 1988; Wang 2000; Urry and Larsen 2011).

In comparison with his earlier records, on *Falco 3* there are more English lyrics, written, most likely by the Bollands, in "Europop English" of the type popularized by Abba. For this reason *Falco 3* disappoints as poetry work. It also contains cover versions of 'Looking For Love', renamed 'Munich Girls', originally performed by the Cars and Bob Dylan's 'It's All Over Now, Baby Blue'. Paradoxically, although understandably, these two songs Falco regarded as the most personal on the whole record. This is because he found them himself and they represent a respectable tradition: the "high shelf" of pop or rock. Falco "borrowed" 'Looking For Love' directly from the leader of the Cars, Ric Ocasek, whom he met during his trip to Thailand and hoped that it would be his next great hit. It is easy to understand why Falco fell in love with this song. It has edginess, even aggressiveness, which the majority of songs written by the Bollands are lacking, as testified by Bork's assessment that such music breaks one's ears. Moreover, its subject of (Munich) girls "looking for love" was close to Falco, who used prostitutes and perhaps needed to romanticize it, to make up for a stigma attached to such behaviour. As a tribute to women who serve men hungry for sex and company 'Munich Girls' precedes Falco's own song, 'Nachtflug'.

'It's All Over Now, Baby Blue' belongs to the most popular and ambiguous songs by Dylan. It comes across as a song about parting with a beloved woman, but in the opinion of some critics its subject is music itself. Both themes were close to Falco's heart, whose love life was marked by impermanence and who on a number of occasions mourned pop music's immateriality, contrasting it with the work of artists such as painters, whose products one can touch. Such a take on pop music renders a pop star a martyr, who sacrifices himself at an altar of ethereal production. Falco needed to create such an image, for the outside world as well as for himself, to counter the perception of him as a greedy seller of (material) records and tickets for concerts, particularly strong at the time of *Falco 3*. For this reason, he tended to finish his concerts with 'It's All Over Now, Baby Blue', as if to ask his audience to carry it and him forever in their hearts. The mournful tone of the song was amplified by Falco's slow, jazzy, "drunken" performance. It feels as if the singer cannot leave the past behind while knowing that it is all over. Finishing *Falco 3* with 'It's All Over Now, Baby Blue' proved prophetic because after that it was, in a sense, all over for Falco – he reached the peak of his career and for the rest of his life had to deal with his past success, which he was unable to match.

The lack of a distinct identity of *Falco 3* is confirmed by its bland title, which announces that it is a third record in Falco's career, and an unimaginative cover, both in some measure reflecting the fact that it was put together in haste. This is the only Falco album released during his life where there is no photograph of the singer on it, only his signature on a red background. The connotation is that there is no unifying image, or message to the record. The only element which gives it unity is Falco himself, yet reduced to a logo, to what he himself described with sarcasm as a "corporate identity".

Falco 3 was a global success, but it failed to impress critics, especially in the English press. This was in part affected by the fact that the singer got drunk during his session with the leading music journalists in Britain and offended many of them, which they revenged, writing, for example, that 'Falco achieves the rare feat of being wildly talentless and almost unbearably arrogant in the space of one record' (Quantick 1986: 18). Another example is a review in *NME*, republished on Facebook:

> It's small wonder that Tottenham's recent form has been so poor when you consider their centre-forward has been messing around in the recording studios making daft records in foreign languages. As a matter of fact I've warmed enormously to Falco (or can I call him Mark?) following a series of interviews which make Steve Sutherland sound moderate. Anybody who's rude to the *NME* can't be all bad.
>
> In the light of this extraordinary behaviour, even the foolish recent hot single 'Rock me Amadeus' can be tolerated. You might even make a case for it being a bit of a tack classic, combining the blissful opportunism of Gary Glitter and Malcolm McLaren and magically turning it into a Eurovision Paul Hardcastle. Benidorm hits always somehow sound so more acceptable in winter and assuming you were pissed enough; 'Rock me Amadeus' was just about bearable. Educational too – I never knew Mozart was a freemason.
>
> This goodwill is, however, very rapidly exhausted as Falco decimates a dozen mixing desks, raps a bit, waffles on about Munich and Vienna and gives me a rather severe migraine. It takes trash to new extremes well below sewer level and if this is album number three, it's already given me nightmares that the postman will turn up on my doorstep tomorrow morning and present me with the first two.
>
> I note with horror that poor Bob Dylan, who gets the blame for everything these days, is credited with 'It's All Over Now, Baby Blue', the track which mercifully brings the torture to an end but the maudlin garbage presented here bears no relation to any Dylan song of that title I know.

I would like to look in detail at this feat of malice as it tells volumes about the heavily guarded hierarchies in pop music, as well as about the specific circumstances of pop music and music criticism in the 1980s. First, it betrays the Englishman's outrage that a foreigner, especially from the "Hitlerland" (although this can only be guessed), dares to be rude to him. Second, the review pronounces that if the record was in a foreign language it had to be daft, because only in English can one express worthy messages. Such a claim presupposes the hegemony of English as a "non-foreign" or "native" language in every context. Of course, by labelling the language Falco uses "foreign", the author of the review betrays his own inability to speak German. The third criticism concerns the record's musical and textual heterogeneity. Heterogeneity was at the time already widely praised by postmodern literary and film critics; the high status of authors such as Salman Rushdie and directors like Jean-Luc Godard was largely to do with their ability to "falconize": mix everything with everything without worrying about creating a proverbial modernist "coherent whole". But the author of the review comes across as conservative – purity, "authenticity", realism à la Bruce Springsteen constitutes for him the positive standard. Fourthly, in his eyes the record was bad because it made one want to dance and dancing equals tacky tourism in Benidorm (Ibiza was not used in this context, most likely because it was dignified by Mick Jagger and his ilk). Fifthly, while normally a critic regards it as his or her duty to inform him- or herself about the author of the reviewed work by studying his or her earlier productions, on this occasion ignorance is presented as a virtue. This might betray the common British disrespect of German culture (perhaps revealing deep-seated jealousy), but also testifies to the fact that in the 1980s popular music was construed in the journalistic discourse as a collection of individual songs, not an expression of a specific worldview of an auteur-star, as was the case with Dylan, mentioned in the review. Such a reading is confirmed by what Bork tells about touring with Falco through the States at the peak of his career, promoting his record. Although the songs were well known, Falco remained practically anonymous: he was usually identified by journalists as "this guy from Australia".

The question arises whether Falco was in a position to overcome the structural obstacles and cultural prejudices and sustain his global career. Perhaps his manager, a man of good intuition, sensing that Madonna would survive this decade of meteoric successes, came up with the idea of putting "Falco in bed with Madonna", metaphorically speaking, by making them sing a love song in duet. But Falco, who despised American culture, perceived himself as a romantic and had a fetish for tall women, categorically refused to have anything to do with the short American "material girl". Instead, soon afterwards he agreed to a duet with a tall, European and, I dare say, no less material a girl, Brigitte Nielsen, in 'Body Next to Body', a song conveying messages not different from those of Madonna, but with less irony and undermining Falco's standing as a "cool" star.

Falco 3 was followed in quick succession by two albums, *Emotional* (1986) and *Wiener Blut* (1988). The speed with which they were released was a consequence of Falco signing a three-record deal with the large label Sire. Such a move proved financially advantageous for the artist in the short run, but its long-time effect is more difficult to judge. The negative result of this speed was over-saturation and burnout. After *Emotional*, Falco practically disappeared from the global stage, in common with the 1980s logic of discarding "hot stars" when they cooled off a bit. Perhaps it would have been better if he had given his fans more time to anticipate something new and reinvented himself.

Emotional and *Wiener Blut* followed the same recipe as *Falco 3*, but with less success. *Emotional* was an attempt to capitalize on the American success of *Falco 3* by including songs which continued, either musically or thematically, those from *Falco 3*, most importantly 'Coming Home', which is the second part of 'Jeanny', and 'Cowboyz and Indianz', which can be regarded as the follow-up to 'Männer des Westens'. Again, the songs are about real and cultural travelling: for tourism, work, colonial expansion or just to kill time. Yet, they also contain new motifs. First, the whole record comes across as a tribute to American popular culture, especially black music and film noir, in 'Emotional', 'Crime Time', and culminating in 'The Sound of Musik'. In the last song Falco not only mentions Cole Porter, James Brown and Otis Redding, the latter "sitting on the dock of the bay", but pronounces black music to be the origin of all pop music. This is a well-known fact, yet conveniently "forgotten" by white rock musicians, such as Led Zeppelin, failing to acknowledge their debt to their black predecessors (Cook 1995–96). The record is also dominated by rap; contrary to some opinions that Falco did not want to be considered as a rapper, it demonstrates that he not only embraced this style, but created his own variations of rap.

On this occasion, his rapping can be compared to the work of an off-screen narrator in noir film, commenting on what happens on screen. Another novelty is the epic dimension of some songs, most importantly 'The Sound of Musik' and 'The Kiss of Kathleen Turner', the latter which lasts about seven and a half minutes and is the longest song in Falco's career. There is an interesting combination of motifs in 'The Kiss of Kathleen Turner' and 'Crime Time', which reminds me of *Prénom Carmen* (1983) by Jean-Luc Godard, a film about a young and beautiful woman, a member of a gang which robs hotels under the cover of making low-budget films. Godard's Carmen enters the scene as a memory of her younger self – as a representation of what does not exist and perhaps never existed – an idea. The gang is a symptom of "casino capitalism", a criminal system whose rules are obscure and in which the vast majority of players lose.

'The Kiss of Kathleen Turner' also celebrates the eternal female beauty – eternal, because not real, only copied, "simulacra-nised", made available for consumers of the mass media. Such beauty is only a cover-up for the ugly world of greed and militarism, evoked by the procession of names, symbolizing man-made catastrophes, such as Hiroshima and Chernobyl. The screen persona of Kathleen Turner, one of the greatest stars of the 1980s, who acted in *Body Heat* (1981) and *Prizzi's Honor* (1985), films about killing and gambling, epitomises the intermingling of perfect beauty with utter greed and ruthlessness. In this sense she perfectly embodies neoliberal "casino capitalism" with its deadliness and timeless, "noir-ish" charm.

Juxtaposing discussion about celebrities with references to "proper" politics is a common trait in rap. In this respect 'The Kiss of Kathleen Turner' can be regarded as a predecessor and a mirror reflection of Eminem's 'Bagpipes from Baghdad' (2009). While in Falco's song musing on Kathleen Turner is revealed as a cover-up for the reflection on the crimes against humanity committed in different corners of the world, in Eminem's the expected meditation on the Iraq war turns out to be an outpouring of love and hatred for fellow singer Mariah Carey (or rather her media representation). Both rappers could be praised for a subtle transmission of (proper) political messages under the guise of supposedly trivial squabbling about celebrities or criticized for trivializing serious issues by putting them side by side with the tabloid stuff.

'Crime Time' and 'The Kiss of Kathleen Turner' are not only over average length, but come across as pieces of larger wholes, which due to the lack of adequate pop music terminology I will call "rap overtures". Rather than being bored by their length, I feel a desire to carry on, to learn more about the world sketched in these songs. This is a remarkable achievement, suggesting a new direction in Falco's work. And yet, overall, *Emotional* betrays a hesitance, a lack of direction, encapsulated by its unfortunate title, which promises what it does not deliver, because it connotes sentimentality, even kitsch, while the songs, with a few exceptions, are not sentimental. The title track is suspended between irony and seriousness, parody (by its nature critical), (neutral) pastiche or tribute and this impression is strengthened by the character of the video. It begins when Falco gets out of a limousine and literally enters the scene surrounded by a group of black musicians who provide a background for his performance, received by hysterical female fans, like the audience shown in the documentaries on the Beatles or Watkins's *Privilege*. Falco plays the star, but unlike in 'Rock Me Amadeus' the star is "Falco as Falco". He is even dressed in "Falco" – the pattern on his jacket shows a man wearing sunglasses and he is himself wearing sunglasses. We get a sense that the singer is locked in a hall of mirrors – wherever he looks, he sees his own reflection, again not unlike Eminem some years later. Falco sings that he is an "emotional man", but this appears to be only a declaration, as there is no reason to be emotional, no story moving us to tears. But maybe this is the point of the song: we do not need reasons to be emotional. Under the condition of postmodernity, affects do not need causes, signifiers can exist without the signified. Shooting the film in black and white adds to the impression of being locked in a self-reflexive world. What is black in the film is a reflection or negative of what is white there. The white sunglasses on Falco's jacket are the negative of the sunglasses he is wearing or his black T-shirt, which is a negative to the white shirts worn by the black musicians.

A similar effect is created by the background, filled by people playing instruments while standing on a chequered-patterned construction. It is difficult to say whether they are real or not, because they are reduced to silhouettes. They look like matchbox people literally locked in match boxes, unable to break their confinement and oblivious to what is going on in the neighbouring box. Instead of trying to suture the various planes of action – Falco surrounded by the black singers, the "matchbox musicians" and the hysterical audience – the video underscores their distance. Falco does not look at the audience, as if singing for himself; the audience comes from another film, and the background musicians communicate only with their partners from the same box. It feels like a perfect illustration of Terry Eagleton's summary of postmodern art: "If art no longer reflects it is not because it seeks to change the world rather than mimic it, but because there is no truth there to be reflected, no reality which is not itself already image, spectacle, simulacrum, gratuitous fiction" (Eagleton 1992: 93).

The sense of unreality and disconnection culminates in the ending of the video, when the light is switched off so the background goes black, and we see only Falco moving in the background. The huge neon-lit letters "FALCO", a reference to one of Elvis Presley's records, are moved to the foreground, and Falco, reduced to matchbox size, eventually perches among them. It is difficult to find a more economic and touristy way to convey the simulacra character of pop music and perhaps life under late capitalism, with its sense of dislocation and unreality. The ending of the video comes across as a metaphor of Falco's status at the time he made this record – of a man who became thwarted by his name and tried to break free from the confines of the industry. Meaningfully, the image of Falco rendered minute by his name was also used for the cover of the record, as an ominous sign of Falco's subsequent struggle to break free from his image and become three-dimensional again.

There is, however, a different way to interpret the "emotional" of 'Emotional', as referring to the power of music to affect our emotions. Such interpretation is encouraged by the wealth of references to music in the mise-en-scène of the video and the lyrics, which play on the double meaning of "soul": as both the reason why we are emotional and the musical style. Such an interpretation is supported by the subject of the biggest hit of the record, 'The Sound of

Musik': music as a universal language, cultural leveller and an object of world-wide affection. "Sei es Rock, Punk, Heavy Metal, Politics or Classical, it's all Musik to me", sings Falco. Popular songs are, of course, awash with such messages, an example being 'Thank You for the Music' by Abba.

'The Sound of Musik' offers a musical equivalent of Noah's Arc, as if the challenge for its authors was to squeeze the maximum amount of references to different styles of music into a four-minute song. Evoked are soul, rock, punk, classical music, and specific songs, such as Otis Redding's 'Sitting on the Dock of the Bay' and Falco's own 'Rock Me Amadeus'. Such an approach can be compared to what Josh Kun labels "audiotopia", borrowing from Michel Foucault's concept of heterotopia understood as a juxtaposition of several spaces, several sites that are themselves incompatible (Foucault 1998; Kun 2005: 23). Kun regards audiotopia as an enacted, real, livid, utopian space created by hybridizing different types of music and musical traditions in opposition to privileging one type of music linked to nation-building (Kun 2005: 23–4). It can be suggested that such a programme was also close to Falco's heart.

Yet, the principal hypotext to this hypertext, as indicated by the title of the song, is *The Sound of Music*, the famous musical known to most people from its cinematic version, directed in 1965 by Robert Wise, with Julie Andrews and Christopher Plummer in the main parts. Wise's *The Sound of Music* concerns Maria, a young Austrian nun travelling to the house of a rich widower, Captain von Trapp, to be the governess of his seven children and eventually his wife. The dashing Captain does not want to hang the Nazi flag even after the Anschluss in 1938 and on every step he defines Austrian identity by its difference from Hitler's ideas. Although the content of the film is Austrian, its form is American, as the dialogues and songs are in English, its generic form is a Broadway musical (in its theatrical incarnation) and a Hollywood musical (in the cinematic one). Wise's film thus connects Austrian culture with American, while offering a robust rejection of Nazism and an affirmation of Austrian nationalism, understood as distancing itself from Hitler's pan-German project.

Austrian and American were also the cultures which Falco attempted to bridge in his career and especially during the period of making and promoting *Emotional*. In this sense 'The Sound of Musik' mirrors Wise's film. However, his work is different in that it not only bypasses the question of Austrian–German difference, but suggests that Austria and Germany are practically the same thing; ironically as Hitler pronounced during the Anschluss. Falco's 'The Sound of Musik' is also (as is the case with videos), more condensed and "touristy" than its hypotext, preserving from it only the setting in the Alps and the idea that music overcomes all divisions and "softens" the hardest of men.

It changes the main character in the video from the Austrian nun to Falco, who in the first scene emerges from the waves in royal costume, like a cross between Aphrodite and King Ludwig II of Bavaria. This connotation is confirmed by the sound of Wagner, opening the song and a brief image of Schloss Neuschwanstein, the most famous of Ludwig's castles. In common with Falco as Amadeus, Falco's Ludwig is an exaggerated and updated Ludwig thanks to a ridiculous hairstyle and sunglasses. Like in 'Rock Me Amadeus', Falco also immediately transforms into a man in a tuxedo, who with his typical self-confidence moves forward, passing people in Bavarian and American costumes and even a man in a kilt (played by Gerd Plez from a West Berlin band Hong Kong Syndicat). Then miraculously Falco is transported to the world of Western subcultures, where he meets punks, hippies and skinheads, all in one space, a metaphor of popular music in the 1980s, which in a populist gesture absorbed and hybridized different styles. Similarly, in the Bavarian part of the video, Falco comes across as a flâneur: he is in the crowd, but not of the crowd, which is conveyed by his mock-Habsburg red jacket. Falco's march through epochs culminates in a party in a large dance hall (in reality Vienna town hall), where people from different epochs and planes of action dance with each other. The two most prominent characters in this episode are Falco and Helmut Zilk, the mayor of Vienna, standing on opposing sides of the hall. The latter behaves like a cross between a dancer and conductor who, however, is not in control of the spectacle. Zilk, who came from a Bohemian family and had a colourful life, including surviving an assassination attempt and being accused of spying for communist Czechoslovakia, can be regarded as a symbol of Habsburg culture. His meeting with Falco in a video-world, as well as, on numerous occasions, in reality, renders Falco as an heir of this eclectic, eternally postmodern culture.

And yet, the mood finishing the video is not cheerful but ominous, even morbid. One reason is that everything here is out of proportion. Several women have over-ripe bodies with large breasts jumping out of their corsets, men are overweight, costumes are outrageous. There are also numerous references to Venice carnival, with faces being covered by masks and huge metronomes. In a quick shot we see a man being pushed off a wheelchair and somebody on the verge of losing consciousness. The people appear less celebrating than desperately trying to escape something horrific. The clear cinematic reference point is the work of Luchino Visconti, the most celebrated European *matteur of decadence*, who made the film *Ludwig* (1972), as well as *Death in Venice* (1971). In such a world music serves merely as a palliative, allowing for temporary escape, which concurs with Falco's view on the role of music, as pronounced in interviews. Falco's audiotopia is thus very fragile and most likely leads to catastrophe.

It is a paradox that after achieving his greatest successes as a rapper and especially after his virtuoso rap performance in 'The Sound of Musik', Falco's next record was made according to a specific recipe: less rap, more melody, closer to the mainstream. The result was, however, the opposite – an album which was born in pain, marked by a conflict with the record company, which rejected the majority of material provided by the first team of producers, Guenther Mende and Candy Derouge, and Falco's humiliating return to the Bollands, who filled out the gaps with previously discarded songs. The record, entitled *Wiener Blut*, damaged Falco's career.

Wiener Blut was meant to be called *Aya*, from the last three letters of "Himalaya", a reference to one of its songs and, perhaps, Steely Dan's album, *Aja*. Such a title suggests a hippie paradise, achieved either by literal travel to India or, as Bauman calls it, postmodern fânerie, for example going to a shopping mall. The best known example of a musician who attempted to reach hippie heaven was George Harrison, who befriended an Indian guru and popularized the sitar in Western pop music. Falco, in a postmodern fashion, did not want to go as far. If anything, India was meant to be only an echo, as suggested by using only the ending of the word "Himalaya". But even this echo was reduced to an echo of an echo as the record did not materialize and the one which came in its place bears witness to different influences. 'Sand am Himalaya' concerns travels undertaken through drugs, dreams, maybe psychoanalysis, as Freud is mentioned in the lyrics. The main point is that the travels are ultimately impossible, as we are searching for the wrong things: "sand in Himalaya" and "snow on Playa". The music, which in an exaggerated manner invokes "Harrison's India", underscores the ironic message.

The first track, which provided the title of the album, was written during the time of *Falco 3*. It harks back to this period by using the word "Vienna" in the title, bringing to mind 'Vienna Calling' and 'Rock Me Amadeus'. In common with 'Rock Me Amadeus' it evokes Austrian music tradition, as 'Wiener Blut' is also the title of an operetta of Johann Strauss. The lyrics point to Viennese high society being in fact a form of mafia capitalism, marked by illegal deals and prostitution. There is a specific reference to Club 45, an exclusive male club set up in 1973 and attended by the high officials of the Austrian Socialist Party (SPÖ), which became the hotbed of nepotism and corruption in Austrian politics and business. Among the people who attended the club was Udo Proksch, the man behind the sinking of the ship *Lucona* in 1977 as a result of an explosion of a bomb in the Indian Ocean, with six fatalities. This was part of of an insurance fraud – Proksch hoped to collect the insurance worth $20 million following the sinking of *Lucona*, but in 1991 was convicted of murder. With him sunk several prominent Austrian ministers.

Falco wrote the lyrics to 'Wiener Blut' before the full story of *Lucona* was revealed and he does not refer to it specifically, but we get from the text a sense that in contemporary Austria, not unlike in the Habsburg monarchy, business, politics and crime come together. As a shorthand for this connection serve images of people playing roulette, prison walls and prison guards, a mortuary, people in Billa clothes (Billa being the largest supermarket chain originating in Austria), a hall where a politician addresses his followers and suitcases full of money. The spaces of these activities overlap. The casino where people play roulette is in a prison; the hall, where politicians work or the club, where they meet, arises from the prison and leads back to it and a money-laundering operation takes place on a building site. Everywhere we see beautiful women who can be regarded as prostitutes, as suggested by references to the "Gürtel" and the "Prater" (respectively a street and a park in Vienna notorious for prostitution). Not only different spaces, but also different temporal orders merge, as suggested by Falco walking through prison corridors in the suit of Napoleon.

Such blending of spaces is typical in music videos and especially in Falco's work, as I showed in my discussion of 'Rock Me Amadeus', but on this occasion it also points to the porous border between the activities and institutions which should be kept separate: politics and business, politics and prostitution, legal and illegal work. Yet, they are not, because, as Falco suggests, the story concerns Vienna – the Viennese have in their blood a belief that it is acceptable and advantageous to cross otherwise strict boundaries. "Wiener Blut" might also be the name of a criminal syndicate, as suggested in an episode where a dead man lying in a mortuary has to his foot attached a tag with the phrase.

In the video Falco navigates between several interconnected spaces, repeating the scenario from 'Rock Me Amadeus' and 'The Sound of Musik'. He walks through a prison corridor in the costume of Napoleon, plays roulette in a prison casino, addresses a group of listeners, as if he was a politician, and finds himself in an open space, behind a car boot where some dodgy deal is being made. Wherever he goes, he is chased by journalists and photographers, as if he was a public figure. As one reader of YouTube observed, Falco looks like a "Yugo gangster", of which signs are sunglasses, shiny clothes, gold jewellery and excessively gelled hair. The singer appropriated such an image on previous occasions, but this time it is heightened and treated with irony, as proved by him wearing ties in the shape of a dead fish. A sign that Falco is both in this world and outside it is him eventually breaking free and joining his (real) wife and child, with whom he poses for the photographers. The last time we see Falco in the video is when he is playing a golden guitar, which – as he mentioned in an interview published in relation to this event – is a symbol of him remaining a musician, as opposed to being merely a celebrity (Falco 1988), although the guitar is meaningfully placed at some distance from the tired-looking Falco. Art and family thus become a refuge from the corrupt world, in the way it is advocated in postmodern discourses.

The video includes an introduction and a coda. In the introduction we see blood poured on a group of angels sitting at a long table. At the end there is more blood poured on them but eventually the process is reversed and the angels become white again. These scenes were inspired by the work of the Austrian performance artist, Hermann Nitsch, whose work Falco admired and collected. In his performances Nitsch used mutilated corpses of animals, to ponder on the idea of sacrifice. Politics, no doubt, is awash with scapegoats, as well as being an arena where people try to present themselves as "whiter" than they really are. The image of angels covered with blood, and then returning to their pure whiteness, succinctly thematizes this concept. The effect of the video is not so much of reducing a complex narrative to its touristy representation, as conveying something which can only be alluded to, as in gossip. The meaning of the lyrics of 'Wiener Blut' is difficult to grasp even for those with a good command of German (on its analysis see Ernst 2010: 129–31).

Ironically, this song, in which Falco attacked the Austrian establishment, was recorded at a time when Falco himself became close to it. The singer's thirtieth birthday, celebrated in "Café Havelka", was attended by representatives of Viennese political and business elites, including the previously mentioned mayor of Vienna, Helmut Zilk and Chancellor Franz Vranitzky, himself a member of Club 45, and ex-Formula I driver, Niki Lauda. Watching the video of this event, which begins with Falco giving his autograph to some young fans, before disappearing behind a closed door, I cannot help but think about the way exclusive clubs, including Club 45, work, in Austria and elsewhere. In his speech, following the receipt of numerous Pop Amadeuses, the Austrian awards for greatest achievements in the music business, Falco emphasized his contribution to the Austrian economy and his role in changing the image of Austria which would help his country to do more business with the rest of the world. One could thus observe a perfect fit between Falco's self-perception as a precious commodity and an advert for other commodities and the way Vranitzky and others wanted to see him. Inevitably, when Falco's value as a commodity decreased, his self-perception changed. In this context *Wiener Blut* can be seen as a watershed.

Another song furnished with a video is 'Satellite to Satellite'. It shows tourist attractions of New York, such as the Statue of Liberty and skyscrapers. Many images are tilted, recalling *Blade Runner* (1982) by Ridley Scott, and by the same token Fritz Lang's *Metropolis* (1927), which was a major inspiration for Scott. As in *Blade Runner*, the surfaces of skyscrapers serve as mirrors and screens reflecting and projecting the reality, in this case an over-sized image of Falco, to be multiplied and transported using advanced (satellite) technologies. The fact that the video is in black and white, with only occasional patches of colour, can be seen as a tribute to the black and white film by Lang.

The touristy exteriors are juxtaposed with images of the interiors, where Falco dances against a background of other dancers. The place comes across as merely a multi-functional club with some dance space, rather than a proper dance hall, as in 'The Sound of Musik'. Like in a port city, we see sailors dancing passionately with scantily-clad women, an image bringing to mind Fassbinder's *Querelle* (1982). In this place Falco is merely a tourist, trying to find a place for himself among the couples oblivious to his presence, a metaphor for the way he was seen (or rather not seen) in America for most of his career. His look comes across as an imitation of an American style. The clearest sign of this is his richly decorated denim jacket with "Texas" written on the back. One would like to think that such a costume constitutes what Susan Sontag describes as "deliberate camp", but most likely it was not the case. Falco, like many Europeans who relocated to the States, adopted such "late Elvis Presley" style without critical distance. We can see him in it on his private photographs and he even sported it on his wedding day, fittingly taking place in Las Vegas, with his wife wearing a similar outfit. Falco from the period of *Wiener Blut*, in his desire to be fashionable, with his carefully tended hair, his 1980s glasses, aged more than his incarnations from any other period.

'Satellite to Satellite' foretells the album *Data de Groove*. The lyrics are about the opportunities and dangers of a mediated, long-distance love. The robotic movements of the singer at the beginning of the song and his over-sized image on the sky-scraper introduce us to a world where simulacra reigns and reality shrinks. Yet, compared to the extravaganza of Falco's earlier productions and visual sophistication of *Data de Groove*, the video gives the impression of being made on a shoestring budget and in a hurry, reflecting the haste of putting the record together.

Although one of the most eclectic in Falco's career in terms of topics covered, musical style and the quality of tracks, *Wiener Blut* reveals some common traits. One is Falco's voice being drowned by the music, even reduced to an echo. As a result the specific "colour" of Falco's voice is lost. Some songs, such as 'Untouchable' and 'Garbo', were written without any input from Falco and it feels like some tracks, especially 'Falco Rides Again', were made even without using his voice; the producers only used his signature to add value to their work. Paradoxically, but typically for Falco, the most "falconized" song on *Wiener Blut* is his cover version of Steely Dan's 'Do It Again'. It was not Falco's original idea to use this song, but he had it in his repertoire when working with Spinning Wheel and he himself produced it. Steely Dan is the rare case of a group which retained its rock/high art status despite limiting itself to studio work; it even dignified studio work as a kind of artistic experiment, which cannot be achieved in concert (Auslander 2008: 89). It could be suggested that Falco attempted to follow their example.

Another feature of the record is laughter. We hear Falco laughing in practically every song, which would be also the norm on Eminem's records. Laughter adds to rap's ambition to capture all noises surrounding city dwellers and through that reflect all aspects of human behaviour, rather than refining the soundscape to some privileged elements. Falco's laughter is not that of joy, but rather of cynical wisdom, even sneer, as when one's worst premonitions are fulfilled and nothing can be done, because things need to run their course. It conveys what I described previously as a "lived apocalypse". 'Do It Again', which is a story of repeated defeat and defiance, shows it very well.

Wiener Blut is Falco's last album from the 1980s, but the description of his career would be very limited without looking at his performance, and especially at what he did with his body, during his concerts, interviews and in videos. Two words which come to my mind to describe his style of performance are "power" and "grace", with the first description suitable especially for his videos, the second to his live performances. In videos we see him frequently walking or dancing between crowds of onlookers and on such occasions the upper part of his body is way ahead of his legs as if he would not tolerate any resistance to his progression. No doubt such movement added to his reputation as being arrogant, which was his 1980s trademark. One can draw a parallel with the movements of Freddie Mercury, perhaps reflecting the fact that DoRo produced some of Queen's videos. Clothes add to Falco's sense of power. The 1980s was a decade of oversized shoulder pads, symbolizing neoliberalism in its heroic, self-confident period; they came to the streets from the television series about ultra-rich tycoons and their feuding wives, such as *Dynasty*. Falco was not immune to such trends. His famous black tuxedo, in which he sang 'Junge Roemer' and 'Rock Me Amadeus', make his arms appear wider than they were.

In a number of videos and concert performances for his 1980s songs such as 'Rock Me Amadeus' and 'Vienna Calling' the vocalized "Oh Oh Oh" or "Cha Cha Cha" are accompanied by Falco's gesturing with his index fingers, which are followed by strong accords and, on occasion, by a change of scenery. The impression is of a wizard able to conjure for us a whole magical world, not just music. Such vocalizes, accords and gestures would practically disappear from Falco's 1990s performances. When the singer was obliged to repeat them, as in his performances of 'Der Kommissar', they looked somewhat out of place, as if done by a wizard no longer able to repeat his tricks.

Figure 9.1: Falco at the peak of his success in 1985

How to locate Falco's manner of dancing against the styles matching his way of singing: rap and disco? It has certainly little in common with hip hop dance as defined in such terms:

> Hip hop dance permits and encourages a public (and private) male
> bonding that simultaneously protects the participants from and
> presents a challenge to the racist society that marginalized them.
> This dance is not necessarily observer friendly; its movement estab-
> lishes immediate external boundaries while enacting an aggres-
> sive self-definition. Hip hop's outwardly aggressive postures and
> gestures seem to contain and channel the dancer's rage (Hazzard-
> Donald 1996: 228).

Falco's dance comes across as the opposite of this attitude – he appears to
be at ease with his audience and the camera, as if knowing that they are in love
with him. In this respect, his dance comes close to disco, which Hazzard-Donald
describes as "the apolitical, slick dance ... [that] gave voice to a newly empowered
economic strata, the yuppie, and the midlevel service worker" (1996: 224). It
reflects Falco's pop star capital, his willing to woo the audience, although simultaneously maintaining a distance from his fans. That said, there are moments
when the artist performed a "dandy rap", as at the Festival of Europe des Cultures in 1983, where he sang and danced 'Der Kommissar'. Dressed immacu-
lately in a tuxedo, with his smooth, short hair, he moved gracefully, yet froze
from time to time in an accented mock-rap pose, as if he was willing to pre-
empt criticism that he was a fake rapper, by being ostentatiously so. Paradoxically, in such moments he came across as most authentic, due to being most
daring in defining his own standard of performance. He can be compared here
to a drag queen, who, aware that he will not be taken for a real woman, does
not behave like a real woman, but a drag queen. In such moments one can see
a similarity between Falco and Bowie, because Falco, like Bowie, moved away
from the idea that a pop artist needed to be "authentic"; instead he marketed
himself as being "artificial" (Frith 1987: 147; Stevenson 2006).

During the period of his greatest success, Falco also frequently appeared
on television, according to Bork, often with a sense of unease, resulting from
his realization that the image which he was expected to project did not accord
with his self-image. Falco's strategy was conveying a sense of being "inside
and outside", to quote his song, playing along but with a sense of only playing rather than being himself. One example is his performance with a singer
and television personality of an earlier generation, Peter Alexander. Falco proposed to the television audience his cover of Peter Alexander's hit, 'Hier ist ein
Mensch' and with Alexander sang fragments of various hits from the 1960s
and 1970s. What one gets from Falco's version of 'Hier ist ein Mensch', as
opposed to his cover of, for example, 'Do It Again', is that he did not attempt
to make it his own. On the contrary, he emphasized that this song belongs to
a different man and a different culture, which he treated with respect, but was
unable to embrace.

Another example worth mentioning is his singing 'The Girl from Ipanema' by Antonio Carlos Jobim on a television show in a duet with the black jazz singer Marjorie Barnes. Rather than trying to compete with Barnes, he conceded that the host of the show, Alfred Biolek, put him in a "tacky situation" and the problem for him in singing in duos is that his partners can actually sing. This can be regarded as a straightforward admission that he is inferior to his singing partners or a subtle way of pronouncing that he represents a genre, which demands different skills – not singing, but, perhaps, rapping, or not jazz, but pop. Falco allowed Barnes to lead, limiting his role to that of singing the chorus and adding a touch of German rap to her performance. In this way he came across as an old style gentleman, who understands that the roles of women and men are different and a friendly observer, rather than co-participant. And yet, looking at the performance from a distance makes one realize that during such cultural travelling, to which he was coerced by the culture industry, Falco developed interests which some years later resulted in songs which sounded 100 per cent "falconisch". The aforementioned 'The Girl from Ipanema' can be seen or rather heard as an introduction to his bossa nova number, 'Bar Minor 7/11 (Jeanny Dry)'.

What was the overall effect of pairing Falco with the representatives of "lighter", "gentler" styles than rap or rock? They made him look gentler: a "family guy", able to entertain a nostalgic granny as well as her teenage grandson. Such an image contrasts with the stereotype of an aggressive, uncompromising, swearing rapper or rocker, rendering Falco a pop performer, as pop is family entertainment (Frith 2001). Falco's take on different musical traditions evokes the concept of "world music", which, like "world cinema", comes across as depoliticized art, whose purpose is to attract cultural tourists by peddling local specialities to anybody who wants to buy them. Fittingly, Philip Bohlman in his discussion of "world music", underscores its commercial character, evoking the idea of shopping arcades, as elaborated by Walter Benjamin and Charles Baudelaire (Bohlman 2002: 133–37). Under these shopping arcades third world music is "appropriated" or "exported" for first world consumption. But if we agree that rap is a quintessential postmodern art thanks to its incessant sampling, stealing and reworking of what was done previously, and offering us the sounds of the global city, then Falco's flirting with different musical traditions made him more of a rapper than the majority of mainstream representatives of this style.

In addition to appearing on television, mimicking the careers of some of his idols, Elvis Presley and David Bowie, Falco also played in two films: *Der Formel Eins Film* (1985) by Wolfgang Büld, which can be translated as *Top of the Pops Film* and *Geld oder Leber!* (1986) by Dieter Pröttel, which means "Money or Liver", where German "liver" (Leber) sounds almost like "life" (Leben). I limit myself to the first, as in both Falco plays practically the same role of a star, met by the female lead. The first film has a thin narrative about a young female car mechanic named Tina, played by Sissy Ketting (who despite her star quality did not make another film), trying to become a pop star. On the road to success Tina joins *Formel Eins*, a German version of *Top of the Pops*, where she encounters Meat Loaf, Pia Zadora, the German punk group die Toten Hosen and, of course, Falco. Falco got more screen time than the other stars and a bit of the story, which can be viewed as a reflection of his high status at the time. As one reviewer observed, his part is the high point of the film (Hannes' Filmarchive 2010), despite the fact that in the episode with Falco the scriptwriters merely recycled the situation from the video to "Brillantin' Brutal".

Tina meets Falco outside the airport in order to bring him to the studio. They do not go there in a normal car, but in Falco's white Cadillac, where the star tells the pretty girl about his recent concerts, where he was greeted with euphoria by thousands of fans. In his self-centredness and arrogance he is different from the other stars of the film, who pay more attention to Tina and even promise to help in her career. The car is full of gadgets, which, however, during their journey cause more problems than pleasure. The critical point is reached when the car breaks down in heavy rain. Falco, standing in tennis shoes in a puddle, tries to get into a taxi, telling the taxi-driver that he is "Falco, der Kommissar", but the taxi driver ignores him. At this moment Tina, taking advantage of her skills as a car mechanic, is patiently mending his car. Eventually they arrive at the studio, where Falco sings 'Rock Me Amadeus', taking this song, already camp in its original version, to the extremes of camp, as he parodies his own performance, immortalized in the video. Every step he takes, every gesture he makes, every face he pulls looks like a re-presentation of a familiar step and gesture. Inevitably, we also get a sense of fatigue, of being blasé, as there is nothing exciting in doing the same routine for the hundredth time.

In this film Falco plays a pop star who plays a pop star – spoilt, narcissistic to the point of autism and representing a star-persona, a "logo", rather than any "three-dimensional" character with a musical talent and a unique story to tell. If in the 1980s "authentic" meant to be self-consciously artificial, quoting oneself quoting a non-existing original, then Falco in this film epitomises this "decade of performance". Watching this film now I cannot help but think about the mountain this young man had later to climb to prove that he could be somebody else – a "serious" artist rather than "multi-storey-camper".

In 1988 Falco's career collapsed, of which the clearest signs were poor sales of *Wiener Blut* and a called-off concert tour, due to lack of interest. Precise reasons for such a downturn of his career are impossible to identify. Bork points to Falco's systematic spoiling of career opportunities and his personal problems, such as the collapse of his marriage and dependence on alcohol and drugs; problems pertaining to a burnout. They were exacerbated by the fact that Falco's life was literally fragmented, with family in Austria, music producers in Holland, business negotiations in the U.S. and Britain and the largest concert tour in Japan. Such a lifestyle would become the norm fifteen or twenty years later, when the advance of neoliberal capitalism would transform millions into itinerary workers. But this would be coupled with advances in technology, alleviating some of the negative aspects of this transformation, which Falco in the 1980s could not enjoy. Another reason for the end of Falco's international career, perhaps more important, is structural. As Will Straw (1993) observes, the 1980s was a decade of great velocity in pop: stars came and went as if on a rollercoaster. Falco was one of such international stars, such as the Human League or Culture Club, pushed aside by a tide of new stars, representing new styles.

After *Wiener Blut* Falco's public image changed – he started to be perceived as a provincial, kitschy version of his old self, unable to propose new trends. Such a "wrong", but strong, image is worse than having no image – it is, to paraphrase Pierre Bourdieu's term, "negative cultural capital". Many Falco fans, even in his own country, deserted him, disowning not only his new record but also his entire oeuvre because he connoted for them badly located emotional investment. However, some of these fans, at least in his native country, returned in the subsequent decade, because he remained there the only star worth its name.

As a consequence of his collapse as an artist and a man, Falco found himself in a "sanatorium", a polite way to describe a psychiatric hospital, which he eventually left, to attempt to regain lost ground. Falco's trajectory mimics that of the Western economy – after the self-confident "heroic" period of neoliberalism, with its conviction that the higher the growth, the greater the speed, the richer the rich, the better for everybody, came a crisis, which in due course was alleviated, but never overcome and kept returning. In due course the singer, with his typical sharpness, realized that big success for him really equalled failure, because nothing passes as fast, nothing diminishes so much any future achievements and nothing leaves as many negative side-effects as great success. As in a Marxist scheme, over-accumulation in one place, the period 1985–88, produced a deficit elsewhere, in the remaining part of Falco's life.

10 The 1990s: return to monarchy

In the 1990s neoliberalism continued its successful march through the world. In Europe it meant co-opting into this system Eastern Europe, which was heralded as "catching up" with the West; in the West radicalization of neoliberal policies by, for example, the financialization of higher education and the health service. The speed of this march was uneven. It was faster in Britain than France, in Estonia than Slovakia. However, everywhere the consequences of neoliberalization were the concentration of income and wealth in the upper echelons of society and the concentration of poverty and insecurity at the bottom. This phenomenon was accompanied by a decline in political and economic sovereignty of nation-states, especially the weaker ones. The "surplus of sovereignty", so to speak, was transferred to an amorphous body that Harvey (2005) describes as "neoliberal elites" and Michael Hardt and Antonio Negri (2000, 2005) label "Empire". Hardt and Negri's term gained popularity in the last decade and not without reason, as it adequately captures the return to the times of colonies, masters and slaves, when the majority of the population is subjugated to the decisions of the capitalist class and aligned to them nondemocratic and secretive institutions, such as the International Monetary Fund and the World Bank, which use "remote control" to avoid confrontation with the disaffected masses. The time of "Empire" means, among other things, that success on the national scale is much less a success than it used to be in the "pre-Empire" period, a fact of crucial importance for Falco's career in the 1990s.

"Empire" and similar terms, such as "monarchy" and "kingdom", frequently appear in Falco's lyrics of the 1990s and they have similar connotations to those in Negri's books: they come across as shady, opaque, impossible to capture, yet omnipresent and powerful entities, controlling allegedly free citizens. This might be regarded as a pure coincidence, but I view it as a sign of sharing a sensibility with authors such as Negri, whose work contains a fair dose of apocalyptic thought.

As mentioned in the previous chapter, in the late 1980s Falco's career declined. After a period of recovering his physical and mental health Falco attempted to regain the lost ground professionally and not only catch up with the newest trends but be ahead of the game in pop music. In 1990 Falco again looked attractive, shedding extra kilos he gained during making *Wiener Blut* and changing his flashy clothes into his classical tuxedo and leather jacket.

More importantly, he made a very original record, *Data de Groove*, produced by Robert Ponger and recorded in 1990 in London. However, neither his image nor the new album tapped into the taste of the wider public. Against the new type of performers from Nirvana, Smashing Pumpkins or Red Hot Chilli Peppers, with their uncombed hair and tattooed bodies, Falco, with his slick image, started to look like a relic from a different epoch. What was his value in the 1980s became his "negative capital" in the 1990s. Consequently, unlike in the 1980s, when Falco managed to successfully integrate elements of high and low art into his oeuvre, in the 1990s the two avenues of his career, high and low, separated, or at least in his public perception. More often than not he became regarded either as an avant-garde poet or a producer of Eurotrash.

But let's begin with *Data de Groove*. It is an album dedicated to the computer age. Although it is not a concept album (Falco never recorded any which merit such a label), it comes across as more coherent than the records produced by the Bolland brothers, due to its focus on language as an active force in creating reality, as opposed to merely a means of reflecting it – an idea linked to Falco's countryman, Ludwig Wittgenstein and in the postmodern age, Michel Foucault. The record investigates what happens to people when computers dominate their lives. The very title suggests that computers are not neutral means to store and process data – they affect our emotions. The word "groove" could be an ironic reference to the hippie culture, as it was one of its key terms and became immortalized in a song by Simon and Garfunkel, 'The 59th Street Bridge Song (Feelin' Groovy)' (1966). Falco proposes, evoking Jean Baudrillard (1994, 2001), that "grooviness" evaporated from the material world, moving to a simulated reality (on Falco's connection with Baudrillard's thought see Bolterauer 2010).

As in a scheme described by Baudrillard, the texts and videos suggest that the advance of technology, leading to replacing representation with simulation, changes our sense of reality, including our identity. The more virtual life gains in importance, the less material life remains for us to enjoy and the less we are anchored. For Baudrillard such a transfer of meaning and *elan*, from (true) reality to simulacra, is dystopian. He claims that televisions and computers overpower and dehumanize us. For Falco, the consequences of the computer age are more ambiguous: there are both gains and losses. Computers impoverish us, make us robotic and fragmented, as the computers, in order to work effectively, have to break down reality into simple elements: digits, bits and bytes (Bolterauer 2010: 86). But these elements can be then reassembled, creating larger objects, to be relocated anywhere we want and stored there for ever. The digital technologies allow a person to inhabit different spaces, to be practically everywhere, and achieve immortality, but at the price of fragmentation, "thinness" and spectrality.

Of all Falco's records, *Data de Groove* demonstrates best that he is an heir to the poets of the Beat Generation, especially William S. Burroughs. His songs bring to mind Burroughs's cut-up technique as a means to achieve unusual juxtapositions, as well as the writer's overall interest in the advancement in sound technologies (Odier 2008: 27–56). They also bring association with earlier paradigms, such as Futurist and Dada poetry, with its theme of the apocalyptic future, due to the war and development of technology, which renders human bodies as inferior machines. As examples I choose fragments from poems by two Polish Futurist poets, Anatol Stern and Tytus Czyżewski. The first, entitled 'Europa' (1929) reads like a premonition of Falco's 'Neo Nothing – Post of All':

> eternity and nothingness – two fattened boxers
> who will always win...
>
> we shall
> lose
> lose
> lose
> as always!

(Stern 1959: 170)

The second poem is entitled 'Hymn do maszyny mojego ciała' (Hymn to the Machine of My Body, 1922):

> one one one
> my heart beats come
> electric heart one
>
> transmission belt
> of my intestines
> two two two
>
> have pity on me
> one two
>
> the telephone of my brain
> dynamo-brain
> three three three
> one two three
> the Machine of my body
> function turn
> live

(Czyżewski, quoted in Carpenter 1983: 27)

Of course, the quoted poets referred to the inventions of their epoch, such as telephones and transmission belts; Falco evokes computer technology. His lyrics, consisting of many simple words, imitate computer language, which sees no difference between verbs, nouns and adjectives and condenses information, trying to get rid of unnecessary material. Many of the words belong to the language of the over-sized "hyper-reality". The two tendencies perfectly coalesce in the title track, 'Data de Groove':

> The MEGA the SCORE
> Desto MONO de CHROME
> ATMO de FORCE
> Is the Atmo at home
> It's got to be the higher the goal
> Desto schwerer Beruf – SAY!
> The deeper the Soul desto
> DATA DE GROOVE
>
> Ich mein: Ich – Mich – Du – Dich – Ich – Mein
> Du dein so allein, so allein zu sein

Another message is that computers make us solipsistic – they teach us to say "I" in all possible ways (ich-mich-mein), rather than helping us to connect with other people. We become for ourselves the main "project": something to elaborate, decompose, reassemble, re-touch. The places occupied by others, our lovers and friends, become supplanted by multiple versions of ourselves. The idea that we do not need anybody but ourselves to make us happy is, according to Slavoj Žižek, a particularly neoliberal concept. For Žižek this trend is encapsulated by edification of masturbation as the highest form of love (Žižek 2008: 25–30). Solipsistic love is both criticized and celebrated by Falco.

The video to 'Data de Groove' elaborates the idea of media-induced solipsism. It shows us an elegant woman leaving a car and climbing metal stairs leading to a building which looks like a power-plant, but which is in fact a highly-powered "media-plant". Such an image harks back to *Vertigo* (1958) by Alfred Hitchcock (who also inspired Dolezal and Rossacher on previous occasions), a film about investigating what is hidden behind somebody's multiple identities. However, unlike in *Vertigo*, it is a woman, rather than a man, who tries to capture the elusive man, played by Falco. She rushes upstairs to find him and fails to notice one of his incarnations – his black figure projected on the inside of the door through which she enters the room. Forcefully opening the door she would have squashed the poor man, if not for the fact that he is already squashed: two-dimensional. Then the woman puts a floppy disk into the computer, takes a seat in front of the screen and starts watching images of Falco. The idea is to show how much a singular image can be transformed and manipulated. Only on rare moments do we see Falco represented realistically. The rest of the time he is fragmented and decomposed: reduced to a contour, which remains unfilled or filled with black matter – it merges with or escapes the ever-changing background. Even when we see the "real Falco", his image is monochromatic, as if to prove that multiplication is paid for by the thinning of the original, which is again a very Baudrillardian concept.

The better computer technologies reproduce our images, the less is contained in a single image and left on the side of the original. Another motif of the video is that of (re)search and spying. The woman who looks at the images of Falco behaves as if trying to find relevant information about him (presumably the eponymous data de groove). The images of the woman surrounded by numerous screens with different versions of the same person/event bring to mind the surveillance culture of CCTV cameras, which started to flourish some years after the album was recorded. The woman both investigates Falco and is surveyed and chased by the police. We are thus thrust into a gigantic panopticon, in which nobody can escape from the circuit of surveillance. The reality created in the video is at the same time ultra-modern (although this is a modernity of late 1980s–early 1990s technology, which is dated now) and retro, as the woman looks like a 1940s/1950s film noir siren, such as Rita Hayworth. The car used in the film also looks old and futuristic at the same time. Although in this video Falco changes his position every second, we get a sense of stasis, of being locked in the never-ending present. This impression is strengthened by the music which is circular and lacking in dramatic effects, as if the composer forbid himself to move beyond tightly defined limits. Even the chorus, which normally serves to counterpoint the spoken word, here is merely an extension of the rapped part.

The second video from the *Data de Groove* album, 'Charisma Kommando', continues with the theme of human diminishing:

> Du denkst nur du wärest wer, doch
> Hier bist du niemand mehr

The vehicle of this diminishing is the "charisma kommando". Such a term, combining a word from the Nazi vocabulary (Kommando) with one from the "discourse of glamour" (charisma), pronounces that pain and humiliation inflicted by a dominatrix can be pleasant. Such ideas inform the whole genre of "Nazisploitation" from which the song borrows, featuring a woman in a quasi-Nazi cap, fish-net stockings and leather boots, a reference to Liliana Cavani's *Il portiere di notte* (*The Night Porter*, 1974). The woman is described in the lyrics as "die Direktorin", but judging by the image, in this world, as in that created in *The Night Porter*, the man is still the boss. We see Falco comfortably sitting in an armchair with a woman standing and dancing around him, attending to his needs, even if these needs are of masochistic character. Their interaction is not a private affair, but a subject of disembodied spectacle, epitomised by huge eyes piercing the walls. Again the media-world is that of a panopticon, which is even more perfect as the walls are more angular and plastic so that Falco and his "Direktorin" are locked in a fish tank whose size can be adjusted to the needs of a spectator. Such a representation on the one hand points to German Expressionism, especially Fritz Lang's films about Dr Mabuse, and on the other to the age of internet sex, where the spectator, in contrast to a viewer of traditional porno shows of older types, has full control over what he sees, while, at the same time, being removed from the physicality of sex.

Throughout the duration of the video Falco moves in a robotic way (maybe because of being drunk during the shooting of the video), as if his material self was following his computer-generated contours, confirming Baudrillard's concept of the domination of the copy over the original. Images are fluid, exceeding what we see in the 'Data de Groove' video, bringing to mind Wong Kar-Wai films from a slightly later period, such as *Chungking Express* (1994) and *Ashes of Time* (1994). The palette of colours is limited to white, blue and red, again conveying the idea that multiplication in one place is paid by impoverishment in another. The fact that the colours of the British flag are used in this video might be seen as an attempt to subliminally appeal to the British public. As with the song 'Data de Groove' the result of the fluid movement is a lack of progress, of being trapped in the present.

Another song which concerns fragmentation, enlargement and displacement of material objects, effected by new technologies, is 'Expocityvision':

> Expo – niert
> Explo – diert
> MA-RA-THON
> King – Size
> Expo – size
> Expo – beat
> City – heat – new prize
>
> Expo – sé
> East – West
> Next – best
> Next – test
> Expo – sition

City – vision
The art TV-ision under
Different condition

On this occasion Falco links fragmentation, enlargement and displacement with producing advertisements. As in 'Junge Roemer', we get a sense of restlessness, of living for the night, which eases the tension of the day. Yet, unlike in the former song, 'Expocityvision' offers a vision of a city which works twenty-four hours a day. It cannot afford any rest because profit has to be made continuously. 'Neo Nothing – Post of All', as the very title suggests, is about the world near its end, almost devoid of material content. We cannot let "nothing" go away, suggests the author, because without "nothing", nothing would remain: everything will be post.

Romantic love, as I previously argued, is rarely a subject of Falco's songs. At best, his songs, such as 'Jeanny', are about love as something to be represented "romantically", played with, rather than consumed. But only in *Data de Groove* does love dissolve into a word play, as in 'Bar Minor 7/11 (Jeanny Dry)' where Falco connects the name of his most famous female creation with the description of a drink (see Chapter 2) and in 'Anaconda 'Mour', a short track closing the record, where "amour" is merely an appendix to or an ornament of "anaconda". 'Tanja P. nicht Cindy C.' is an answer to a song by Prince, 'Cindy C.' from his *The Black Album* (1987); it is thus representation of a representation. In this track, as well as in 'The Kiss of Kathleen Turner', Falco refers to the role of media images of beautiful women, such as Tanja Patitz and Cindy Crawford, in the lives of their consumers, writing with irony

Tanja P. nicht Cindy C.
Es steht fest, in dieser Klinik bist nur du meine Therapie

(Tanja P. not Cindy C.
This is certain that in this clinic you are my therapy)

Falco also points to the link between beauty, celebrity and money, quoting Tanja saying "In mein Budget nur Dollar rein", and ultimately the alienating effect of the celebrity culture on its consumers. The song affirms the superiority of German culture over American, as Tanja is pronounced as more attractive than Cindy (although a touch of irony is attached to such trivial comparisons), but also recognizes that Germans can compete with Americans only on American terms: a reference to Falco's own position as somebody taking part in this contest.

By and large, the album *Data de Groove* perfectly fits the concept of postmodernity as a world dominated by the media, mindlessly breeding its own copies, coreless, soulless, and full of decadent pleasures. However, there is nobody to guide us through this universe, no "Ziggy Stardust of the postmodern age". Falco, who we would expect to take such a position, has a subdued presence as merely one of the victims or beneficiaries of the computer age, unable to stand at a distance from the reality which he describes. Perhaps this is the point of this record. If postmodernity, using computers and the media, dissolves identity, no "unified identity", no embodied narrator is left to tell us why and how it happens. But the lack of the "last man" in this dystopian yet seductive universe might have an alienating effect on the audience. The listeners of popular songs want to anchor their attention on somebody specific, therefore most songs are first-person narratives. Endowing an album such as *Data de Groove* with a distinct narrator might be even more important due to its linguistic and conceptual complexity.

Figure 10.1: Cover of *Data de Groove*

But to be true to his concept of fragmented, disembodied reality, Falco could not give himself a coherent identity. On the record's sleeve we see his head, from which another, smaller head grows and, as we can guess, if the cover was to be extended, we would see another head coming out of the smaller one and so on. The face of the singer is smudged and scratched. On closer inspection, some of the scratches take the shape of zips, plaited belts or perforations, suggesting that the proliferation of identities is paid by subtle bondage and mutilation.

The computerized universe of *Data de Groove* brings association with the work of Kraftwerk, the most popular band that has come from Germany, which in some measure influenced both Falco and Robert Ponger. However, although in both worlds computers rule, the effect is different. Kraftwerk, most importantly in 'The Robots' (1978), produced an impression of humanized robots. Falco, by contrast, offers us robotized humans and by extension a posthuman world, of the type professed by Deleuze and Guattari (1983), Donna Haraway (1991), Friedrich Kittler (1999) and in the previous century, Marx.

Kraftwerk's vision strikes me as ultimately more optimistic, showing faith in technological progress and in this way, perhaps, valorising the dominant ideology ruling postwar Germany, as a country proving its value not through military aggression, but by technological achievements. Falco, by contrast, foretells the world when computer programmes would dominate people, forcing them to work in step with their instructions.

According to Simon Emmerson, there are two principal approaches to electronic or electroacoustic music. One, based historically on developments from *musique concrete* and the French tradition, creates clean, smooth surfaces free of any noise. The goal of this approach is perfection, impossible to achieve using normal instruments. In popular music such an approach is represented by Jean-Michel Jarre. The second approach uses the possibilities of electronic technologies to create a noisy bricolage, the sound of dense, urban, industrial life (Emmerson 2000: 194–95). The goal of artists adopting this approach is realism. Knowing Falco's earlier records and especially his predilection to "noise", one would expect he would follow the second route. Yet, he chose the first one. The sound of *Data de Groove* is clean and otherworldly, as if it was created not by a human, but by a super-talented computer. It is music made to fill spaces of expositions of new technologies, high-tech museums, airport lounges or shopping centres, rather than streets and discos. No doubt this effect was even stronger when the record was released, contributing to its poor sales. Pop music is meant to be personal and intimate, even if, as Adorno argued, its intimacy is cynically manufactured for profit. With its posthumanism *Data de Groove* was so ahead of its time that it missed the spirit of its present day, especially in the German-speaking world, where the main news was the end of communism, die Wende and the fall of the Berlin Wall. Moreover, when Falco with Ponger were busy refining its sound, Berlin experienced the first wave of techno, the style of the active, the extravert, those embracing the noise and even, as its historians, Felix Denk and Sven von Thülen (Denk and von Thülen 2012; Schieferdecker 2012) argue, having a rather optimistic outlook on life, in part effected by these political changes. Falco himself recognized that this record was too cold, conceptual and impersonal to take it to a live audience, as we do not hear it at his concerts.

The failure of *Data de Groove* made Falco reconsider his approach. As in the case of *Junge Roemer*, which was followed by the eclectic *Falco 3*, produced by the Bollands, *Data de Groove* was followed by musically eclectic *Nachtflug*, again produced largely by the Dutch brothers. Yet, while *Falco 3* comes across as a tribute to the robustness of Western music and culture, *Nachftlug* is about its decline and foretells the artist's escape from the West. Such a trajectory is inscribed into the record's structure. The first three songs, 'Titanic', 'Monarchy Now' and 'Dance Mephisto' take us to the West's past. The next two tracks, 'Psychos' and 'S.C.A.N.D.A.L.' (or simply 'Skandal' in later releases) are rooted in the present-day West. The second part of the record offers a sample of different Eastern musical styles, reggae in 'Yah-Vibration' and samba in 'Propaganda'. The final part, consisting of 'Time', 'Cadillac Hotel' and 'Nachtflug', expresses nostalgia for what was lost or left in the West.

'Titanic' is the only track on this album for which a video was made. The song and the video hark back to 'Rock Me Amadeus'. In both Falco sings about Western "decadence", which on this occasion is changed into a verb, "decadance", suggesting that decadence is not a reaction to an unpredictable state of affairs, but an active position: dancing to the tune of disaster. This is what we see on screen: the ship is sinking, which is conveyed by a huge amount of water poured onto the characters, who, not unlike in Fellini's *La Dolce Vita* (1960), are invigorated by its power and dance frantically. Leather braces on women's naked bodies and erotic behaviour of characters bear association with Nazisploitation films, the ultimate genre of decadence. The colours of the costumes are garish, the man who begins the song with the words "The Unsinkable Titanic" and sinks, looks grotesque, like the Penguin in Tim Burton's *Batman* (1989). The camera position is constantly changing, so the images are blurry, conveying loss of a sense of reality on the part of both the characters and viewers. In this decadent world Falco occupies an ambiguous position. He can be regarded as the captain of the sinking ship, due to being placed some distance above the crowd of guests and alone. However, he does not try to rescue it, only "conducts" the sinking operation, while telling us what is going on.

The title of the song inevitably evokes the ill-fated maiden voyage of the *Titanic* and its numerous screen adaptations, of which the most famous, James Cameron's *Titanic* (1997), had its premiere five years after Falco released *Nachtflug*. Although both works can be regarded as products of millennial angst, they are quite different and not only because they represent different genres, but different attitudes to this monumental disaster. Cameron's film carries a message of hope: although the ship sank, some (mostly good) people were saved. By contrast, in the story presented in Falco's video nobody survives, as demonstrated by the ending, showing what looks like the depth of the ocean. Universal decadence produces universal disaster. If the disaster is inevitable, there is no point resisting any pleasures, but make the most of what is still available.

Two subsequent songs, 'Monarchy Now' and 'Dance Mephisto', add to the list of catastrophes: the fall of the Habsburg Monarchy and Nazism. They point to ordinary people's love of their leaders, the leaders' indifference to them and, ultimately, the implication of ordinary people in grand politics. 'Monarchy Now', despite its old-fashioned setting (Orientexpress Konstantinopol-Wien), captures "neoliberal apathy", resulting from the conviction that there is no viable political choice; the only choice, as Falco sings, is between "monstrosity" and "decadence". The title of the song and the chorus, "Monarchie now, alive", illustrate that it concerns contemporary times. Past is used to illuminate the present, as in the famous aphorism by Paul Valèry that "our memory repeats to us what we haven't understood".

In 'Psychos' and 'Skandal', Falco sketches a portrait of a new class, presumably one which learnt from the mistakes of their forefathers: a class constituted of people who indulge in excess, hate "softies" and need no leader: all features linked to a neoliberal mindset. In comparison with the vulnerable *Junge Roemer*, described a decade earlier, it is a hardened group, which does not need a night to escape from the daily duties, but use the day for their nocturnal, excessive and morbid pleasures. 'Psycho' evokes *American Psycho*, a bestselling novel by Bret Easton Ellis, published in 1991, which is a satire on such neoliberal yuppies, whose protagonist is a Manhattan businessman and serial killer. The way his friend presents himself on the first page of the novel concurs with the cruelty and arrogance of Falco's "psychos": "I'm resourceful, I'm creative, I'm young, unscrupulous, highly motivated, highly skilled. In essence what I'm saying is that society cannot afford to lose me. I'm an asset" (Ellis 1991: 3). 'Psychos' includes the line "They gotta say yes to another excess" which is a quotation of the title of an album by Swiss electronic band, Yello, made in 1983, a collection of songs which glorify excess, not unlike Falco's 'Junge Roemer'. According to Raoul Herget, post-*Nachtflug* Falco was interested in collaborating with Yello, but – as with many plans in his life – it was not fulfilled. Unlike 'Junge Roemer', which is imbued with melancholy, mourning the price young Romans have to pay for their successes, 'Psychos' and 'Skandal' show no sympathy for "psychos"; perhaps reflecting the fact that by this point in time Falco left the "yuppie-land" and yuppie culture was no longer "cool". The repetitive choruses of these two songs capture the mundane lifestyle of the "psychos" because nothing gets more boring than everyday excess.

If the West is so despicable and mundane, then let's go to the East. 'Yah-Vibration' and samba in 'Propaganda' are products of such voyages. "Vibration", used in the title of 'Yah-Vibration', belongs to the hippie vocabulary. It connotes political and personal transformation, achieved by peaceful means, free love and rejection of materialism. During the famous Monterey Pop Festival in June 1967 the Mamas and the Papas sang in their probably most famous song, 'San Francisco (Be Sure to Wear Some Flowers In Your Hair)':

> All across the nation such a strange vibration
> People in motion
> There's a whole generation with a new explanation
> People in motion people in motion.

In the film, made at the festival, we see a young woman who expressed an expectation of "vibrations" achieved by a "love-in", a term defined as a peaceful public gathering focused on meditation, love, music and use of psychedelic drugs. The memory of "vibrations" of this kind is present in Falco's 'Yah-Vibration', but its protagonist does not intend to transform the world, only to escape the depressive Austrian winter and cold "yuppie-land". He flies with his girlfriend to Jamaica, the Ganja-Land, where they hope to get vibrations, which

> Makes her feel so high
> Makes her come alive

Falco's song tells us that it is still pleasant to get vibrations, but their effect is rather mediocre in comparison with those described by the Mamas and the Papas. Unlike vibrations of 1967, which were meant to affect the whole generation, leading to illumination, Falco's 1990s vibrations do not bring any lasting effect and are private; they are not even shared by the couple he describes, because after reaching Jamaica they hardly see each other. As is usually the case with Falco, the pleasure has a distinct monetary price. The Rastaman mentioned in the song is not a spiritual leader of the type invited to places like Woodstock, but an ordinary drug dealer, instructing the tourists about the best ways to take drugs.

Such a matter-of-fact, disillusioned take on vibrations points to the temporal distance between the idealistic hippie songs of the 1960s and the down-to-earth neoliberal music production that Falco epitomises. This might also have partly to do with the fact that the East for the hippie generation was the East imagined rather than experienced first-hand. Falco's "Jamaica" is that of a well-informed tourist, for whom it stands for cheap pleasures. The difference is reflected in the style of music. 'Yah-Vibration', more than songs performed at Monterey Pop or Woodstock, with its slow tempo and off-beat, is a proper reggae song.

Falco's song, as it often happened, is a reworking of his earlier song, 'Urban Tropical' and it foretells the work of Eminem, in this case 'Must Be the Ganja'. It is difficult to establish whether Eminem's song talks about the effect of marijuana on the actual behaviour of its protagonist or only on his imagination (which is a perennial ambiguity in Eminem's songs). What is, however, clear, is that the song links marijuana with extreme aggression. Falco with his Jamaican "vibrations" can be metaphorically located in the middle of the road between the innocuous, peaceful hippie-land and the dangerous and surreal ganja-land of Eminem.

'Propaganda', which follows 'Yah-Vibration', has a Latino rhythm and ponders on Cuba's being colonized by rich Westerners, a fact which needs to be covered up by (communist) propaganda. But propaganda means here also all political discourse, everything which politicians say to us. The song expresses distaste of such politics, but without offering an alternative, not unlike in 'Wiener Blut'. This brings to mind the previously mentioned observation of Stuart Hall's that post-1968 the preferred position of the young is to be "radically against *all* parties, party lines and party bureaucracies" (Hall 1988: 181). Such attitude, although it might result from a different impulse than acceptance of the dominant ideology, leads to the same result: political apathy.

The last three songs, 'Time', 'Cadillac Hotel' and 'Nachtflug', are imbued with nostalgia. 'Cadillac Hotel', due to its theme of loss and waiting for love, is regarded as a continuation of 'Jeanny'. However, the language used to express it harks back to the album *Data de Groove*, even using expressions from this record

> Tour – retour
> Acting on l'amour
> Wir spielen das alte Spiel
> Der Schlange Kur – so nah
> Ihr hohes Ziel
> Denn die Zeichen stehen verändert
> Neuer Tendenzen – Konsequenz
> Extravaganza Hi-Tech-Hexen
> And the pressure
> And the pressure
> Is immense!

With the last track, 'Nachtflug', the singer felt a special connection. In this song Falco reflects on his hectic 1980s lifestyle, when only night-time brought him respite from the stresses of his career, and is a subtle tribute to prostitutes who helped him with his predicament. 'Nachtflug', like the tracks from *Data de Groove*, is about mediated love as a medicine for loneliness, but on this occasion Falco does not talk on behalf of a generation or a group, only himself.

The sleeve, showing Falco in a black cape, against a background of clouds or fog, brings association with nocturnal creatures, such as vampires or Batman, known for their dual nature: human and non-human. The image also suggest a flight, hence acts as a premonition of Falco leaving Austria. Not surprisingly, this image was also chosen for Falco's grave.

Commercially *Nachtflug* proved a significant success in Austria and a minor success in German-speaking and some European countries, selling better than Falco's previous record, *Data de Groove*. The record apparently also immensely pleased the singer. But it was a far cry from his mid-1980s successes, sealing Falco's fate as an icon of the 1980s rather than projecting a new image. The rest of the decade Falco spent, on the one hand, trying to shed his old "corporate identity" and move to a new epoch; and on the other hand, trying to make a living by performing his 1980s songs and image.

Nachftlug is the last Falco album with new material released during his lifetime. This, however, does not mean that he did not produce new songs, although most of them were released posthumously. There are two complementary answers to the question, why Falco went semi-underground. One, "mythological", proposed in the documentary *Hoch wie nie* and then perpetuated in other media, was his unwillingness to show to the world anything sub-standard, which led to obsessively painting and repainting, writing and erasing what he wrote, like Kafka or Munch. The other, "historical", is the lack of interest by the mainstream music industry in his work, reflecting his "negative capital" at the time and a critical assessment of his new work from this period.

Either due to internal or external pressures, essentially lack of money, Falco was forced to experiment, both by turning to new producers and exploring new styles. He wrote and recorded songs with his colleagues from the band, Thomas Rabitsch and Thomas Lang, and German producer Thorsten Börger, who was largely responsible for Falco's turn to techno. In one interview from the mid-1990s Falco explained his turn to this style as dictated by his need to respond to the changing tastes of the new and younger audience. In the 1990s techno was played practically everywhere but, as I already mentioned, it was especially popular in Germany (Monroe 1999; Denk and von Thülen 2012). An important site of German techno was music television station VIVA, a German equivalent of MTV, set up in 1991–92, as a means to increase the presence of German pop music in German and European audio-visual space. Falco's video producers, Dolezal and Rossacher, were instrumental in VIVA's design and operations (Hachmeister and Lingemann 1999: 143), facilitating Falco's continuous presence in German houses, although at the price of arguably lowering his artistic standards, becoming a model Eurotrash singer.

I shall add, however, that Falco's "trash series" belongs to my favourite of his productions.

Techno was the style of his last hit, 'Mutter, der Mann mit dem Koks ist da', as well as 'Naked', 'Cyberlove' and 'Krise'. For 'Mutter' he adopted a new alter ego – TMA. These letters, as he explained in an interview to the Austrian magazine *Wiener*, stood for "Too Many Assholes" (Fehringer 1996), which most likely was an expression of the singer's opinion about the music industry or/ and of Falco's favourite word, "Thema" (theme). Giving himself a new name reflected his (or his advisors') conviction that for Falco to exist in the 1990s, he had to cease to be "Falco"; it was better for him to start from scratch than with negative capital. Such a move also reflected the fact that "techno discourages talk of auteurs" and "is rife with musicians who are continually changing their names" (Brackett 1999: 7). This musical style also openly pronounced itself as an expression of a "chemically altered state of mind", which Falco acknowledged both in the lyrics to the song and the video. In a sense techno was also what Falco was doing all his life, mixing rock and roll with rap, disco and electronica and drawing on the experience of his German "cousins", Kraftwerk and Can. Now, however, the mixing was done at higher speed and with new sounds, imitating post-industrial noises. 'Krise', produced by Rabitsch, deserves special attention for at least two reasons. It is the last song recorded by Falco and a culmination of his apocalyptic discourse. I mentioned on previous occasions that in Falco's works apocalypse does not take the shape of an abrupt ending to the old world, but a permanent state of decline, "decadance", slow agony. In 'Krise' this state is domesticated and normalized, as indicated by its title: *Krise* (*Crisis*) and the refrain: *Krise wie? Krise was?*, following the, unusually for Falco, hard-sounding German words.

> Immer tiefer, immer tiefer,
> Immer tiefer in die Krise

The lyrics sound like a caricature of managerial speak, whose purpose is to convince employers and customers that everything is under control and disaster is only a matter of perception. The techno sound roots this crisis in the contemporary, urban environment of speeding cars. One cannot imagine a better closing of the career of this bard of a yuppie and crisis generation than this song.

The second style, in which Falco dabbled in his last years, was rock, writing 'No Time for Revolution', 'Egoist' and 'Out of the Dark', although on each occasion the style is hybridized with a different type of music, such as reggae. In these songs he adopted a personal tone and solemnity which the majority of his earlier songs are lacking. For me, adopting a rock idiom meant donning a costume which did not suit Falco. That said, these songs, in common with 'Krise', fulfilled the function of his artistic and personal testament very well, even if literally they were not his last songs.

'No Time for Revolution' traces back an evaporation of revolutionary spirit from Western society, from the 1960s to the 1990s, dedicating each decade a sentence. Content-wise, it is a typical Falco song, as it adheres to his "small apocalypse" formula, by pronouncing that things declined in the described period, yet claiming that nothing can be done about it – the "ship" with the humanity has to sink:

> Back in the sixties: they stand up and fight,
> Fight for their dreams, fight for their right
> while
> In the nineties: there's a so-called bust generation
> The spirit of the money is the sound of the time

Written entirely in English, it lacks the irony and poetic sophistication which informed Falco's earlier "apocalyptic songs", such as 'Monarchy Now' and 'Titanic'. The same can be said about the music; its emphatic beats and overall loudness render it a pastiche of such machismo acts as Judas Priest or Iron Maiden.

'Out of the Dark' fares better, because it feels more dramatic. There is a contrast between a mournful, almost whispered rap in German, which creates the effect of intimacy with the listener, and the loud, English chorus "Out of the dark, into the light" and it has a prolonged guitar solo, like in Falco's first released single, 'Ganz Wien'. The success of this song relies in part on its prophetic character, to which I return in due course.

Another song from this period is 'Die Königin von Eschnapur', which is the most ambitious of Falco's "oriental tracks". The title harks back to Fritz Lang's Indian epic, whose first part was entitled *Der Tiger von Eschnapur* (*Tiger of Eschnapur* aka *Tiger of Bengal*, 1960). There are many references to Lang in Falco's songs and videos, but on this occasion the connection is more pronounced. Lang, as his *Tiger* testifies, did not want merely to imitate Indian films or smuggle references to Indian culture into his Western productions but to upstage films about the Orient made either in the East or in the West. The means to this goal was *Tiger of Eschnapur*'s epic dimension and the ample use of metaphors, most importantly the main female character, Indian dancer Seetha, with her love of white music and white men, symbolizing the utopian synthesis of the East and West. Due to its linguistic virtuosity, with complex metaphors worth of Fritz Lang and an interesting blending of Eastern sounds with a rock, energetic rhythm, in 'Die Königin von Eschnapur' Falco presents himself as a worthy heir to Lang, albeit working in a different medium. Pity there is not a video to this song as it would be interesting to see how Falco might have handled Lang's legacy. The use of alternative descriptions of the Eschnapur's royalty: "die Kaiserin von Kasachstan" and "das Fürstenkind von Caracas" (perhaps standing for "pet names" given by Falco to the prostitutes) suggests that Lang's dream of hybridizing the West with the East was fulfilled, but at the price of blurring their contours and reducing the East to what is accessible to a tourist or even a virtual tourist, who samples the East in his own hometown.

Finally, Falco tried a relaxed, jazzy singing in a new timbre of his voice in 'Ecce Machina'. The song, written by Falco and Thomas Lang, the drum player in his band, for Lang's record, *Mediator* (1995), but later credited only to Lang, can be seen as an ironic comment on Lang's relation to his instrument, because some critics regard him as such a precise drummer that he is more drumming machine than man. Its theme is the similarity between man and machine, as explored in *Data de Groove*; the crucial term, the "temple of code", would perfectly suit Falco's earlier album.

Falco's live performances in the 1990s belong to two contrasting types. One leans towards "high art". It comprises Falco's concert in June 1993 during Donauinsel Fest, with an audience of about 100,000, and his performance with a symphonic orchestra conducted by Raoul Herget in Wiener Neustadt in June 1994, for an audience of 10,000. Both events were public events, and they acted as proof that Falco could still pull in the crowds, at least in his homeland. The concert in Wiener Neustadt, which was part of the celebrations of the city's 800th anniversary, was of special importance, as it rendered Falco a follower of a noble classical tradition, associated with Mozart. Falco tuned to this role and for most of the concert behaved more like an opera singer than a pop star, singing in an elegant suit, merely walking about on the stage and at times putting his hand on his heart. Thanks to elaborate arrangements, and short instrumental inserts, all written by members of Falco's band, Thomas Rabitsch and Peter Paul Skrepek, the songs, most of them written in the 1980s by the Bollands, gained epic dimensions. 'Rock Me Amadeus' shed its "rocky" character and sounded like an updated "classical piece", as opposed to a contemporary song about the old times. Herget, who apart from being a conductor, is a distinguished jazz player and erudite, invited Falco to Wiener Neustadt to read there poetry of authors such as Charles Bukowski and Ernst Jandl. In due course, Falco gave lectures in Schule der Dichtung in Vienna, whose founder, Christian Ide Hintze, championed Falco as a distinguished poet, leading to serious research on his work by literary scholars (Hintze 2010).

Figure 10.2: Falco and his band during the concert tour in 1993

Figure 10.3: Falco and Raoul Herget in Wiener Neustadt

If Falco limited himself only to performances of this type, he would not only have preserved but strengthened his standing. However, he played much more in the 1990s, because, as Skrepek claims, "stage was his life" and he needed quick money, which concerts ensured. Often these performances took place in venues and under circumstances that not only failed to add to Falco's mystique, but rendered him as a fallen star. One reason was their geographical locations, which can be traced from Castaldi's memoirs. In a nutshell, it was not the West or the Far East (Japan), as in the 1980s, but provincial Austria and the "near East", Eastern Europe and Russia. One can guess that Falco treated these places as substitutes of sites where "real stardom" was performed, such as London or New York. Most likely he was perceived there as a stand-in for "real stars", such as Kurt Cobain or the eternal Mick Jagger. But it is also likely that he was so popular in "Europe's backyard" beyond the 1980s because Eastern Europeans construct their cultural identities differently to Westerners. They were more likely to know and appreciate Falco as an *auteur* because he sang about their world – their "empire", in a language which was familiar to them.[17]

These late performances were not meant to be preserved for posterity, but the availability of video cameras and YouTube allow us to access them now. The best known is Falco's concert in Sylvester Gala in Excalibur City in 1997–98, a large commercial centre in Austria near the border with the Czech

Republic, set up and owned by Falco's friend, "duty-free millionaire", Ronnie Seunig. Such a postmodern "temple of consumption", where the myth of Excalibur is evoked alongside Chinese history, can be regarded as a recreation of a typical setting of Falco's song with its frequent motif of excessive consumption and virtual tourism, leading to the loss of a sense of history. But it is one thing to sing about it and another to be in it not only metaphorically but also physically, embracing and advertising it, as happened on this occasion. Falco in Excalibur City was an artist entirely integrated into the capitalist order, selling his fare among those who sell alcohol or cosmetics, not unlike Steven Shorter in Watkins's film. In this context it is difficult to treat seriously Falco's self-presentation as a nonconformist romantic. Falco's position in Excalibur City, epitomising his position post-*Nachtflug*, demonstrates that Falco's neglect of professional opportunities in the name of doing what he wanted to do at the peak of his career in the 1980s did not lead to greater artistic autonomy, but on the contrary, to losing the remnants of his autonomy and a greater dependence on the system.

The concert itself makes for uncomfortable viewing and, judging by the comments published on YouTube, tests the loyalty of Falco's fans. What makes the spectacle particularly embarrassing is Falco's gravity. Such an impression results not only from the fact that Falco at this point was already forty, when jumping on stage is more difficult, but that he attempted a more energetic dancing than ten or so years previously. It looks as if music is in control of him and he is barely able to catch up with its flow, unlike on earlier occasions when he was in charge of the show. There is a gap between the energetic techno rhythm on the one hand and the sense of the singer's breathlessness, perhaps exacerbated by alcohol. Another factor which affected negatively Falco's performance was the lack of support from other musicians. Although Falco was known as a solo artist, a crucial aspect of his concerts was the music of his band and his interaction with its members, many of whom exerted a quiet charisma of their own. It was against the background of these men (the intellectual Thomas Rabitsch, the Harry Potter-like Skrepek, the energetic and "cool" Lang, the jazzy virtuoso Bernhard Rabitsch, to name those in one of the last configurations of his band) that Falco appeared to be a real star. One can also deduce that the proximity of these men with cooler heads often prevented him from some disasters on- and off-stage. By contrast, in Excalibur Falco is supported merely by zombie-like female dancers, with whom the singer seems to have no rapport, appears to be lonely and exposed to the reaction of a hostile and voyeuristic audience, as if he was a lion in a cage. But, viewed differently, for the same reasons, it is a great show, because fallen stars are more human and individualized than rising stars, who come across as very similar to each other. One can think about

Elvis Presley's late shows, for which he is today more loved than for his performances in his prime. As with many of Falco's performances, his Excalibur show got a second life by providing material for the video for 'Push Push', shot posthumously. The video, assembled with wit and sensitivity, on the one hand, dignifies the original performance, but on the other, prolongs the pain of watching the "fallen Falco".

In an interview given in 1994 Falco ridiculed Michael Jackson for his reclusive lifestyle. Yet, two years later he followed him, although on a smaller scale, moving to the Dominican Republic. There Falco acquired objects which connoted a need for extra security: a house with a swimming pool in a secluded villa resort, inhabited mostly by German-speaking ex-patriots, a Mitsubishi Pajero, a car of the type described as "a gated community on wheels", and a gun. Falco in the Caribbean, among fellow rich Germans and Austrians, served, in all ways, also sexually, by an impoverished local population, can be seen as a fulfilment of Hitler's dream of having colonies, yet acquired by the power of money, as opposed to military means. On the other hand, in comparison with many English and American pop stars, such as Brian Ferry, Eric Clapton and Madonna, who not only surrounded their much more lavish country houses with fences and walls, but engaged actively in protecting privileges of the rich, such as the right to fox hunting, Falco in his Dominican adobe comes across as a paragon of modesty and normality.

His relocation to the Caribbean was also a sign of his embracing hippie culture, summarized by Timothy Leary's phrase "turn on, tune in, drop out". The singer described his decision as prompted by his desire to escape a noisy and meaningless existence, intrusive media and depressing Austrian winters. The fact that the Dominican Republic is regarded as a mecca for cheap drugs reinforces a "hippie reading" of this move. It is worth mentioning that some years earlier Falco was thinking about moving to Los Angeles. Falco's move to the Dominican Republic can be seen as a logical conclusion to his claim that the West is finished – the future belongs to the (cultural) East.

11 Into the light

Falco lived in the Dominican Republic less than two years. He died on 6 February 1998, following a collision of his car with a bus near Porta Plata. He died shortly before his forty-first birthday, on the verge of leaving his youth behind and entering middle age. His death is presented as an accident rather than suicide and I am myself of this opinion. I even believe that he died when he was enjoying life more than at any other moment of his adult life. His photos and video recordings from the Dominican Republic, showing the slightly overweight singer in comfortable trousers, polo shirt and a baseball cap, bring association with the great hedonist Marlon Brando in the tropical heat, rather than with the neurotic James Dean, to whom Falco is typically compared. However, accepting that his death was a tragic accident does not preclude treating it as a consequence of his deeper death wish, as manifested in his heavy drinking, taking drugs and driving a car in a state when it was unwise to do so, including on this occasion.

Falco's death has all the right ingredients of the "romantic death": the young age, abruptness, taking place on foreign soil in a state suggesting utter loneliness and emotional turmoil (on romantic death of pop stars see Gregory 2011). As an author of his death, Falco upstaged many of his predecessors and followers, such as Jim Morrison, Michael Jackson or Amy Winehouse and even romantic poets, maybe with the exception of Lord Byron, because it was very abrupt, in a car crash, in a young age, on a foreign soil and was related to taking drugs. The other deaths did not include all these ingredients. It allowed for casting him as a tragic figure and revived his career.

However, before I move to Falco's afterlife, let's pause to consider what happened around this time. In politics, it precedes only three years what is known as 9/11 (2001) – a date rendered as a "time of apocalypse" for the West, although apocalypse which proved unable to lead to any new beginning, only to further crises. In the history of music, it coincides with the death of Frank Sinatra. Sinatra was one of Falco's favourite artists, as testified by mentioning him in 'Männer des Westens' as among the greatest "men of the West". This allure might be due to the elegance of Sinatra's songs, despite or because of their lack of deeper messages. Such a lack, in Falco's opinion, was a crucial ingredient in the formula for a perfect song. Falco's pronouncement that he lives his life "between depression and megalomania" sounds like a repetition of Sinatra's confession that "having lived a life of violent emotional contradictions, I have an over-acute capacity for sadness as well as elation". But Sinatra sustained such a life for much longer than Falco and seemed to be more content as years went by. Perhaps it would also have been Falco's case, had he changed his car for a bike.

Figure 11.1: Falco's fatal car crash

Falco also died shortly before the second album of the most successful rapper of all times, Eminem, *The Slim Shady LP* (1999). Eminem proved once and for all that being white is not an obstacle in a successful rapping career and that rap is not a minor style within pop music, but the avant-garde of pop. One could speculate that if Falco started his career some years later and was better advised he might become "Eminem before Eminem". My belief in such a possibility is based on many parallels between the work of these two artists. They tackle in an unsentimental way the same problems (drugs, fame, solitude, living in the mediated world, saturated with the images of celebrities) and reveal linguistic virtuosity of the highest order by playing with words and bending the rules of grammar. They are great rap poets, because their skill is fully appreciated only when their lyrics are rapped, as opposed to seen on paper. Although Eminem sings only in English, he is also a cultural traveller, ostentatiously stealing from many music encyclopaedias. But there are also differences – Eminem's authenticity is based on his working-class roots, complete with a broken family and coming from de-industrialized Detroit, misfortunes which he amplifies in his songs. Falco betrayed his working-class background in the opposite way, by projecting himself as a dandy. Eminem invades our space and insults his audience (female audience, especially, including his own mother and wife), correctly assuming that such insults would provoke a strong reaction. Falco protected his space and hid from the public behind sunglasses, but ultimately also in hope that he would woo us. Eminem is "not afraid to take a stand" and "walk this world together through the storm", reflecting, even if in a subtler and more unsentimental way than those from the first generation of rappers, the emancipatory ideology of rap. Showing solidarity with the suffering and the oppressed was hardly on Falco's agenda and he refused to "take a stand". However, this is also a position worth investigating for its revolutionary potential, as constant listening to the claim that everything remains the same provokes thinking about the possibility of change.

Part IV

Falco Lebt: Mourning and Melancholia

12 Life beyond death

In Falco's song which also provided the title of his first posthumous record, 'Out of the Dark', we find the words, "Muss ich sterben, um zu leben" (Do I have to die, in order to live). In due course these words became repeated ad nauseam by people writing about Falco. We find them on the back cover of Falco's biographies, written by Peter Lanz (2007) and Beatrice Castaldi (2012), and in numerous articles and comments to Falco's songs, published on websites. Although I would like to avoid clichés, I am not able to distance myself from these words, when writing about Falco's afterlife.

Let's first put these words in context. Typically and prosaically they are explained by Falco's resentment of the musical establishment and his countrymen, who deserted him, of which the clearest sign was his difficulty in releasing the material which he recorded in the second half of the 1990s and which was released posthumously. But in addition they evoke the idea of gaining eternity through art, harking back as far as Seneca's "non omnis moriar" and can be linked to Mahler's Symphony No. 2, known as the *Resurrection Symphony* and to some other works by Mahler, such as his Symphony No. 5 (Greene 1984; Cooke 1988: 81). The overall theme of the Second Symphony, according to Deryck Cooke, is "finding some assurance in the face of human immortality; and the resolution is a reaffirmation of the Christian belief in resurrection" (Cooke 1988: 52). There are other motifs, foregrounded by Mahler himself, appropriate in this context, such as the very pain of living and questioning its meaning. Cooke quotes Mahler as saying:

> Why did you live? Why did you suffer? Is it all nothing but a huge, frightful joke? We *must* answer these questions in some way, if we want to go on living – indeed, if we are to go on dying! ... When you awake from this dream [of happiness], and have to return into the confusion of life, it can easily happen that this ever-moving, never-resting, never-comprehensible bustle of existence becomes horrible to you, like the swaying of dancing figures in a brightly-lit ballroom, into which you look from the dark night outside – and from such a great *distance* that you can no longer hear the music. Life strikes you as meaningless, a frightful ghost, from which you perhaps start away with a cry of disgust (quoted in Cooke 1988: 53).

It is impossible to establish whether Falco knew these words or even listened to Mahler. What is certain is that he was encouraged to do so by the erudite Raoul Herget, the conductor at his Wiener Neustadt concert, who during the period of their collaboration filled the singer's head with much information about Austria's most famous late romantic and Austrian rich modernist heritage (as he filled my head later on). The second connection is with Mozart's opera, *The Magic Flute*, which also charts the road from the darkness to the light. If there was a conscious attempt to emulate ideas presented in these works, this would confirm my point that Falco was a romantic artist, because resurrection (of a person or a country) is a common motif in romantic works.

Mozart and Mahler are both posthumous stars – they were never as popular during their lifetime as they were after their deaths. This cannot be said about Falco – his afterlife fame does not match the one from the mid-1980s. Nevertheless, his status is considerably higher than in the last years of his career. This is because death gives a different inflection to facts from the artist's life, especially if he or she died romantically, as was his case. It amplifies his or her successes and changes straightforward failures into unfulfilled opportunities, for which the artist is no longer to blame, but cruel fate or those who did not love and appreciate him or her enough when he or she was still alive. Death requires making up for loss and guilt by engaging in commemorative rites. This part will be devoted to such rites, performed by his official heirs, such as members of his family and friends, fellow artists, who adapted Falco's works, and his fans. And all of them are bound together by the culture industry through using its tools: commercial record productions, film studios, publishing houses, YouTube platforms etc. Their goal and those of the culture industry also overlap: they want the memory of Falco to go on, even if, ultimately, for different reasons. For them, the ideal mourner is not a mourner in the Freudian sense, who after acute suffering from the death of the beloved one moves on, beginning a new life, but a melancholic, a prolonged mourner, who is unable to detach him- or herself from the object of his or her loss, who is thus potentially an insatiable producer and consumer of the objects related to the dead person (Freud 2005: 203–18). Their task is thus to feed their own and others' appetite but not to quench it entirely. Digital technologies help to provide the food for a melancholic, as they allow the traces of the deceased person's presence to be easily recomposed. Thus, although, as Jacques Derrida (1994), the (god)father of modern hauntology maintains, every period has its ghosts (and ghost scholars), the digital epoch has more of them and they multiply with a speed unknown to their ancestors. This part will be devoted to some of Falco's mourners, and the methods and fruits of their memory work. I am interested in how Falco is represented or rather recreated or simulated in their work: who or what is Falco beyond Falco.

13 Torch bearers and vampires, or mourning and earning

Falco's posthumous successes, as measured in the release of his new records, as well as such manifestations of public remembrance as naming a street after him in Vienna, erecting his monument in Gars am Kamp, publishing biographies, staging musicals, shooting a biopic and making documentaries devoted to him, happened thanks to the effort of many individuals who invested time, energy and money in keeping his memory alive. Let's look at some of them.

Falco's death brought to the centre stage Falco's mother, Maria Hölzel, who became literally and figuratively his main heiress, following the artist's paternity test and change of his will, which led to disinheriting his daughter.[18] With a biblical name and mournful look, she became a perfect Dolorosa, dignifying her son's life, presenting him as a Christ for postmodern times – somebody who, as she put it, was devilish, but in a saintly way. In such a role she did not lock herself up in her mourning, but embraced a contemporary notion, related to authors such as Pierre Nora and Jacques Derrida, that remembering prolongs life and the most effective remembering is through creating material and virtual sites of memory. As long as health allowed her, we could see her present whenever public remembering of Falco took place. To ensure that her son was remembered correctly, Mutter Maria also engaged in discursive cleansing, by criticizing or silencing voices which did not agree with her. One such voice was that of her ex-husband, Alois, whom she denied the right to participate in Falco's inheritance. She also criticized those spreading rumours that Falco's death was a suicide (Graf and Hicker 1999a). Falco's mother also set up the "Falco Foundation" with the businessman Ronnie Seunig as its chairman, who by the virtue of this role became the main stand-in for Falco.

Other principal memorists include Falco's collaborators: the producers of Falco's most successful songs, the Bolland brothers, his video producers, Rudi Dolezal and Hannes Rossacher (DoRo), his band leader and again music producer, Thomas Rabitsch and manager, Horst Bork. They are responsible for releasing Falco's posthumous records, films and music videos, books about him and presenting Falco to the public in interviews. Their commemorative work is both praised and criticized, and I would like to address here some of the criticisms directed at them.[19]

Figure 13.1: Falco spectral

Figure 13.2: Falco haunting in Vienna

One concerns extracting profit out of Falco (Köpf and Wictora 1999; Graf and Hicker 1999b; Oberhuber 2008). Ironically, such an impression was facilitated by Rudi Dolezal, who in the wake of Falco's death described himself as Falco's "Blutsbruder" (blood brother), most likely unconsciously (but according to Freud, what is unconscious, is the truest) conveying a desire to perform a metaphorical transfusion of blood from the barely cold body of his "brother" to his own, like a vampire, which according to the legend, sparks a whole vampirish chain; not unlike the operation of capital according to Marx.

No doubt in death Falco allows others to enrich themselves materially, but why is this deemed inappropriate? Most likely because the critics give into the "myth of disinterested mourning", assuming that mourning can be sincere only when it does not coincide with financial gain. But in reality the opposite is the case. We mourn most those from whom we inherited the most, such as parents who left us their houses and bank accounts, as well as immaterial goods, such as education, professional skills or good manners, precisely because they passed to us these goods, which help us to survive and develop ourselves. If we received from them nothing, we might be less grateful. I see nothing out of the ordinary in the activities of Falco's artistic heirs. The second issue is whether they should benefit from their memory work, as opposed to Falco's "more rightful heirs". For me, they are his rightful heirs, because they were co-authors of his earlier successes, including his songs and his public image. They probably invested in him more than he invested in them, according to the rule of asymmetry in dividing profit in the music business (the star takes disproportionally more for a unit of his or her work than any backstage personnel) and under capitalist regime at large. If Falco's death allowed this asymmetry to be readdressed to an extent, then I applaud it. The same goes for his lovers, who decided to share their secrets with the public – it is morally right to do so because it was their shared life, not solely Falco's.

Another argument concerns the inappropriate character of certain commemorative work, created against the artist's expressed or assumed will or of quality and character which undermines his achievements. Such criticism is not easy to assess because, unlike for example Vladimir Nabokov, who instructed his wife and son to burn his unfinished novel, which was subsequently published under the title *The Original of Laura*, Falco most likely did not ask his music producers to erase his unreleased songs. On the contrary, he wanted these songs to reach an audience – it was the record companies which prevented this from happening. But for this reason the duty of the heirs should be to explain the status of this work as precisely as possible, for example by saying whether a specific "new" song consists of fragments put together by a producer, and is thus really a mashup, or whether a specific title was given to a song when Falco was still alive or only posthumously. Otherwise the charge of taking advantage of his posthumous vulnerability becomes justified.

As for the quality of memory work, this is, of course, a matter of taste, which is culture-specific. For my taste, the DVD *Falco Symphonic* is a success both on account of its aesthetic quality, the way it dignifies Falco's voice and the openness with which it presents itself as a memory work and the medium it uses. I also welcome those "memory works" which develop Falco's musical or visual inheritance in an unexpected way, such as covers of his songs produced in the style of industrial techno and mashups produced by DJ Schmolli, which I will discuss in detail.

Finally, there is an argument that the "true" Falco is lost in the cacophony of texts. As I already indicated, I am sceptical about such a concept and rather than defending the rights of "true Falco", I would like his legacy to be continued in a way that makes one want to return and reflect on Falco's music and phenomenon. It would happen only by "upgrading" technically the "original" Falco, as happened in *Falco Symphonic*, or performing his works in a new, iconoclastic way. By contrast, poor clones of Falco, such as sloppily produced "new songs" or biopics which naïvely try to retrace his life, might undermine Falco's original achievements. That said, perhaps bad memory is still better than no memory at all, as it encourages us to engage with it, while silence leads to silence.

14 Burial and grave

The first event of importance for Falco's posthumous career was his funeral rites. They were conducted in a typical Habsburg way, which was also Falco's way – mixing elements that are normally kept separate. The funeral was staged as a public event, bringing to mind the funeral of Diana, Princess of Wales, which took place half a year previously, and in an Austrian context that of Princess Zita of Bourbon-Parma, the last Empress of Austria, who was buried in Vienna in April 1989. Ordinary people queued for hours to be able to pay respect to the deceased artist and the guest list read like Austria's "Who's Who". Among the public figures attending the funeral was the mayor of Vienna, Helmut Zilk, while Falco's coffin was carried by the rockers from the band Outsider Austria, who played in the video for 'Rock Me Amadeus', somewhat undermining the seriousness of the event, not unlike Elton John performing at Diana's funeral. On this occasion, however, Falco 'performed himself', singing one of his favourite songs, Bob Dylan's 'It's All Over Now, Baby Blue', in this way beginning his complex self-haunting operation.

Comparing Falco's and Diana's funerals (both televised) one can reach the conclusion that Falco was for Austrians what Diana was for English people, the object of their love and identification. Such an idea is conveyed in Falco's entry in "Uncyclopedia", an online encyclopaedia priding itself on being "free of content", yet rich on insights, where we can read the slightly exaggerated statement: "Also in attendance at his funeral was the entire populace of Austria, and it was reported that they have never recovered from the loss of their only awesome person".

Falco's funeral also points to the singer's intermeshing with the world of Austria's very rich. His coffin was transported from the Dominican Republic to Vienna in a private jet, provided by Niki Lauda, who subsequently named one of his planes "Falco" and his grave was paid for by his other rich friend, Ronny Seunig, the owner of Excalibur. Such acts can be seen both as manifestations of mourning on the part of these friends, as well as a means to gain respectability by presenting themselves as charitable capitalists. In a wider sense, this privatization of Falco's funeral points to a colonization of pop music by capital. It was, of course, always the case, but not in such a conspicuous way.

Falco's grave in Zentralfriedhof, designed and produced by an Austrian monumental mason, Erich Zechmeister, consists of three parts – an ordinary tombstone, commemorating Falco as a private person; an obelisk, which is a monument to Falco as an artist; and a plexiglass quarter-circle with a larger than natural photo of Falco and the titles of his greatest hits – a representation of a broken record. The plexiglass construction dominates the grave rendering it unusual, even in Vienna's Zentralfriedhof, where the heterogeneity and the spirit of extravagance, permeating the Habsburg Empire, are magnified. Glass, better than stone, allows for a mimetic reproduction of a person. Against a transparent background, Falco, clad in a black cape, looks almost alive, as if he was a vampire haunting his own grave and inviting us to visit him. Unlike stone, glass does not erode, suggesting that Falco's art will likewise resist the corrosion of time.

Figure 14.1: Falco's grave

The grave tells us that contrary to some common truths, even after death people are not equal; death tends to magnify previous differences. The fact that Falco, being merely a pop star, after his death usurped himself the place of a demigod (or allowed others to grant him such a place) attracted some amusingly malicious comments, such as this one: "FALCO is buried in a grave that rivals that of many of the great Pharaoh's tombs in size, scope and obelisk construction" (Granger 2012). I shall add that in reality (or my perception of it) Falco's grave does not have monstrous dimensions. It is the shape, not the size, which makes it unusual. Falco's grave, predictably, became the site of fans' pilgrimage, as demonstrated by candles, flowers, letters and stone hearts left there. It became also a source of inspiration for serious artists (at least in intention, if not in execution), as exemplified by an exhibition entitled "FALCOS Grab" (Falco's grave) by a Berlin-based artist Stephan Gripp in Galerie Kai Hoelzner. In the introduction to this exhibition we could read that

> Taking Falco's grave in Vienna's Zentralfriedhof as his starting point, Gripp presents a portrait of Hans Hölzel's subconscious. This is achieved not by idealizing his aura but rather in terms of a psychography. Stephan Gripp's preferred materials for his sculptures are chipboard, plastic panels, mirrors and decontextualized materials such as neon tubes and woollen thread. It is not just the choice and utilization of material in his work which points towards the kind of interior most commonly associated with discotheques or swinger clubs. They can also be seen symbolically as part of the decor found in young people's rooms and places for sexual or cultural privacy. Chains, tubes, expressionist jaggedness and again and again monolithic black and clinical white all hone the effect created by his sculptures to produce a psychological mood in which fear and trauma prevail. Whereas classic psychoanalytic theory considers the possibility of sublimating instinctive impulses and perversions by diverting libidinous energy towards cultural activity, Stephan Gripp's work demonstrates how such redirected affects can lead into neurotic or psychotic structures. Like reflections in a mirror they remain phantasms that form an imaginary frame, as for instance in the case of the three penises of FALCO and his stillborn brothers, shown in the form of plastic tubing lying intertwined on the floor. Or in the mirror tiles which can be seen in the place of Hans Hölzel's face at the top of a column, reflecting not infinity but merely the ceiling tiles of the gallery. Thus, the heavens remain unattainable both for Hölzel and for the viewer, at least for as long as the world believes in the clichés of his productions and carries on perpetuating them (Gripp 2007).

While I cannot help but smile reading about "the three penises of FALCO and his stillborn brothers, shown in the form of plastic tubing lying intertwined on the floor", I do it with an awareness that initiatives of this kind can be seen as a continuation of Falco's own practice of cannibalizing high art for low art purposes. Moreover, my own way of looking at Falco has much in common with such projects and is thus equally open to ridicule.

15 The culture industry looks back at Falco's career

Falco's death also sparked a trail of biographies. I want to focus here on three, written by people who knew him in a specific capacity, therefore can shed a light on Falco from a distinct perspective. Authors of these biographies remained in an ambiguous relationship with Falco. They were close to him, liked or even loved him, but also felt disappointed by him and perhaps also felt that they themselves owe something to Falco.

The first is a biography of Falco, written by his manager, Horst Bork: *Falco: Die Wahrheit* (*Falco: The Truth*) (2009). The word "truth" in the book's title can be dismissed merely as an advertising gimmick, whose purpose is to maximize its readership, as well as a need to find a way to differentiate Bork's version from those who already used the term "biography". And yet, I find it meaningful that his manager, who in principle was with the singer in a merely professional realm, attributes himself knowledge of the "real Falco", thus having a deeper knowledge than his family and friends. Such a position, however, reflects human relations under neoliberalism, where money making dominates all aspects of life, and in this process transforms personal relations into professional ones and professional, by default, into personal; a situation captured by the term "affective labour" (Gregg 2011). It suggests that what the manager knows, and by extension, what the managerial class knows about its employees, is the most trustworthy version of their external and internal existence. In this concrete case it reflects Bork's belief that he had access to Falco's most secret thoughts, was his closest friend, which for a considerable time was also a view shared by the singer.

Bork and Falco's collaboration began when the former spotted Falco performing 'Ganz Wien' with Drahdiwaberl in 1981 and invited the singer to visit him in his office in Hamburg. The next time they met Falco brought with him a demo tape of 'Helden von heute' and 'Der Kommissar'; the latter becoming a great hit and leading Bork to devote his efforts entirely to managing the singer's career. During their period together Falco became a star and a millionaire and Bork enjoyed a comfortable life thanks to their successes. Their close relationship, however, finished, when it stopped being profitable in a literal sense: "the goose stopped laying golden eggs", or at least the eggs ceased to be sufficiently large.

Bork's writing style is balanced, even dry, which makes us trust his version. This trust is augmented by the way the author presents himself in the photos inserted in the book. He comes across as a likeable, yet somewhat grey man, baldish and bespectacled even in his youth: a man born to manage others, work behind the scenes rather than take centre stage. Falco, as shown on the same pages as Bork and his wife, comes across as a jester, making faces, as if unable to take life seriously and stick to one identity. Yet Bork, even if he is unaware of it, produces a highly ideological work – his is the voice of a neoliberal economy, believing in its absolute rationality. His narrative is thus a story of a man who attempted to instil reason in his employee, for – as he believed – mutual advantage.

In a sense the manager of a pop star is not like the manager of a factory: the normal power relations are in this case reversed. The singer chooses his or her manager, rather than the other way round and can sack him or her at will or even whim. Moreover, the manager usually earns less than his or her client – only ten percent of their salary or so, unlike a factory manager, whose wages exceed those of the workers. But this apparently subservient position of the manager of a pop star only reflects a wider rule of class struggle, as presented by Marx in *Capital*, that in the situation of a shortage of labour force, the workforce can gain some privileges from capital. High-skilled workers and especially those who monopolized certain skills (those with a high human and cultural capital, as Pierre Bourdieu would say) can afford advantages ordinary workers do not enjoy, for example demanding an unusual pattern of work, being capricious and even insulting their employers. This reflect a wider rule that money gives power over fellow human beings and Falco, in common with other stars, was keen to take advantage of this power.[20]

However, despite the special case of being a pop star, he or she has to adhere to the demand of generating maximum profit. Bork's objective as Falco's manager was always simple – making money – and his affective labour, his friendship with Falco, was a means to this goal. There is no deliberation in the book on how much money was enough for Falco and by the same token for the manager. There was never enough because it could always be more. Bork's book even reads like Marx's *Capital* for the age of immaterial labour, namely a manual about increasing the rate of profit when the produced commodities are immaterial. Bork writes, for example, about attempts to sell the singer in all possible media. For this reason, he performed in music videos and films which, in the words of Bork, were a far cry from an ambitious "Autorenfilm". Falco was encouraged or compelled to "colonize" the globe with his music, from Vienna to Tokyo. We also gather that in his best years (1985–87), which also can be regarded as his worst years due to their leading to his physical and mental collapse, the singer spent more time promoting his music than making it, reflecting the idea that under advanced capitalism, production becomes subsumed by commerce, which is assisted by the image-making industry.

Bork writes about a requirement of Falco to perform practically continuously during a concert tour, because touring is investment-intensive. Taking a day off means paying for the unused technical support, hotels etc., hence losing money. Pop stars are a particularly precarious position not only because their non-working life is so costly, but also because they – despite the myth of an easy life of touring musicians – work in difficult conditions: away from home, changing location every day and not knowing how much they will earn in the end. Falco's touring life reminded me of the case of Mary Anne Walkley, described by Marx in the first volume of *Capital*:

> twenty years old, employed in a highly respectable dressmaking establishment, exploited by a lady with a pleasant name of Elise... These girls work, on an average, 16 and a half hours without a break, during the season often 30 hours, and the flow of their failing "labour-power" is maintained by occasional supplies of sherry, port or coffee (Marx 1976: 364).

The girl quite simply died from overwork.

Many will argue that this is a bad analogy, as Mary Anne Walkley was practically a slave, while Falco was a free man and had many more rewards for his extraordinary performance than the poor dressmaker. Yet, dying from overwork is not something that is confined to the nineteenth century, and nowadays "many people's lifetimes are shortened through the overwork they suffer or from the work conditions they encounter" (Harvey 2010: 143). I see Falco as such a case. On both occasions the working day had practically no limits, rest overlapped with work and all workers needed performance drugs to allow them to work to the required level. Falco was so concerned with the effect of his lifestyle on his health that he travelled with his personal physician, who was also his psychiatrist – a fact treated by Bork with derision, as a sign of the singer's hypochondria and a waste of money. Furthermore, although Falco enjoyed personal freedom, he was enslaved to the myth of an easy and exciting life of a star, as somebody who practically does not work and never does mundane tasks.

From Bork's book we learn that the manager did everything in his power to circumvent Falco's scope of manoeuvre, by making sure his schedule was full and even his physical freedom was limited. We read that following a night of "fun" (drinking, drug-taking and possibly paid sex) Falco missed his plane to London, where he and Bork were meant to have had a meeting with the Virgin boss, Richard Branson. As a result Falco had to apologize to a deeply-hurt Bork and in due course they both decided that from then on they would sleep in adjoining suites, to prevent the rowdy singer from wandering off. Bork's story is that of a subtle disciplining of an unruly worker by pointing out to him over and over again that money should come first and if he earns enough money, other goals would be taken care of. An example is tempting Falco to move to the States by showing him a beautiful house in Los Angeles in special evening light (an image reminiscent of the biblical story of Jesus tempted by the devil) – a perfect place for the singer to relocate with his young family, but paid for by agreeing to work even more. Bork can regard himself as a top manager – he managed to transform Falco into the most successful pop star from a German-speaking land of all time. And yet, even when the manager describes their best years, his narrative is clouded in frustration. In Bork's view, Falco was always lazy, unreliable and missing out on opportunities due to a stupid sense of pride or a fear of losing something of non-monetary value. He mentions Falco's refusal to sign a contract with the record company A&M because its boss, Herb Alpert, did not allow the singer to smoke in his house. Ultimately, their story could not have a happy ending because for the culture industry, as for other segments of capital, there is always a gap between the workers' potential for creating profit and the profit they actually create. Bork, with all his gentleness and sympathy for Falco, accepted this rule.

That Bork's voice is a voice of the culture industry we can also deduce from his bourgeois values, saturating his narrative. He edifies Falco's wife Isabella as the only woman whom Falco really loved and subtly, yet for that more effectively, illuminates the link between the artist's failure to reach his earning potential and his inability to fulfil an ideal of a stable family life. If Falco was a happy family man, Bork believes, he might have had a more successful career and ended his life differently. Yet, he avoids reflecting on the difficulty of fulfilling this ideal, while having to sustain the pressures (and pleasures) of being a pop star, although Falco's life reads as proof that family and fame do not fit together. A telling example is his wife's decision to leave him when he was touring in Japan. It appears that the culture industry wants it both ways: employees accepting intolerable working conditions, which force them to forfeit their right to time off and neglect their families, yet having wives and children, as a sign of fitting well into the capitalist project.

There is, however, a counter-narrative running through the book, that of Falco himself, not unlike the thwarted voice of Lolita undermining the voice of her master Humbert (also, incidentally, a German) in Vladimir Nabokov's famous novel. The connection is the more pervasive as for most of the book Bork describes Falco as if the singer was a child: immature and prone to emotions, with Bork and his wife (most likely a childless couple) as Falco's adopted parents, providing the young man with the family and home he was lacking.

Bork even mentions that although the difference of age between them was less than ten years, Falco treated him as if he was a much older man. This counter-narrative is a story of a child gradually disentangling himself from the tentacles of his father-manager and show business at large. The signs of his independence were growing intervals between making records, his loss of interest in being in the media spotlight and finally moving to the Dominican Republic. Falco's frequent alcohol abuse and antics in hotels can also be viewed this way, although, as I indicated earlier, I treat them as a means to cope with the pressures of being a pop star. Did the disobeying of his manager make Falco more autonomous as an artist and a human being, or less? On the one hand, one gets the impression that Falco post-Bork had more time and personal freedom. On the other hand, he desperately attempted to hold onto his position as a star (and its perks, such as money), which forced him to be less choosy and accept less dignified jobs. Either as an autonomous being or as a failed artist Falco had no value for Bork and they parted ways. The manager admits that Falco perceived their separation in terms of Bork's betrayal, but points out that such a betrayal is only natural in his profession, where ultimately profit not friendship rules.

16 Mourning as therapy

While Horst Bork embarked on a fact-finding mission about Falco, the books written by Katharina Bianca Vitkovic and Beatrice Castaldi, respectively Falco's daughter and lover, were meant to fulfil a different function: that of therapy. Using such a word obviously points to a trauma suffered by their authors, but it is not so much a pain caused by Falco's death itself, as a certain unfinished business, which they needed to address. Although Vitkovic's memoir was published before Castaldi's, I will discuss it later, as Castaldi's memory work sheds some light on what Vitkovic is writing.

While the style of Bork betrays the dry, yet tender hand of a businessman dealing with delicate objects, Castaldi's work comes across as a work of passion, as one might expect from a book written by a lover. True to its genre, it focuses on sex and intimate secrets, although ultimately there is nothing especially revealing or unexpected. The language is full of journalistic clichés, perhaps attesting to the author's lack of literary training, her lack of deeper insight into her lover's inner life or the wider phenomenon of media affecting the way we think about ourselves. The last hypothesis is confirmed by the fact that Castaldi often writes about both Falco and herself as if they were images, constructed by the media, as well as discussing the role of the media in Falco's life. As Castaldi admits with a disarming honesty, if Falco had read her memoir, he would have said that it is not a book deserving a Pulitzer prize (Österreich-Interview 2012). But its rawness makes it easier to identify some crucial points.

Let's, again, begin with the title: *Falco lebt* (*Falco is alive*). Castaldi is not a conspiracy theorist, trying to convince us that Falco carries on living incognito. Her title is metaphorical: Falco is alive, because he lives on in her memory or even, during the time of writing her book, was infused with extra blood as Falco became more vivid in her memory. Her commemoration of Falco, like those of others, is not entirely disinterested. She uses the memory of her affair with Falco to come to terms with the failure of her marriage to an Italian millionaire, Giovanni Castaldi. Remembering publicly the supposed charisma of Falco, as a lover and as a man, is meant to humiliate her ex-husband, whose callousness is described in the first chapter of her book, and help Beatrice regain self-respect. We also can detect a more subtle mourning or melancholia at play here: her mourning for unfulfilled love and by the same token an unfulfilled life.

But when we assess somebody's love life, we inevitably, although implicitly, judge it against our own standards of love. The standard I want to use comes from a recent book, *In Praise of Love*, by Alain Badiou, a philosopher already quoted in this study, in which he argues against reducing love to the types advocated in neoliberal discourses: either to "zero-risk" love, epitomised by a well-planned marriage, based on semi-scientific research provided by internet dating sites, or rampant hedonism, devoid of passion. Instead, he proposes to understand love as "an existential project: to construct a world from a decentred point of view other than that of my mere impulse to survive or re-affirm my own identity" (Badiou 2012: 26). Badiou talks about "Two scene" (2012: 29); love understood in such terms involves partnership, not manifested merely in sharing kitchen duties or childcare, but also through willingness to embrace and enjoy the other person's point of view.

Castaldi's marriage, as described in the first chapter, did not pass "Badiou's test" or even less demanding standards of love, as he was a bully, and she did not love him. But what about her relationship with Falco? Was it true love on both sides? There is no simple answer to this question, only some clues in the text. The proper story begins, of course, when the to-be-lovers meet for the first time. Its setting, a sauna, which, like a nightclub or especially its sub-category of a strip club, another common setting of Falco's life, is a liminal space, situated between an innocent zone of rest and a brothel. Strip club or sauna courtship tends to be short and lacking in sophistication; it is geared towards people who do not have an entire lifetime to fall in love, but need to get to the business of lovemaking as soon as possible. Respectively, alcohol and drugs, and heat and nudity, facilitate this goal.

Falco met all his girlfriends in saunas, nightclubs or similar establishments, such as hotel lobbies, and the intervals between their first meeting and sex tended to be short, often only several hours. In Castaldi's case (whose name at the time was Zohmann), it was several days, not because Falco took more time to court her than other women, but because he was busy with preparation for his Dounauinsel concert. It goes without saying that it was the singer who chased the girl, rather than the other way round. One day the singer told her that he liked her, a couple of days later he sent a car to take her to his concert and straight after the concert announced to the press that they were a couple. With some pride Castaldi confesses that their relationship was sealed by Falco forbidding her to socialize with other stars at the event. Jealousy, leading to exclusiveness on the part of the man, was thus interpreted by the author as a sign of his love, rather than his patriarchal mindset.

What follows is the description of their shared life, which most likely can serve as a matrix for most, if not all, of Falco's relationships with women and, I believe, those of many other men with money and power. It was full of tenderness and pleasant surprises for the beloved woman, beginning with a free pass to his concert and booking a "wedding suite" in a hotel in Graz, a highly satisfying sex life (no doubt, emphasized as the main selling point of her book), yet based on inequality of rights and duties, exacerbated by an age gap, with Falco being seventeen years older than his lover. Falco was always "himself": he drank excessively and often disappeared without warning, yet he expected his girlfriend to put up with his behaviour, smoothing the process with bunches of roses, presents and love confessions. His schedule was Beatrice's schedule rather than the other way round. She gave up for him her studies to become a vet; he did not give up practically anything for her. He also publicly admitted, offending modern standards of gender relations, that he expected his woman to walk half a step behind him. Even if, as Castaldi claims, pronouncements of this kind were merely a means to create a public persona of an arrogant macho, and had little in common with his private behaviour (yet which, as she shows, was not exactly the case), it raises the question why the singer wanted to convey such a public image, humiliating his lovers.

As a "modern man" (a term used by Falco in some interviews, to describe his relationship with women), he did not insist on marriage with Beatrice or with any of his lovers (although Castaldi mentions his desire to marry her and have a child), nor protested when they left him. On the contrary, the freedom to leave was their foundation of being together: the woman could choose either to conform to his lifestyle or leave and eventually all of his girlfriends left him. One can guess that this fact did not devastate my protagonist. Immediately after one woman left him, he went to a nightclub or sauna and picked up another woman and the story repeated itself. The only difference was a faster turn-over of lovers – while with his early partners he remained for three to four years (the record appears to belong to Sylvia Wagner, whom he also singled out as being of best character), he was with Beatrice Castaldi for less than two years, and with his last "great love", Caroline Perron, for around a year, reflecting these women's difficulty in putting up with his behaviour. Another change concerned the growing age gap, most likely adding to the man's sense of power over his lovers that he needed, feeling increasingly disempowered in his professional life. This was also reflected in the fact that, as Castaldi confirms, he tended to negotiate with her parents, rather than herself, the conditions of their relationship.

Falco himself near the end of his life explained that the fiasco of his relationships was due to women looking for the wrong man in him. Such an answer is convincing – most women (as, indeed, men) look for partners who would consider their needs, views and, to use Badiou's language, enjoy constructing a shared world from a decentred point of view. He proved unable to conform to such an expectation – he was the wrong man for a plethora of good women, being, as he pronounced in one of his last songs, an egoist. In the light of the pattern described, it is not surprising that Castaldi, asked in an interview how she compared to Falco's other women, replied, with an insight lacking in her book, that such comparison is pointless – for the singer there was only the current woman. All of them – to use a fairy-tale language – were his true loves or none was.

In the documentary *Hoch wie nie*, the most touching fragment shows Maria Hölzel displaying the photographs of Falco, no older than nine years of age, with his cousin, both in wedding-like clothes. On one of the photos the young couple are even kissing. The cousin, in his mother's words, was an object of Hansi's great love; he wanted to marry her. Such uncanny photos, which I believe one could find only in fiction films about sexual perverts, from the vantage point of Falco's entire love-life, act as a symbol of a gap between high romantic ideals most people cherish and the somewhat thwarted, prosaic love lives they choose, not least, because as Badiou claims, love understood as an existential project requires hard work. They can also be seen – as Falco's mother wants to see them – as a sign that Falco simply did not meet the right woman: one who had the power to make him look at the world her way.

Yet, although Falco's love of Beatrice Castaldi fell short of Badiou's and most likely of her own ideal, she still mourns him, because in the light of disappointment of her later life, he appears to be an angel. Her mourning thus encourages a somewhat clichéd feminist reading about the "glass ceiling", which forces many women to choose a degrading existence of an appendix to a man's life. Yet I refrain from such an interpretation, because, on the one hand, becoming a career woman is not getting any easier and, on the other, breaking the "glass ceiling" comes across today as a less appealing option than it used to be, as testified by information that so-called career women constitute the most unhappy strata of Western society. Against the complex slavery of contemporary work, the old-fashioned and light bondage of living with a rich man, especially of the type described by Castaldi, seems like a better choice. She confirms this opinion, by saying that she is happy to be defined as Falco's ex-girlfriend, and – as her book demonstrates – she attempts to extract surplus value from this fact.

17 Mourning as an act of revenge and forgiveness

In contrast to the title of Castaldi's book, which is in the present tense, that of Katharina Bianca Vitkovic's *Falco war mein Vater* (*Falco was my father*), is in the past tense. There is an ambiguity to such an expression. Either Falco was her father because he died, so cannot be any longer, or because the relationship changed during his or her life. Both of these things happened; before Falco died, he took a paternity test, which showed that he was not Katharina Bianca's biological father and on the basis of that literally and metaphorically disinherited her. She did not get a penny from his will, and she stopped seeing him, although he saw her occasionally, when she could not see him, when she was playing in the school yard and talked to her on the phone.

The discovery that the child he fathered was not biologically his is presented by Falco's biographers and friends as a sign of the artist's tragedy; it rendered him lonely in a deeper, metaphysical sense. Instead, relatively little concern was given to the daughter's position, despite her being much more vulnerable to the changes in such circumstances than an adult man. Equally, the plight of Katharina Bianca's mother, taken by surprise by this discovery, was rendered unimportant. She was even (re)presented as a cheat, as well as proof that Falco was unlucky with women.

The pain of learning about her genetic make-up, as Katharina Bianca admits in her book and interviews, is largely in the past. The question she asks in her book is a different one: should she still regard Falco as her father, after the harm he inflicted on her, or should she "disown" him? This is not the first time she took such an active stance in relation to Falco – even when he was still alive, she decided to change her surname, from Hölzel, to her mother's maiden name, partly to avoid being bullied at school as Falco's "daughter" and partly to punish him. As she claims, this decision made Falco very angry, pointing to the fact that he wanted to be in control of the relationship with his family (especially his women), but did not want them to enjoy the same right.

The fact that she poses the question "was Falco my father?" reverses their relationship – she is no longer the object of an investigation (the crude blood test) by her father, but investigates Falco, unearthing memories of their shared life, trying to figure out his motives and assessing the role of his death in her relationship with him, enjoying the power of discursively cleansing him, if she wishes to do so. The ambiguous title leaves the answer to this question suspended, but the very fact that Vitkovic wrote her book, as well as the fact that her room or apartment looks like a shrine to Falco, and her admitting that she has no feelings towards the man who most likely was her biological father (the first husband of her mother), suggests that she still loves Falco and even loves him more than when he was alive. This is because the passing of time helps us forgive and it is easier to forgive and "retain" a father who was a celebrity than one who is an ordinary man, as a celebrity father constitutes some kind of cultural capital, as confirmed by the fact that Katharina Bianca found a publisher for her memoirs.

Although Vitkovic knew Falco from a different perspective and in a different period than Castaldi, her account concurs with that of Falco's lover. She presents him as a man who wanted others to interact with him on his own terms. In her case it meant learning to play music and speak English, in order to follow in her father's footsteps. Katharina Bianca, however, showed no signs of being his female version; she was neither musical nor interested in foreign languages, and it is difficult not to guess that this in part prompted Falco's decision to test his paternity and deny her inheritance. Paradoxically, as an adult (as some YouTube users' noted), she shows a striking resemblance to Falco's own mother.

Falco's attitude towards Katharina Bianca contrasts with the behaviour of many current celebrities, such as Madonna or Angelina Jolie, who regard adopting children as their civic duty and, as cynics say, a means to look fashionable. A particular case is Eminem, who adopted his wife's daughter from a different relationship and a daughter of his wife's sister. Such a decision could be seen not only in the context of "playing a celebrity", but also in relation to the idea of a black family as an extended unit, where women pull forces to care for their children from different relationships, as well as of those belonging to other members of the family. This is in part a legacy of the times of slavery and the loss of status of black males, following de-industrialization. Eminem, of course, subverts this idea because he attributes himself the role of the caring "super-mother". Falco, by going the opposite way, also gestured to a specific custom – of a disgraced German tradition of prioritizing blood over culture. One can only hope that if he lived longer he would have changed his thinking.

18 Falco Symphonic

The second peak of commemorative work of Falco (the first followed his death) took place during the tenth anniversary of his death. One of them is the release of his concert with a symphonic orchestra in Wiener Neustadt in 1994, on a DVD titled *Falco Symphonic*. The reconstruction of the Wiener Neustadt concert could not happen straight after Falco's death due to psychological factors and technical constraints. Thomas Rabitsch told me that he was not able to undertake this work immediately after Falco's death because he needed time to come to terms with it: a time for "raw" mourning. Moreover, as he explains in a documentary, added to the DVD, the work on the concert proved difficult due to the scarcity and poor quality of the material at hand, which consisted of one VHS tape with a recording taken by three cameras and one audio cassette.

It required new technology to achieve the standards acceptable in the twenty-first century. By 2007 these conditions were fulfilled, because new computer programmes were available to allow for the upgrading of technically sub-standard material to an acceptable level and new, young specialists were able to use them, most importantly Dietz Tinhof, known for his work in the Vienna Symphonic Library, a state of the art digital resource for music producers. The task of sound editors, or rather "sound archaeologists", was to extract Falco's voice from the sound recorded during the concert, using a version of software known as Algorithmix Renovator, used for forensic purposes (Tinhof 2008). This involved painstaking work, comparable to rescuing a rare original from the layers of dust and dirt of history, which was justified only by the special status of Falco in Austrian culture. Such reconstruction, as the "archaeologists" conceded, is never complete – as in a literary translation, some aspects of the original are lost, some are added, reflecting the choices of the translator. In several cases, when the voice was not recoverable, Tinhof and his collaborator, Dorothee Badent, searched Rabitsch's archive for comparable live-takes from Falco's voice, mostly from his 1993 tour and matched/lip-synched Falco's own performance syllable by syllable (ibid.). In this way the "simple" past of 1994 became enriched by earlier layers.

The rest of the sound, recorded during the concert, was discarded and recorded again in 2007 by the principal protagonists of the 1994 concert: members of Falco's band and the orchestra from Wiener Neustadt. The musicians had to repeat in the studio what they played live in 1994, adjusting their new performance to the voice of Falco. The past thus was imbued with the present, memory replaced history and the live performance seamlessly merged with music created in the studio. To make up for the lack of voices of the public, typically heard on concert albums, Rabitsch invited Falco fans to the studio and recorded their singing. In this way the public played a more active role in producing the record than is normally the case. *Falco Symphonic* thus became in part a tribute to Falco by his fans.

Similar and different problems emerged during work on the visual material. The image was of low quality, the camera was out of focus and presented the singer with limited perspectives and there was no close-up on instruments, which is expected in films showing the performance of a symphonic orchestra. Here the challenge was to upgrade the quality and have more images. To get more material, Rabitsch appealed in a newspaper advert to the public to provide him with videos made by them during the concert and several people came forward, offering their films. In due course, such material was incorporated into the final version. The video producers also shot members of the orchestra playing their specific instruments: violins, flutes, trumpets, to add their close-ups to the film. The film thus merged the past (the time of the concert) with the present (the time of its reconstruction) and attributed the audience a role of amateur historians or "memorists", adding their "mini-narratives" to the larger story of Falco's performance. It also rendered Falco a people's artist, not only serving his audience, but being created by it.

Figure 18.1: Falco in Wiener Neustadt

The DVD, which is the main result of the reconstruction of the concert, wears its character of a memory work on its sleeve, so to speak, by including a documentary about its production. It introduces the main people behind the concert and its reconstruction, such as the mayor of Wiener Neustadt, Peter Wittmann, Herget, Rabitsch, Skrepek, other musicians from Falco's band and the sound and video editors. They all talk about the challenges of their work and, especially, about their desire to foreground Falco's presence in the final product which also testifies to his poignant absence at the time they completed their work. We can learn about the specific role each of them played, but the overall impression is that it is a product of collaboration: the sum is larger than each individual element.

The main film, presenting the concert, equally emphasizes its constructed character. One means is to frequently split the screen into two or three parts. This allowed the use of the lower quality material, as low resolution of an image is less of a problem when the image is smaller. The juxtaposition of the images, recorded in 1994 with images from 2007, point to the past being interwoven with the present: old voice with the new instruments. Part of the film is in colour, part in black and white. This is not an uncommon practice in film and video art, but the usual way is to show the past in black and white, which are the colours of old chronicles. On this occasion, however, there is no clear rule regarding the use of colour. One moment we see Falco in black and white, the next in colour, as if he was navigating between the past (of the concert) and the present (of the reconstruction). From time to time we also see Falco in slow motion, the sign of an effort to capture him and prolong his presence.

Although *Falco Symphonic* is a product of collaborative work, even the main authors of this production are conspicuously absent on the cover of the DVD and CD: we only see on it Falco. This reflects the fact that Falco was always positioned as the star of his records and that *Falco Symphonic* is a monument, and monuments do not show portraits of their creators, even if there would be no monuments without them. On the cover we see Falco in a black tuxedo, white shirt and a bow tie. This is not the costume he wore during the concert in Wiener Neustadt, but one with which he was most associated during his career: the costume of a dandy, but also of a "classical" musician, as shown in the video of 'Rock Me Amadeus'. The message is that the material contained on the DVD offers a synthetic image of Falco: as a musician, a poet and a public figure. This image is split; the cover presents two almost identical pictures of Falco, of which neither shows him in full. This might suggest that the work offers us two Falcos: one from 1994, one from 2008, and neither is complete. In a sense they are the same, because Falco was no longer alive in 2008, therefore on a photo he is no different than in 1994, but the posthumous Falco has a different aura. While in 1994 the listeners can assume that there will be more opportunities to see him performing live, from 1998 this is no longer the case. The lacuna left in Austrian music by Falco's death is reflected in the fact that *Falco Symphonic* proved commercially very successful, in Austria receiving the status of a Platinum record and a Platinum DVD, as well as very good reviews.

19 Falco schmolli-ed

Another anniversary work which I decided to consider here is a series of mashup songs and videos, entitled *Falco Re:loaded* and produced by an Austrian DJ who goes by the moniker DJ Schmolli. They constitute a sustained piece of work, comprising of thirteen mash-up tracks and mashup videos, and offer a distinct perspective on Falco and his heritage. Schmolli's take on Falco also coincides with the way I see the singer. The genre which Schmolli uses is still relatively new and there is not much academic work devoted to it. Video mashups can be compared to found footage films, except that in mashups there is practically only found footage – the author juxtaposes fragments of music videos and songs, without adding any new material which she or he recorded. William Wees argues that thanks to situating fragments of an old film in the "tissue" of a new film, its richer implications become apparent and the film becomes open to new and unexpected readings (Wees 1993: 17). A similar idea is proposed by Michael Serazio in his discussion of music mashups. He observes that they have the potential to transcend borders and formats as a means of resisting narrowly imposed cultural parameters, most importantly those relating to music genres. Serazio's crucial example is 2 Many DJs' 'Smells Like Teen Booty', which is a hybrid of Nirvana's 1991 'Smells Like Teen Spirit' and Destiny's Child's 'Bootylicious' (2001). This is an ironic work, as it "peels off Kurt Cobain's iconic, angstful lyrics, subverts what had been Cobain's genuine lament and erases originally coded meanings and readings. Instead of a growling 'I feel stupid and contagious', the listener hears, 'Is my body too bootylicious for you, baby?'" (Serazio 2008: 83). 'Teen Booty' works, argues Serazio, because rather than going deep (what Nirvana desires), it stays shallow and takes pop at its face value. Not surprisingly, Dave Grohl of Nirvana reportedly found 'Smells Like Teen Booty' "wretched" (Serazio 2008: 84). That said, every act of mashing-up, be it of music, fragments of films or music videos, is also an act of recognition of the value of the material at hand, is a tribute to it by taking the trouble to think about it in an inventive way.

This is also the case of Schmolli's mashups – they explore meanings of Falco's music, performance and videos which were undiscovered or played down during his lifetime and reveal their hidden potential. Schmolli reads Falco's songs subversively and re-enacts Falco's missed opportunities. One such example is "Falco vs Jennifer Lopez", where the author mixes Falco's 'Jeanny' with Lopez's 'Jenny from the Block'. Apart from the main characters having similar names, the two songs are different. In 'Jeanny' the narrator is male and the woman is merely an object of his narration. In 'Jenny from the Block' the narrator is female and she sings about herself. We are encouraged to treat it as Lopez's autobiographical story. Falco's 'Jeanny' is full of drama; 'Jenny from the Block' is much more mundane. Falco sings about somebody extraordinary; Lopez represents herself, provocatively, as a "girl next door". Bringing these songs together points to the fact that Falco was always at the centre of his performances and women were marginalized and objectified in them. It also offers a possibility (for some viewers real; for others only imaginary) to post-humously overcome this limitation by organizing a duet of Falco and Lopez. The question arises whether by hybridizing 'Jeanny' with 'Jenny' Schmolli also undermines the seriousness and art-ness of Falco's song, in the same way the author of 'Smells Like Teen Booty' undermined the seriousness of Nirvana's work. For some listeners it might be the case, but I believe not to the same extent as for the fans of Nirvana, because Falco's 'Jeanny' did not have the same level of depth. Among others, Horst Albrecht (1993: 14) and Alice Bolt-erauer (2010: 88) observe that Falco's 'Jeanny', in common with many of his earlier songs, was a kind of mashup song already in its original version, made up of romantic clichés, "simulations" of reality, and inviting "deconstruction". For me it is a camp song.

Other Schmolli's mashups betray a similar agenda. In 'Whenever Young Romans Get Into the Groove', which is a variation on 'Junge Roemer', he offers us iconic images of 1980s Madonna. Juxtaposing Falco with Madonna evokes the fact that Falco refused to sing a duet with her, which can be viewed as symbolic for his unwillingness to engage positively with music created by women for women, as well as American music. On the other hand, in 'I Won't Be Crying Out Of The Dark' Falco's last hit, 'Out of the Dark', is juxtaposed with a song by a Danish dance band, Infernal, 'I Won't Be Crying', which also brings memory of Falco's duet with a Danish performer, Brigitte Nielsen. Schmolli attempts to imagine Falco's music as offering more scope for collaboration with female performers, while simultaneously demonstrating that this aspect was underdeveloped in his work.

Another feature of Schmolli's take on Falco is linking him to the tradition of black American rap, most importantly in Falco vs Luniz vs Nelly – 'Mash Me Amadeus', where 'Rock Me Amadeus' is combined with the work of Luniz and Nelly. Again, such juxtaposition points to the fact that Falco was a rapper and by the virtue of that he deserves to be placed in the company of hip hop artists. But, again, this mashup shows Falco's unfulfilled potential as a rapper, a potential Schmolli fulfils in his place, so to speak.

According to Schmolli's website, the artists who contributed to his spe-
cial Falco album include AC/DC, Afrika Bambaataa, Amerie, Ashanti, Beyonce,
Bob Marley, Cevin Fisher, David Guetta, Dr. Dre, Eric B. & Rakim, Fatboy
Slim, Jan Delay, Jay-Z, Jennifer Lopez ft. LOX, J-Kwon, Luniz, Madonna, Mis-
teeq, Nelly, O.K., Queen, Sean Paul, Shakira, Snoop Dogg, Steely Dan, Stevie
Wonder, The Chemical Brothers, The Pussycat Dolls, The Temptations, W.A.
Mozart, Wu-Tang Clan plus a few others (DJ Schmolli 2008). This list can be
read as a list of Falco's metaphorical "cousins", some of whom he encoun-
tered in his career and some of whom he was unable to meet. The album
finishes with a track and video entitled 'Okay Falco'. This work is of special
importance because there is something very Falco-like in its title. Falco, like
many non-English speaking people, overused the word "OK". We hear it often
at his concerts when he alternates "OK" with "all right", rather than using its
German equivalents. Secondly, Schmolli inserts the most famous quotations
from Falco, so the video has a quality of personal testament of the artist. The
choice of quotes points to the fact that Falco, as I already argued in the first
part, presented himself, particularly in his interviews, as a romantic artist:
lonely, unique and sacrificing himself at the altar of his art. I also mentioned
that there was a considerable gap between Falco's self-projection on the one
hand and the commercial character of his music and his artistic trajectory
on the other. Schmolli is able to present this gap economically by juxtaposing Falco's lofty discourse with the video of one of his arguably most trashy
and intentionally commercial song, 'Naked'. Perhaps this juxtaposition was
meant to expose Falco as a hypocrite who wanted to be seen as an idealistic
artist while producing trash. For me, however, it rather demonstrates that he
was able successfully to broach boundaries between pop and rock, high and
low art, commercial and autonomous art, etc. 'Naked', which I regard as one
of his most sophisticated songs and videos, despite being accused of trashi-
ness, demonstrates it very well. The mashup video finishes with words said
off-screen that Falco must be a great artist to be honoured with such an excellent tribute. These words are uttered by Rob Bolland, Falco's music producer
and co-author, together with his brother, in an official tribute to Falco, entitled
'Falco Super Star'. For those who know the Bolland's tribute and recognize the
voice, its inclusion in the mashup is imbued with irony because of the dubi-
ous artistic quality of the Bollands' own tribute and Rob Bolland's naïve self-
exposure as somebody yearning to be honoured in place of the more famous
and tragic Falco. Yet, ultimately, I take seriously the claim that Falco was a
great artist and a cool guy to be honoured in such a way, because Schmolli's
tributes capture Falco's work very well, develop it and, in a wider sense, demonstrate that art can be enhanced by fun, rather than undermined by it.

20 In a shadow of the original: *Falco – Verdammt, wir leben noch!*

The film *Falco – Verdammt, wir leben noch!* (2008), directed by Thomas Roth, was another symptom of Falco anniversary fever. Biopics do not belong to genres favoured by film historians and critics, being too bound by the demand of telling the truth to merit them as a form of art. But telling the truth in film is not easy either, as the average film lasts 100 minutes, while the life of an artist, even if it is below the population's average, is several decades. There are additional problems with biopics of contemporary people. Unlike actors playing Napoleon, Mozart or Edvard Munch, who at best can be compared to their painted portraits, actors playing Presley or – as is the case here – Falco, have to compete with the originals, immortalized by cameras and cine-cameras. This poses a dilemma for the filmmakers: imitate, telling as good as they can the story, already well known from the documents, or construct, offering a version nobody has told before. The authors of *Falco – Verdammt, wir leben noch!* chose the first option, providing the pleasures of recognition. They aimed at maximum authenticity in recreating the famous utterances by Falco, events, in which he took part, videos etc. They succeeded in recreating the 1980s as a period of "heroic neoliberalism", when it was cool not only to be rich but also show it, being flamboyant, gaudy, artificial, arrogant and silly. They were less successful in giving the characters any psychological depth.

The main victims of this failure are Falco, and Manuel Rubey who plays the main part. An actor from a different generation than Falco (born in 1979), most likely with different taste and values, he could have updated Falco, "mash him up" with the new Viennese rappers and rockers, in the way Forman and Falco updated Mozart in their work. Instead, Rubey was reduced to putting on Falco's old mantel, doing karaoke, rather than singing Falco's "new" songs with a new attitude. Rubey repeats exactly what Falco said, therefore his words come across as quotations rather than spontaneous expressions. In the part with Falco as a child, his mantel of the future artist comes across as dustier than "authenticity" demanded, because it draws heavily on Truffaut's *Les quatre cents coups* (*The 400 Blows*, 1958), set in the period of postwar austerity rather than the more colourful late 1960s. Little Hansi's first encounter with a prostitute harks back to an even earlier period in cinema's history: the times of Jean Renoir, rather than Truffaut. The fact that the future singer at the end of the 1960s watches in a cinema with eyes wide open Oskar Werner's performance as Mozart in Karl Hardt's film from 1955 adds to the impression that Roth places the young Falco in the wrong decade and, to pack maximum information, takes shortcuts.

The adult singer is reduced to a pathetic alcoholic, who drinks irrespectively of whether he is at the top or bottom of the charts, in his own home or in a brothel, before or after the concert. The scenes of boozing are juxtaposed with Falco miraculously appearing on stage or in a video, as if there was no middle ground between drinking and performing – no work on the part of the singer to present himself favourably to the audience. All it took was to sober up and go on stage or on a film set, where he was a puppet remotely controlled by some invisible forces. Horst Bork and some of Falco's acquaintances, such as Edek Bartz (Kralicek and Nüchtern 2000) claim that this was indeed the case – Falco was a puppet, although with the right qualities for meteoric success: good voice, good looks and youth. But this does not make for an original or even interesting film.

Perhaps Roth could have made up for the boredom of watching bottles of Jack Daniels being emptied by Falco if he focused on those who put this puppet in motion: music producers, video makers, make-up artists, stylists, photographers, as did Peter Watkins in *Privilege*. They are, however, not included in the narrative. The DoRo duo, responsible for Falco's videos, are completely omitted from the film, and the Bolland brothers are reduced to a disembodied voice from the telephone and an image of the massive music studio, a castle which Falco is not even allowed to enter. Falco's discoverers, Markus Spiegel and his manager, come across as old-fashioned pen-pushers with no creative input.

Another victim of Roth's quest for "authenticity" and popularity are Falco's women. The girlfriends have no personalities of their own and their role is limited to providing Falco with sexual services and nagging him to stop drinking and go to bed early. Such an approach betrays the fact that Roth failed to consult the singer's lovers, satisfying himself with an opinion that there were many and they conformed to a certain "type". But it can also be seen as a nod to a theory of the fin-de-siecle Viennese philosopher, Otto Weininger (2005), who in the book *Geschlecht und Charakter* (*Sex and Character*) argued that while men (with an exception of Jews) are rational, women operate only at the level of their emotions and sexual organs.

Giving Falco's wife Isabella a pretentious (in the Austrian context) name of Jacqueline suggests that she is a composite character, encompassing a number of Falco's lovers and representing his favourite type: blond, tall and slim. Jacqueline is also the name of a character played by Diana Scott, played by Julie Christie in a film within John Schlesinger's film, *Darling* (1965). Diana Scott/Julie Christie's Jacqueline is a heroine in a cartoonesque horror, who dies in the first five minutes of the film without uttering a word. Schlesinger's inclusion of Jacqueline's story was his ironic commentary on the way women are treated in the movies. No such irony can be found in *Falco – Verdammt, wir leben noch!*; the film naïvely endorses the attitude to women criticized by Schlesinger. While the lovers are all "dumb blondes", Falco's mother adheres to the "castrating mother" type. She is a bitter woman, who following her husband's departure gives herself the task of eliminating other women from her son's life.

Yet, even in the middle of this disappointing film, there is a profound moment, worthy of Josef von Sternberg's *The Last Command* (1928). In this Emil Jannings plays an ex-tsarist general, now a poor old man in Hollywood, who applies for work as an extra and is cast to replay his glorious former self in the film-within-the-film. Such a meta-cinematic moment in *Falco – Verdammt, wir leben noch!* consists of casting in the role of a barwoman who witnessed Falco's death, Grace Jones. Jones bears many similarities to Falco, as she enjoyed a peak of popularity in the 1980s, while in the 1990s she suffered a downturn. At the top of her career she connoted excess and was regarded as a performance artist, a persona, rather than merely a singer. She also enjoyed a comeback around the same time as Falco, although – in contrast to my protagonist – this happened when she was still alive. Her playing in a film about a fellow fallen star raises the question of what role Falco would have played had he reached old age – would he be cast as an extra in a biopic about his own life or on other, more successful artists, because, had he survived, they would be no biopic about him?

21 Falco (dis)covered

Another way of commemorating Falco is through producing cover songs. Dai Griffiths divides covers into "renditions" and "transformations". Rendition is a straightforwardly faithful version of the original, carrying with it some of the connotation of performance in classical music, transformation being a more determined claim on the original – at certain times it would be better even to speak of an "appropriation" of the original. However, he concedes that a rendition, a "straight" cover with little alteration, can alter the original meaning simply because of the specificity of the historical or cultural context of the performance or its recording (Griffiths 2002: 52); which is a view taken by other authors writing on this subject. For example, Alexander Sebastian Dent argues that "the cover song represents a form of musical translation in which the performer signals previous authorship, thus layering, or laminating, these moments of authorship in performance. All this partakes of history through previous performance contexts, and puts these layers to use in the new situation" (Dent 2005: 209). For the purpose of my study, I assume that every cover is both a rendition of an original song and its transformation and appropriation; it is a new work, but also a comment on the old work, its place within the music and cultural history and, in some cases, a means to fulfil its unfulfilled potential. Again, there is no place to discuss here every cover version of Falco's songs. I am only interested in mapping the main directions of this memory work.

Predictably, the most frequently covered are the most popular Falco songs, such as 'Rock Me Amadeus', 'Der Kommissar' and 'Jeanny', and the bulk of the new versions are released by German-speaking artists. These covers belong to different genres. One is industrial techno and metal. A German metal group, Megaherz, released in this style in 1998 'Rock Me Amadeus' and recently an Austrian artist Thomas Rainer, known for his project Nachtmahr, recorded 'Titanic'. In addition, Norwegian band Sturmgeist covered 'Rock Me Amadeus'. Although I am not particularly fond of this style, I am fascinated by these examples, because they confirm my reading of Falco as a 'bard of apocalypse', not unlike Nick Cave (Boer 2012).

These artists take Falco's apocalyptic discourse to the extreme, changing its mood. While Falco renders apocalypse bearable, almost unnoticeable and even pleasurable, because smoothed with champagne and caviar, it is not the case with Nachtmahr's 'Titanic', which comes across as a song of hungry masses stranded in a postindustrial landscape.

The second style is German punk, represented by its queen, Nina Hagen. Hagen recorded a tribute song, 'Poetenclub', using fragments of Falco's interviews and performed 'Ganz Wien' at Vienna festival in 2005. In her take on Falco, not unlike the industrial techno artists, Hagen renders him somewhat more serious than he was during his lifetime. Her "heroin" in 'Ganz Wien' comes across as more deadly and full of pathos than Falco's drugs ever were. Paradoxically, although Hagen is a female artist, and during her performance we can see her in a short skirt and with flowers in her hair, she does not feminize Falco's song, in a way, let's say, Roberta Flack feminized Bob Dylan's 'Just Like a Woman'. Hagen's shrilly voice rather points to the softness and vulnerability of Falco's original performance.

Thirdly, Falco's songs were covered by rappers. One such example is a version of 'Jeanny' by MC Basstard, a Berlin rapper of Iranian origin. Basstard's 'Jeanny' paints a milieu of a distinctly lower class than Falco's 'Jeanny'. It is set in underground passages, not like the grandiose *The Third Man's* tunnel in the original version, but of the type one can find in more run-down parts of postindustrial cities. The new Jeanny looks plainer than Theresa Guggenberger, who played the original Jeanny, and her character comes across as less innocent. She goes to clubs, clearly looking for sex, most likely with a man who would become her assassin. Basstard's character, with his unshaven face and loose tie, looks scruffy in comparison with Falco. At times, his 'Jeanny' video evokes 'Mutter, der Mann mit dem Koks is da', suggesting that the latter song is a more seedy version of 'Jeanny'.

Another Berlin rapper, Fler, covered 'Rock Me Amadeus' as 'Neue Deutsche Welle 2005'. Fler has a reputation of being a leading German "gangsta rapper", with the right cultural capital, due to his past of a troubled teenager with an inclination to violence. Unlike Basstard, Fler wrote completely new lyrics for 'Amadeus', in which he expresses aggressive German nationalism and rejection of American culture, epitomised, somewhat predictably, by Britney Spears. It is ironic that Fler recycles the gentle hymn to the classical and cosmopolitan genius from Vienna, sporting a T-shirt with Falco's image, to put across such messages. Yet, although Fler pronounces to be German through and through, and his poetry is addressed to a German audience, including those who do not understand "Ami-rap", he also "falconises", smoothly moving from German to English in one line, as in:

> Mit dem Basie in der Hand, so crazy ist der Mann
> Ihr habt es nicht geschafft, doch ich hab jetzt das Game in meiner Hand

174 Falco and Beyond

Falco was also "covered" in countries such as the United States, France, Poland, Norway and the Czech Republic. He thus proves to be a posthumous ambassador of German music, while during his lifetime he was an ambassador of world music. Commercially some of the most successful cover versions of Falco songs were produced by a popular Polish pop band, Ich Troje, and individually by its members, including the frontman, Michał Wiśniewski. While industrial techno performers took Falco's heritage to its apocalyptic end, Wiśniewski dragged Falco's legacy to its trashy extreme. He did so by covering 'Jeanny' and producing its Polish "clones" in a way that emptied the song of any "meta" quality, ambiguity or even romanticism, rendering it as an explicit story of murder and rape. In one of his numerous performances of 'Jeanny' we see Wiśniewski bare footed, in pyjamas covered in blood, with a teddy bear in his hand, singing about Jeanny in a drunken, dishevelled, melodramatic voice. Wiśniewski not only appropriated and transformed Falco's songs, but positioned himself as the Polish Falco: somebody of a specific image and a brand of distinct monetary value. Like in the case of Falco, hair is an important part of Wiśniewski's image, but in his case the distinctiveness results from his frequent change of its colour, from garish red to green and back. Currently he is better known for his life as a celebrity than his singing. His frequent marriages, divorces and numerous children (one of whom was even meant to be called Falco Christian, but was – literally and symbolically – miscarried), fill the pages of the Polish tabloid press and gossip websites. Wiśniewski's appropriation of Falco's songs and publicly professing his affinity to the Austrian singer attracted some negative comments from the Polish fans of Falco, who find such memory work disrespectful of their idol. I also felt embarrassed when I first watched Wiśniewski covering Falco, perhaps more so due to never listening to the Polish star prior to learning about his connection with the Austrian singer. But I realized that my embarrassment did not result from the fact that Wiśniewski has nothing in common with the original Falco but, on the contrary, that he bears an affinity to him, being like Mr Hyde to Falco's Dr Jekyll. He shows what Falco could have become if he had been stripped of his urbane veneer, romantic mantel and intertextual playfulness: what could have happened to him after the undignified performance in Excalibur City and other such venues.

The styles of covers suggest that Falco was a rapper, a Neue Deutsche Welle and apocalyptic artist, but he was on the periphery of these movements, offering their softer versions in comparison with what we normally associate with those musical paradigms. They also can be seen as more or less successful attempts to democratize or even "proletarize" Falco's music. By contrast, none of the performers tried to emulate Falco's dandy style. Perhaps this means that it is impossible to go further down the "dandy route" because Falco rendered this figure perfect. It might also be seen as a reflection of living in non-dandy times. When protests and riots are on the rise, it is difficult to regard a man "in a crowd, but not of it" as a serious public figure.

22 Falco commented on by his fans

In the last two chapters I will look at the fans' responses to Falco's songs and phenomenon, following his death: comments on YouTube attached to his songs as well as my own take on Falco. Of course, it would be impossible to discuss every comment on every song as there are sometimes several thousand for one song. What I have tried to do, however, over a period of about six months of reading them, is to divide them into specific themes. Such divisions are, again, never neutral, but are prompted by the researcher's own interest. Inevitably, I was inclined to pick comments which coincided with the way I organized my own work on Falco and ignored those which did not fit my favourite discourses. However, to counteract such bias, I also looked at the YouTube comments on other artists comparable to Falco, such as Kraftwerk, Eminem, David Bowie, Michael Jackson, to ensure that my bias is kept at bay. As many comments convey a certain flair, and are short, I decided to quote them, only slightly correcting their spelling or grammar in some cases.

Being a multi-lingual artist is perceived as at the core of being Falco and appreciating this fact is central to "Falco-ism". A large proportion of comments concern the type of language he uses, which lead to discussions about cultural identities of specific ethnic groups, and their mutual relations, often in a context of either asserting or rejecting nationalism, learning German and expanding one's cultural horizons and the meaning of pop music as a universal or national language. Here are some comments fitting this discourse:

> My German is not very good – but this song is so fucking amazing that i spent about 10 hrs to translate the lyrics for my own – and now I've got the proof – Falco is epic.

> Comment: This is the first German (Austrian) song I heard. Falco is a superstar.
> Response: You mean it's the first Austrian (German) song you ever heard.

> Comment: Proud to be from Austria.
> Response: Greetings to all proud Austrians.
> Response: I'm proud to be American but Falco helped me love Austria!

Falco's multilingualism is also reflected in the large number of languages used, and the importance their authors attribute to presenting themselves as citizens of a specific country and linguistic community, often reflected in writing about Falco in their own language, rather than in English. Some of the comments about Falco's many languages lead to discussions about the Second World War, Austria's role in it and the war's legacy. While a minority of fans (or non-fans, who use YouTube as a forum to express their hostility to Falco and what he stands for) regard Falco's language and image as a re-enactment of Nazi-speak and image, the prevailing opinion is that his music and persona helped foreigners to move away from reading Germany and Austria in Nazi terms. One such humorous comment, which both points to the role of Falco in overcoming the Nazi perspective on Austria and a difficulty to free itself from, is:

> Is this Hitler's secret son?

Many fans not only acknowledge that Falco made Austria famous in a new way, but also that he "personalized" Vienna for them. They link their trips to Vienna with listening to his songs, especially 'Vienna Calling'.

> I found love in Vienna. This city has a very special meaning to me.
> My thoughts are always in a small apartment where I discovered
> that love exists, and in the streets where I walked hand in hand with
> the girl of my life.

Another context is Falco's authenticity. For his YouTube fans, he stands for authenticity and originality:

> Falco was the most subversive singer of the 80s.

> The 80's music is a peak of innovation. All the rest coming after that
> is just crafty plagiarism.

Such singling out the 1980s as a decade of authenticity does not mean that there was something essentially authentic about it, merely that the standards of authenticity in pop are located in the past. Not surprisingly, if in the 1980s Falco was often seen as somebody who was prepared to exchange artistic quality for a specific quantity of money, the opposite is the case today – he is seen as the one who did not sell out and put quality first:

> This is real music where the singers actually give you a part of what
> they're going through no matter if you understand it or not, some-
> thing that artists in this day have forgotten and instead focus on the
> cash in.

The artistic integrity of the "real" Falco is compared with those who have privileged access to his legacy, namely music producers releasing his posthumous songs. The listeners engaging in such discussions either condemn such practice tout court or suggest that it is acceptable if it leads to worthy results. All, however, point to the need for giving the background to such "new songs", especially where there is a doubt about whether Falco participated or at least was aware of their production or whether they are just mashups.

> Another fake Falco song. The line "Extravaganza" is from *Cadillac Hotel*, and as noted by someone else, "Er war der Mann" is from *Genie & Partisan* (which was already stolen for the fake *Fascinating Man* on *Verdammt...*) Give it a rest, guys! Let Falco rest in peace!!

> This is totally fake. Sampling one spoken word Falco said and then putting whatever crap music around it doesn't make it a Falco song! If you know any of his music, he wouldn't produce crap like this!!!

> Interesting song – yeah! Seems to be a demo or a mix of other songs, but well done. I am wondering that it wasn't released on CD? Is this from the Bollands like *Where are you now?* More material on tapes??

> I am happy to hear "new" songs.

> Baah, don't give up posting such stuff, please!! Better fake-songs of the falcon, than bad other stuff ... keep on.

Falco is also seen as "the one to look at". Most commentators emphasize the timeless character of his beauty, even when it is obscured by clothes which aged.

> It would be amazing if time travel actually existed, I could only imagine how many ladies would be taking the trip to Vienna, Austria circa 1984 or perhaps even the Dominican Republic, circa 1996–97, Falco was sexy at any age!

> He dressed like a 80's yuppy stock broker. Fucking awesome. And yes Falco, I would love to buy some stuff. Man.

> I love you Falco man and I am Jeannie ... und du kannst mich anmachen wenndu willst.

> I'm an American and Falco has always been the definition of sexy cool to me, I would have had a heart attack if I had ever been lucky enough to actually meet the man in person. Hot!

> He was handsome in an old school way!

Many authors of the comments mourn Falco's death, on some occasions revealing a deep psychological bond with Falco and a need to pronounce it publicly:

> Great song, great performance. My son was born in 1991 and is named after him. Falco. In all these years I still find it terrible that he was deceased by that car accident. R.I.P. Falco.

> This Thursday I have to get my Falco tattoo better (it's a little grey). They have to add more black to the tattoo. But I need a text from one of his songs.

Adorno, no doubt, would attribute comments of this type to the success of the culture industry to integrate the audiences in its unworthy project of capitalism. I disagree with this opinion as I see no contradiction between having a Falco tattoo and engaging in emancipatory struggles or even having a Falco tattoo as a reminder to fight for a better future. That said, I suspect that indeed for most people who write comments on YouTube this activity is in place of any overt political activity. It is also telling that Falco's political messages are practically ignored by his fans. But, as I learnt studying the comments about songs of other artists, it goes for others as well, even those whose political agenda is articulated in a clearer way than in the case of Falco.

Comments I quoted in the most part lack development or historical contextualization that I am trying to provide in this study. This is a consequence of their genre – they belong to what is called "ephemeral media". However, while brief they make up for this with their wit, humour, off-hand poetry and love. My hope is that people will keep posting, in this way maintaining the fragile community of Falco fans and offering new perspectives on his life and music.

23 Falco and I

Academics are reluctant to admit that private passions prompt their research, most likely out of anxiety that it will diminish their claim to objectivity and reduce them to the level of "ordinary" fans. This situation, however, is changing, reflecting, among other things, the influence of Foucault's thought and feminism on humanities, which demystified the "objective" character of knowledge as articulating merely a dominant ideology. But here I do not want just to confess that if it were not for my private passion for Falco, I would not have embarked on this study, but to explain its character and maybe shed some light on a wider phenomenon of fandom.

I believe that we fall in love with stars only when it is right for us. The same song and its performer can move us to tears when we are twenty, deeply embarrass us when we are twenty-five, make us indifferent when we are thirty and make us fall in love again when we are forty. This relationship reflects a wider rule, as described by Nelson Goodman that aesthetic experience is an epistemological experience (see Part I) or, as Deleuze and Guattari claim, that "each of us was several" (Deleuze and Guattari 1988: 3). My life with Falco confirms this opinion. It consists of only two short periods: one in the mid-1980s, in Poland, at the peak of Falco's career, and one beginning in January 2012, in Britain, fourteen years after his death. In the first period, when I was a philosophy student at Warsaw University, I only familiarized myself with Falco's greatest hits, most importantly 'Rock Me Amadeus'. Then the music and its performer (whom I might not have seen aside from on photographs) not only failed to charm me, but awakened my hostility, as confirmed recently by my Polish friend, who reminded me of my criticizing her for listening to music of "this type". It is not difficult for me to explain my reaction. I justly categorized the songs as dance music and hits, and I wanted to stay away from both types of music due to construing myself as a (budding) intellectual of original taste, rather than the follower of a crowd. I do not remember whether Falco's mixing of languages was an issue for me then, but if it was, I would have counted it as another argument against him, seeing him not as perfect material for Wittgensteinian analysis, but a dangerous self-colonizer, polluting the beautiful German language with second-class English. This was because at the time I was an ardent consumer of New German Cinema, and identified myself with the mourning of German colonization by American culture.

In 2012 when I started my research none of the reasons which put me off Falco existed any more. Falco is no longer fashionable, especially in Britain where I live, and even if he was, it would be less of an issue for me as I care less about having original taste. Besides, in the meantime I learnt that taste is culturally constructed. If somebody does not share my taste in music, this merely means that his or her cultural trajectory is different from mine rather than that one of these tastes is superior. My attitude to specific music genres also changed. Now I regard it as the highest gift of a musician to make his listeners dance as opposed to only listen. My attitude to mixing languages also changed. I gained a special interest in and affinity to artists mixing languages and regard Wim Wenders's purist attitude to German language and culture as a reactionary gesture, betraying latent German xenophobia.

But such a change of identity alone would not explain why I started to listen to Falco and got "hooked". A crucial factor was my then eight-year-old son singing 'Dr Zaius', after watching an episode entitled "A Fish Called Selma" in *The Simpsons*. I suggested that I would show him the original on YouTube and we both liked it, in my case much more than I expected. 'Rock Me Amadeus' took me to other Falco songs and videos, which I found catchy, intelligent, funny and in tune with my mood and Weltanschauung at the time. In due course it also took me to Falco's biographies, to Vienna, to his collaborators, fans, other Austrian artists, and to writing this book.

My experience reflects the common route in which we currently get in contact with artefacts: through adaptations, samples, snippets or simulacras, as confirmed by somebody on YouTube confessing to reaching the "original Falco" through the same door as me: "Simpsons brought me here. From watching a Falco spoof of 'Rock Me Amadeus' it made me seek the original. I liked it, listened to more Falco and found this". However, there is still a certain guilt or shame attached to reaching what becomes an important part of our lives through such means, reflecting the fact that even if we stopped studying anything comprehensively, as apparently did men and women of earlier generations, there is still a sense that we should do so and "YouTube university" is of a lower order than a proper one.

What does it mean for me to be a Falco fan? In a nutshell, two things. The first is the sensual pleasure of listening and looking at Falco, which can be shared, but cannot be easily explained. The second is a satisfaction of understanding, of being able to imagine the world from Falco's perspective. This might not be a different pleasure to that which happens when we meet somebody who charms us and we want to know more about them. But in reality knowing somebody attractive might lead either to a desire to be friends or lovers with her or him, or discovering that there is such a huge gap between our values and worldviews that there is no point in carrying on. In the case of

Falco I discovered that almost everything divides us – in the unlikely case of meeting him I would find his views and lifestyle intolerable, as most likely he would find mine not to his taste. There is a possibility of bridging such gaps, but I would not like to change Falco even if I had a chance, because it would be tantamount to emptying him of what I find so attractive in him as an object of my fandom: his difference, his exoticism, his contradictions. Neither would I like to change my ways for him. For this reason it is a bonus for me, rather than a handicap, that I never met Falco and he was already dead when I began this study. In my contentment with dealing merely with "Falco the text", the collection of his traces, as opposed to the real person, I might be untypical, for example due to being over-exposed to film directors and actors, who used to disappoint me in direct contact. However, I sense that the majority of Falco fans also lack the desire to cross the boundary between their more ordinary world and that of the star. Falco understood this mechanism and rather than "going down" to meet his fans, he "went up", amplifying their difference, and projecting himself as somebody unattainable.

Perhaps for people like myself, who are happy to remain just fans, stars act as a depository of the features which they try to purge from their world, but want to retain in some safe fantasy world as a means to colour their more mundane existence. However, in common with many other mysteries of Falco I was unable to solve, I will leave it to the pupils of the "Viennese quack" to explain this mechanism.

Notes

Introduction

1. Recently a similar idea was put eloquently by Alain Badiou, a philosopher whom I will recall more than once in this study. He writes that philosophy requires its practitioners of either gender to assume the roles of savant, artist, activist and lover (Badiou 2012: 2).

Part I

Chapter 1

2. Problems of integration of popular culture and specifically popular music into the dominant, capitalist system, are discussed by many authors, including Dick Hebdige (2003: 90–99) and Thomas Cushman (1991). A similar argument in relation to popular culture and music under state socialism and postsocialism are discussed also by Cushman (ibid.) and Anna Szemere (2001).
3. The very distinction between rock and pop is a subject of controversy. I side with authors such as Philip Auslander, who regard the difference between these types of music as principally ideological, not stylistic (Auslander 2008: 81).
4. I noticed that the most effective way to convince my friends that Falco is high art and deserves serious thought is by showing them the two, nicely published, volumes devoted to his poetry and the 6-DVD luxurious edition documenting his career.
5. Falco's song, 'Rock Me Amadeus', was also used in a car advert, in a way which can be seen as an example of détournement, because the car advertised was a Japanese Subaru, presented as "the Japanese car the Germans wish they made". In this case the subversion, however, concerns merely national colours of capitalism, rather than accepting or rejecting capitalism.

Chapter 2

6. It is therefore worth differentiating rap from hip-hop, regarding the former as a specific type of performance, the latter as a specific culture originating in the black ghetto and articulated, among other things, by rap (Krims 2000: 10–12). Accordingly, I will treat Falco as a rapper but not a hip-hop artist.

Part II

Chapter 3

7. According to Carl E. Schorske, in fin-de-siècle Vienna the position of an artist, due to the complexities of the Austrian way to modernism, was distinctly higher than elsewhere in Europe and the gap between high-brow and low-brow art was rel-

184 Falco and Beyond

atively small. Arthur Schnitzler and Otto Wagner perfectly represent this trend (Schorske 1979). Most likely even in contemporary times Austrian artists, including Falco, benefited from this tradition.

8. Falco's father also shared a name, Alois, with Hitler's father. I wonder if I am the only Falco fan who noticed this.

Chapter 4

9. Falco's mixing of languages (German Mehrsprachigkeit) is the most discussed aspect of Falco's work. In *Falco's Many Languages* practically the whole volume is devoted to this problem, which includes locating Falco's language within the context of other users of German who mixed languages (Ernst 2010: 132), going as far back as the beginnings of German language (Zimmermann 2010: 23), as well as to the overall intertextual character of his oeuvre (Bolterauer 2010; Hintze 2010).

10. In Germany such a defence of German culture against American invasion was undertaken most famously by the directors of the New German Cinema, especially Wim Wenders.

11. The majority of filmgoers do not know that Schwarzenegger is Austrian, so for them he does not project any image of this country. For those who know, including myself, this image is negative – it is an image of pathological physicality and violence, as conveyed by the fact that on websites he is often described as a "Nazi". Austria's image as a "weird-land" and a "land of violence" is also, to a large extent, a self-image, perpetuated in the most influential cultural documents about this country, such as the films of Michael Haneke and Ulrich Seidl and the autobiography of the world's most famous victim of paedophilia, Natascha Kampusch.

12. My comparison of Falco and Adorno is paradoxical, as Adorno most likely would find in Falco (his art and his persona) many of the features he despised in American culture, such as kitsch and the loss of historicity. But it also shows that judgements about one's culture always reflect not only the character of this culture, but also our own position.

Chapter 6

13. Whether Falco was indeed the first European rapper is a subject of debates conducted on various websites.

Chapter 7

14. These words are also used in the advertising material of ING bank, testifying to the previously mentioned talent of capitalism to incorporate any view, tradition or artefact into its project of multiplying capital.

15. Abba's affluence was an important reason why the group was widely criticized in its own country. This reflects the fact that they came from a country that cherished egalitarian values more than any other European country and that their greatest successes were in the 1970s, which was a time of acute ideological struggle between the radical left and the new (neoliberal) right (on Abba's reception

in Sweden see Broman 2005). Falco properly started his career when the war between left and right was already lost by the left (see Chapter 6).

Part III

Chapter 9

16. A strategy of omitting "minor signifiers" was also used by the Bollands in their most famous song, bar 'Amadeus', 'In the Army Now', performed by Status Quo. This is an anti-war or protest song, whose origin can be traced to the Bollands' origins from South Africa, a country with conscription, and being children of a mining engineer, a profession with a strong colonial aura, factors which most likely affected the way the young musicians felt about military life. Yet, there is nothing specific about Ferdi and Rob's history in this song; instead it deals with the universal condition of being a soldier. These arguments show that pop music is not made by "morons for morons", as its critics often want to see it. On the contrary, it requires great talent to render universal issues successfully, typically by making up for simplicity in one area with complexity in another.

Chapter 10

17. My research on reception of Falco in Poland confirms this opinion. On the Polish websites I found some of the most sophisticated discussions of his work, often by representatives of a younger generation of fans, who are able to appreciate him not because they have no access to English or American hits (everybody has such access these days), but because in their view his music provides a worthy alternative to such hits.

Part IV

Chapter 13

18. Appraising Falco's life from a moral perspective is not the main purpose of this book. Nevertheless, in my eyes he was wrong to disinherit his daughter. She should have benefited financially from what he left in his will, no less than Falco's mother, irrespective of her genetic make-up, solely on the grounds of their social ties, in the same way adopted children inherit from their non-biological parents.

19. I contacted some of them during the writing of this book, most importantly Rabitsch and Rossacher, and benefited from their help. Aware of the problems which might result from such personal connections, I thought this issue over before talking to Falco's collaborators and prepared the first draft of this part before meeting them.

Chapter 15

20. This aspect of Falco's behaviour is mentioned in an interview with Falco's father. He says that Falco treated his manager and collaborators appallingly, with Falco justifying himself by saying that they are paid to endure insults (Graf 1999).

Discography

Albums

During his lifetime:

EINZELHAFT (1982)

Zuviel Hitze 4.34 / Der Kommissar 3.52 / Siebzehn Jahr 3.54 / Auf Der Flucht 4.13 / Ganz Wien 5.06 / Maschine Brennt 3.38 / Hinter Uns Die Sintflut 3.16 / Nie Mehr Schule 4.36 / Helden Von Heute 4.07 / Einzelhaft 4.01

JUNGE ROEMER (1984)

Junge Roemer 4.30 / Tut-Ench-Amon (Tutankhamen) 4.30 / Brillantin' Brutal 3.47 / Ihre Tochter 4.26 / No Answer (Hallo Deutschland) 3.37 / Nur Mit Dir 4.27 / Hoch Wie Nie 4.21 / Steuermann 3.44 / Kann Es Liebe Sein 4.06

FALCO 3 (1985)

Rock Me Amadeus 3.22 / America 3.56 / Tango The Night 2.28 / Munich Girls (Lookin' For Love) 4.17 / Jeanny 5.50 / Vienna Calling 4.02 / Männer Des Westens – Any Kind Of Land 4.00 / Nothin' Sweeter Than Arabia 4.46 / Macho Macho 4.56 / It's All Over Now, Baby Blue 4.41

EMOTIONAL (1986)

Emotional 4.53 / Kamikaze Cappa 5.09 / Crime Time 4.23 / Cowboyz And Indianz 5.46 / Coming Home (Jeanny Part 2) 5.31 / The Star Of Moon And Sun 5.19 / Les Nouveaux Riches 4.30 / The Sound Of Musik 4.57 / The Kiss Of Kathleen Turner 7.31

WIENER BLUT (1988)

Wiener Blut 3.31 / Falco Rides Again 4.44 / Untouchable 3.17 / Tricks 3.52 / Garbo 3.49 / Satellite To Satellite 5.14 / Read A Book 3.55 / Walls Of Silence 4.40 / Solid Booze 4.31 / Sand Am Himalaya 4.01 / Do It Again 5.15

DATA DE GROOVE (1990)

Neo Nothing – Post Of All 4.45 / Expocityvisions 4.08 / Charisma Kommando 4.47 / Tanja P. Nicht Cindy C. 3.35 / Pusher 4.25 / Data De Groove 4.38 / Alles Im Liegen 5.04 / U.4.2.P.1. Club Dub 3.41 / Bar Minor 7/11 (Jeanny Dry) 3.45 / Anaconda 'Mour 0.57

NACHTFLUG (1992)

Titanic 3.56 / Monarchy Now 4.10 / Dance Mephisto 3.28 / Psychos 3.16 / S.C.A.N.D.A.L. 3.56 / Yah Vibration 3.35 / Propaganda 3.34 / Time 4.03 / Cadillac Hotel 5.11 / Nachtflug 3.15

After his death:

OUT OF THE DARK (INTO THE LIGHT) (1998)

No Time For Revolution 3.51 / Out Of The Dark 3.36 / Shake 3.41 / Der Kommissar 2000 3.47 / Mutter, Der Mann Mit Dem Koks Ist Da 3.38 / Hit Me 3.45 / Cyberlove 3.33 / Egoist 3.26 / Naked (Full Frontal Mix) 6.02 // Geld 3.46 (Matth. Xl 15)

VERDAMMT WIR LEBEN NOCH (1999)

Verdammt Wir Leben Noch 5.14 / Die Königin Von Eschnapur 4.29 / Que Pasa Hombre 4.14 / Europa 5.07 / Fascinating Man 4.00 / Poison 4.22 / Ecce Machina 5.31 / We Live For The Night 3.52 / Krise 3.54 / From The North To The South 3.11 / Der Kommissar (Club 69 Radio Mix) 3.40 / Verdammt Wir Leben Noch (Remix) 4.26

THE SPIRIT NEVER DIES (2009)

Return To Forever 2.08 / Nuevo Africano 4.56 / Jeanny 5.50 / Coming Home (Jeanny Part 2) 5.31 / The Spirit Never Dies (Jeanny Final) 4.57 / Que Pasa Hombre 4.41 / Poison 4.57 / Sweet Symphony 4.24 / Kissing In The Kremlin 3.53 / Dada Love 4.27 / The Spirit Never Dies (Jeanny Final) (The Special Remix) 5.00 / Forever 2.18

Remix albums

During his lifetime:

THE REMIX HIT COLLECTION (1991)

Der Kommissar (Part 2, Club Mix) 5.35 / Rock Me Amadeus (Club Remix) 6.47 / Jeanny (Harold Faltermeyer Remix) 7.07 / Data De Groove (Club Mix) 6.48 / Vienna Calling (Spencer Tobie Remix) 4.03 / Junge Roemer (Bingoboys Remix) 6.05 / Wiener Blut (Club Remix) 6.00 / Emotional (Harold Faltermeyer Remix) 6.05 / Coming Home (Jeanny Part 2) 5.31 / Falco Megamix 6.00 / The Sound Of Musik (Extended Rock 'N' Soul Version) 10.00

After his death:

FALCO SYMPHONIC (2008)

The Sound Of Musik 4.43 / Vienna Calling 4.48 / Jeanny & Coming Home (Jeanny Part 2) 6.22 / Titanic 4.22 / Rock Me Amadeus 4.12 / Les Nouveaux

Riches 3.26 / Nachtflug 3.17 / Dance Mephisto 3.27 / Monarchy Now 4.15 / Der Kommissar 4.30 / Die Königin Von Eschnapur 3.58 / Europa 5.31 / Helden Von Heute (Live) 5.21 / Junge Roemer (Live) 4.22 / Ganz Wien (Live) 5.20 / Helden Von Heute Reprise (Live) 1.40

Live albums
After his death:

LIVE FOREVER (1999)
Excerpts from live concert recorded on 27 October 1986 in Berlin, Eissporthalle
The Sound Of Musik 5.20 / Jeanny 6.32 / Der Kommissar 5.03 / Emotional 5.20 / Junge Roemer 4.46 / Auf Der Flucht 4.00 / Coming Home (Jeanny Part 2) 5.14 / Hoch Wie Nie 4.32 / Ganz Wien 4.58 / Vienna Calling 4.41 / Helden Von Heute 4.27 / It's All Over Now, Baby Blue 7.23 / Rock Me Amadeus 6.04

FALCO DONAUINSEL LIVE (2004/2008)
Live concert recorded on 27 June 1993 in Vienna, Donauinsel
Les Nouveaux Riches 3.41 / Junge Roemer 4.31 / Auf Der Flucht 4.13 / Der Kommissar 4.21 / Ganz Wien 5.03 / Jeanny & Coming Home 6.07 / Männer Des Westens – Any Kind Of Land 3.53 / The Sound Of Musik 5.08 / Titanic 4.20 / Vienna Calling 4.29 / Nachtflug 4.29 / It's All Over Now, Baby Blue 5.33 / Helden Von Heute 6.33

Singles
During his lifetime:

That Scene (1981)

Der Kommissar (1981)

Maschine Brennt (1982)

Junge Roemer (1984)

Nur Mit Dir (1984)

Kann Es Liebe Sein (with Desiree Nosbusch) (1984)

Rock Me Amadeus (1985)

Vienna Calling (1985)

Jeanny (1985)

The Sound Of Musik (1986)

Coming Home (Jeanny Part 2, Ein Jahr Danach) (1986)

Emotional (1987)

Body Next To Body (with Brigitte Nielsen) (1987)

Wiener Blut (1988)

Satellite To Satellite (1988)

Data De Groove (1990)

Charisma Kommando (1990)

Titanic (1992)

Dance Mephisto (1992)

Nachtflug (1992)

Mutter, Der Mann Mit Dem Koks Ist Da (1995)

Naked (1996)

After his death:

Out Of The Dark (1998)

Egoist (1998)

Push! Push! (1999)

Verdammt Wir Leben Noch (1999)

Europa (2000)

Die Königin Von Eschnapur (2008)

Bibliography

Adorno, Theodor W. 1974. *Minima Moralia: Reflections from Damaged Life*, trans. E. F. N. Jephcott. London: NLB.

—1975 [1963]. "Culture Industry Reconsidered". *New German Critique* 6: 12–19.

—1978 [1938]. "On the Fetish-Character in Music and the Regression of Listening". In *The Essential Frankfurt School Reader*, ed. Andrew Arato and Eike Gebhardt, 270–99. Oxford: Basil Blackwell.

—2004 [1970]. *Aesthetic Theory*. London: Continuum.

Albers, Patricia C., and William R. James. 1988. "Travel Photography: A Methodological Approach". *Annals of Tourism Research* 15: 134–58.

Albrecht, Horst. 1993. *Die Religion der Massenmedien*. Stuttgart: Verlag W. Kohlhammer.

Anderson, Mark. 1992. *Kafka's Clothes: Ornament and Aestheticism in the Habsburg Fin-de-siècle*. Oxford: Clarendon Press.

Augé, Marc. 1995. *Non-Places: Introduction to an Anthropology of Supermodernity*. London: Verso.

Auslander, Philip. 2008. *Liveness: Performance in a Mediatized Culture*. London: Routledge.

Badiou, Alain. 2007. *The Century*, trans. Alberto Toscano. Cambridge: Polity.

—2012. *In Praise of Love*, trans. Peter Bush. London: Serpent's Tail.

Banks, Jack. 1996. *Monopoly Television: MTV's Quest to Control the Music*. Oxford: Westview Press.

Barker, John. 2006. "Intensities of Labour: From Amphetamine to Cocaine". *Mute* 2, no. 3. http://www.tamute.org/editorial/articles/intensities-labour-amphetamine-to-cocaine (accessed 6 June 2012).

Barthes, Roland. 1992 [1957]. "The Face of Garbo". In Gerald Mast, Marshall Cohen and Leo Braudy (1992), *Film Theory and Criticism*, 4th edn, 628–31. Oxford: Oxford University Press.

Baudrillard, Jean. 1994 [1981]. *Simulacra and Simulation*, trans. Sheila Faria Glaser. Ann Arbor: University of Michigan Press.

—2001. *Selected Writings*, 2nd edn, ed. Mark Poster. Stanford: Stanford University Press.

Bauman, Zygmunt. 1994. "Desert Spectacular". In *The Flaneur*, ed. Keith Tester, 138–57. London: Routledge.

—1996. "From Pilgrim to Tourist – or a Short History of Identity". In *Questions of Cultural Identity*, ed. Stuart Hall and Paul du Gay, 18–36. London: Sage.

Beaujour, Elizabeth Klosty. 1995. "Bilingualism". In *The Garland Companion to Vladimir Nabokov*, ed. Vladimir E. Alexandrov, 37–43. New York and London: Garland.

Benjamin, Walter. 1983 [1976]. *Charles Baudelaire: A Lyric Poet in the Era of High Capitalism*, trans. Harry Zohn. London: Verso.

—1992. "The Work of Art in the Age of Mechanical Reproduction". In *Art in Modern Culture: An Anthology of Critical Texts*, ed. Francis Frascina and Jonathan Harris, 297–307. London: Phaidon.

—2007. *Illuminations*. New York: Schocken Books.

Bernstein, Basil. 1975. *Class Codes and Social Control: Theoretical Studies Towards a Sociology of Language*. New York: Schocken Books.

Bertens, Hans. 1995. *The Idea of the Postmodern: A History*. London: Routledge.

Boer, Roland. 2012. "Some Routine Atrocity, or, Letting the Course of God Roar: Nick Cave and Apocalyptic". In *Anthems of Apocalypse: Popular Music and Apocalyptic Thought*, ed. Christopher Partridge, 1–12. Sheffield: Sheffield Phoenix Press.

Bohlman, Philip V. 2002. *World Music: A Very Short Introduction*. Oxford: Oxford University Press.

Boltanski, Luc and Eve Chiapello. 2005 [1999]. *The New Spirit of Capitalism*, trans. Gregory Elliott. London: Verso.

Bolterauer, Alice. 2010. " 'Lost in Translation' – Zur Funktion des Mehrsprachigen Zitats bei Hans Hölzel alias Falco". In *Falco's Many Languages*, ed. Christian Ide Hintze, 85–100. Vienna: Residenz Verlag.

Bork, Horst. 2009. *Falco: Die Wahrheit*. Berlin: Schwarzkopf & Schwarzkopf.

Bowman, Wayne D. 1998. *Philosophical Perspectives on Music*. Oxford: Oxford University Press.

Brackett, Nathan. 1999. "Foreword" to Dan Sicko, *Techno Rebels: The Renegades of Electronic Funk*, 7–8. New York: Billboard Books.

Broman, Per F. 2005. "'When All Is Said and Done': Swedish ABBA Reception During the 1970s and the Ideology of Pop". *Journal of Popular Music Studies* 1: 45–66.

Carpenter, Bogdana. 1983. *The Poetic Avant-Garde in Poland, 1983–1939*. Seattle and London: University of Washington Press.

Castaldi, Beatrice. 2012. *Falco lebt*. Wien: Edition A.

Chambers, Iain. 1985. *Urban Rhythms: Pop Music and Popular Culture*. Houndmills: Macmillan.

Cook, Nicholas. 1995–96. "Music Minus One: Rock, Theory and Performance". *New Formations* 27: 23–41.

—1998a. *Music: A Very Short Introduction*. Oxford: Oxford University Press.

—1998b. *Analysing Musical Multimedia*. Oxford: Oxford University Press.

Cooke, Deryck. 1988. *Gustav Mahler: An Introduction to his Music*, 2nd edn. Cambridge: Cambridge University Press.

Covach, John. 1997. "Progressive Rock, 'Close to the Edge', and the Boundaries of Style". In *Understanding Rock: Essays in Musical Analysis*, ed. John Covach and Graeme M. Boone, 3–31. Oxford: Oxford University Press.

Cushman, Thomas. 1991. "Rich Rastas and Communist Rockers: A Comparative Study of the Origin, Diffusion, and Defusion of Revolutionary Musical Codes". *Journal of Popular Culture* 3: 17–61.

Dassanowsky, Robert. 1996. *Phantom Empires: The Novels of Alexander Lernet-Holenia and the Question of Postimperial Austrian Identity*. Riverside: Ariadne Press.

Deleuze, Gilles, and Félix Guattari. 1983. *Anti-Oedipus: Capitalism and Schizophrenia*, trans. Robert Hurley, Mark Seem and Helen R. Lane. London: Athlone Press.

—1988. *A Thousand Plateaus: Capitalism and Schizophrenia*, trans. Brian Massumi. London: Athlone.

Denk, Felix, and Sven von Thülen. 2012. *Der Klang der Familie: Berlin, Techno und die Wende*. Berlin: Suhrkamp Taschenbuch.

Dent, Alexander Sebastian. 2005. "Cross-Cultural 'Countries': Covers, Conjuncture, and the Whiff of Nashville in *Mu'sica Sertaneja*. Brazilian Commercial Country Music)". *Popular Music and Society* 2: 207–27.

Derrida, Jacques. 1994 [1993]. *Specters of Marx: The State of the Debt, the Work of Mourning, and the New International*, trans. Peggy Kamuf. London: Routledge.

DJ Schmolli. 2008. "DJ Schmolli Presents Falco Re: Loaded", 20 March 2008. http://falcoreloaded.blogspot.co.uk/ (accessed 15 October 2012).

Dolezal, Rudi, and Hannes Rossacher. 1998. *Falco: Hoch wie nie. Romanbiographie*. Wien: Kremayr and Scheriau.

Dyer, Richard. 1998. "Resistance through Charisma: Rita Hayworth and *Gilda*". In *Women in Film Noir*, new edn, ed. E. Ann Kaplan, 115–22. London: British Film Institute.

Eagleton, Terry. 1992 [1985]. "Capitalism, Modernism and Postmodernism". In *Art in Modern Culture: An Anthology of Critical Texts*, ed. Francis Frascina and Jonathan Harris, 91–100. London: Phaidon.

Einstein, Alfred. 1947. *Music in the Romantic Era*. London: J. M. Dent & Sons.

Ellis, Bret Easton. 1991. *American Psycho*. London: Picador.

Emmerson, Simon. 2000. "'Losing Touch?': The Human Performer and Electronics". In *Music, Electronic Media and Culture*, ed. Simon Emmerson, 194–216. Aldershot: Ashgate.

Ernst, Peter. 2010. '"Falconisch" – Falco und seine Sprachverwendung'. In *Falco's Many Languages*, ed. Christian Ide Hintze, 125–35. Vienna: Residenz Verlag.

Falco. 1986. "Mit Madonna würde ich gern ein Duett aufnehmen". *Bravo* 45. http://www.falcoworld.net/falcoextrablatt/extra/?cat=1&paged=26 (accessed 19 December 2012).

—1988. "Böses Blut". *Musikexpress*, 8. http://www.falcoworld.net/falcoextrablatt/extra/?cat=22 (accessed 24 August 2012).

—1996. "Koks und Kohle". *Musikexpress*, 6. http://www.falcoworld.net/falcoextrablatt/extra/wp-content/uploads/2009/02/me0696r.jpg (accessed 9 April 2012).

Fehringer, Andrea. 1996. "Fast wieder Mensch – Falcos neuer Höhenflug". *Wiener* 12: 127–29.

Fiske, John. 1986. "MTV: Post-structural Post-modern". *Journal of Communication Inquiry* 1: 74–79.

Forman, Murray. 2000. "'Represent': Race, Space and Place in Rap Music". *Popular Music* 1: 65–90.

Foucault, Michel. 1998) [1986]. "Of Other Spaces", trans. Jay Miskowiec. In *The Visual Culture Reader*, 2nd edn, ed. Nicholas Mirzoff, 229–36. London: Routledge.

Freud, Sigmund. 2005 [1917]. "Mourning and Melancholia". In Sigmund Freud, *On Murder, Mourning and Melancholia*, trans. Shaun Whiteside, 201–19. London: Penguin.

Frith, Simon. 1981. *Sound Effects: Youth, Leisure, and the Politics of Rock'n'Roll*. New York: Pantheon.

—1987. "Towards an Aesthetic of Popular Music". In *Music and Society: The Politics of Composition, Performance and Reception*, ed. Richard Leppert and Susan McClary, 133–49. Cambridge: Cambridge University Press.

—2001. "Pop Music". In *The Cambridge Companion to Pop and Rock*, ed. Simon Frith, Will Straw and John Street, 93–108. Cambridge: Cambridge University Press.

Goodman, Nelson. 1968. *Languages of Art: An Approach to a Theory of Symbols*. Indianapolis: Bobbs-Merrill.

Gotye. 2012. "Gotye to Release an Entire Album of 'Somebody That I Used To Know' Remixes". http://www.nme.com/news/gotye/64093 (accessed 2 September 2012).

Graf, Edda. 1999. "Ewiger Zank um Falco". *News* 38/99: 316–17.

Graf, Edda, and Ossi Hicker. 1999a. "Maria Hölzel über die Zeit seit dem Unfall: 'Manchmal glaube ich noch an einen bösen Traum'". *News* 5: 185.

—1999b. "Tod und falsche Moral". *News* 5: 187–88.

Granger, Matt. 2012. "Falco's Grave and Other Enduring Monuments to His Genius". *The Granger Bros Blog*, 5 November 2012. http://www.thegrangerbros.com/blog/falcos-grave-other-enduring-monuments-to-his-genius/ (accessed 7 November 2012).

Greenberg, Clement. 1973. *Art and Culture*. London: Thames and Hudson.

Greene, David B. 1984. *Mahler, Consciousness and Temporality*. New York: Gordon and Breach Science.

Gregg, Melissa. 2011. *Work's Intimacy*. Cambridge: Polity.

Gregory, Georgina. 2011. "'Stairway to Heaven': Grieving, Loss and Popular Music". *International Journal of the Humanities* 10: 327–38.

Griffiths, Dai. 2002. "Cover Versions and the Sound of Identity in Motion". In *Popular Music Studies*, ed. David Hesmondhalgh and Keith Negus, 51–64. London: Arnold.

Gripp, Stephan. 2007. "Falcos Grab". http://www.kaihoelzner.de/artists/gripp/gripp-falco.html (accessed 15 August 2012).

Guilbault, Jocelyne. 2001. "David Bowie" and "Abba". In *The Cambridge Companion to Pop and Rock*, ed. Simon Frith, Will Straw and John Street, 196–200. Cambridge: Cambridge University Press.

Hachmeister, Lutz, and Jan Lingemann. 1999. "Das Gefühl VIVA. Deutsches Musikfernsehen und die neue Sozialdemokratie". In *VIVA MTV! Popmusik im Fernsehen*, ed. Klaus Neumann-Braun, 132–63. Frankfurt am Main: Suhrkamp.

Hall, Stuart. 1988. *The Hard Road to Renewal: Thatcherism and the Crisis of the Left*. London: Verso.

Hannes' Filmarchive. 2010. http://www.yllr.net/filmarchiv/movie/id%2C171/Der+Formel+Eins+Film.html (accessed 12 June 2012).

Haraway, Donna J. 1991. *Simians, Cyborgs and Women: The Reinvention of Nature*. London: Routledge.

Hardt, Michael, and Antonio Negri. 2000. *Empire*. Cambridge, MA: Harvard University Press.

—2005. *Multitude*. London: Hamish Hamilton.

Harvey, David. 1990. *The Condition of Postmodernity*. Oxford: Blackwell.

—2005. *A Brief History of Neoliberalism*. Oxford: Oxford University Press.

—2006. *The Limits to Capital*, new and fully updated edition. London: Verso.

—2010. *A Companion to Marx's Capital*. London: Verso.

Hazzard-Donald, Katrina. 1996. "Dance in Hip Hop Culture". In *Droppin' Science*, ed. William Eric Perkins, 220–35. Philadelphia: Temple University Press.

Heath, Joseph, and Andrew Potter. 2006. *The Rebel Sell: How the Counterculture Became Consumer Culture*. Chichester: Capstone.

Hebdige, Dick. 2003. *Subculture: The Meaning of Style*. London: Routledge.

Hertl, Wolfgang. 1996. "Ich bin ein absoluter Sucht-Typ", *Musikexpress*. http://www.welt. de/kultur/musik/article13925874/Ich-bin-ein-absoluter-Sucht-Typ.html (accessed 12 April 2012).

Hilburn, Robert. 1986. "Here's Falco: From Vienna with Whimsy". *Los Angeles Times*, 6 April. http://articles.latimes.com/1986-04-06/entertainment/ca-24741_1_falco (accessed 15 April 2012).

Hintze, Christian Ide. 2009. "Vorwort: Falco Lesen". *Falco: Lyrics Complete*. Vienna: Residenz Verlag.

Hintze, Christian Ide, ed. 2010. *Falco's Many Languages*. Vienna: Residenz Verlag.

Hobsbawm, Eric. 1995. *Age of Extremes: The Short Twentieth Century 1914–1991*. Abacus: London.

Holt, Grace Sims. 1972. "'Inversion' in Black Communication". In *Rappin' and Stylin' Out*, ed. Thomas Kochman, 189–208. Urbana: University of Illinois Press.

Holton, Milne, and Herbert Kuhner, eds. 1985. *Austrian Poetry Today*. New York: Schocken Books.

Horkheimer, Max, and Theodor W. Adorno. 2002 [1987]. *Dialectic of Enlightenment: Philosophical Fragments*, trans. Edmund Jephcott. Stanford: Stanford University Press.

Huber, Michael. 2012. "Der 'Austropop' und die Entstehung einer österreichischen Jugendkultur in den 1970er Jahren". In *Die Ära Kreisky in Österreich und die Normalisierungsperiode in der CSSR. Politik und Kultur*, ed. Gerald M. Sprengnagel, Niklas Perzi and Michal Stehlík. Wien: Lit-Verlag.

Jameson, Fredric. 1991. *Postmodernism, or, the Cultural Logic of Late Capitalism*. London: Verso.

Jameson, Fredric. 2003. "Future City". *New Left Review*, 21. http://www.newleftreview. org/?view=2449 (accessed 21 September 2011).

Kael, Pauline. 1965. *I Lost It at the Movies*. London: Jonathan Cape.

Kaplan, E. Ann. 1987. *Rocking Around the Clock: Music Television, Postmodernism, and Consumer Culture*. London: Routledge.

Kastberger, Klaus. 2010. "Neo Nothing – Post of All, oder: Warum Falcos Texte k(eine) Dichtung sind". In *Falco's Many Languages*, ed. Christian Ide Hintze, 67–83. Vienna: Residenz Verlag.

Keightley, Keir. 2001. "Reconsidering Rock". In *The Cambridge Companion to Pop and Rock*, ed. Simon Frith, Will Straw and John Street, 109–42. Cambridge: Cambridge University Press.

Khort, Wolfgang. 1986. "Mit Stimmbändern Würde erdrosselt" and "Ist Falcos *Jeanny* ein Protestsong?" *Junge Welt*. http://www.falco-calling.com/jeanny.htm (accessed 15 May 2012).

Kittler, Friedrich. 1999. *Gramophone Film Typewriter*, trans. Geoffrey Winthrop-Young and Michael Wutz. Stanford: Stanford University Press.

Köpf, Thomas, and Stefan Wictora. 1999. "Aasgeier über dem Falken". *Wiener* 2: 24–29.

Kralicek, Wolfgang, and Klaus Nüchtern. 2000. "Ganz allein am Flughafen". *Falter* 12: 22, 50–60.

Krims, Adams. 2000. *Rap Music and the Poetics of Identity*. Cambridge: Cambridge University Press.

—2002. "The Hip-hop Sublime as a Form of Commodification". In *Music and Marx: Ideas, Practice, Politics*, ed. Regula Burckhardt Qureshi, 63–78. London: Routledge.

Kun, Josh. 2005. *Audiotopia: Music, Race, and America*. Berkeley: University of California Press.

Lanz, Peter. 2007. *Falco: Die Biographie*. Wien: Ueberreuter.

Larkey, Edward. 1993. *Pungent Sounds: Constructing Identity with Popular Music in Austria*. New York: Peter Lang.

Leary, Timothy, Ralph Metzner and Richard Alper. 2008. *The Psychodelic Experience: A Manual Based on the Tibetan Book of the Dead*. London: Penguin Modern Classics.

Loos, Adolf. 1998. *Ornament and Crime: Selected Essays*. Riverside, CA: Ariadne Press.

Lyotard, Jean-François. 1984. *The Postmodern Condition: A Report on Knowledge*, trans. Geoff Bennington and Brian Massumi. Manchester: Manchester University Press.

Marcuse, Herbert. 1964. *One-Dimensional Man: Studies in the Ideology of Advanced Industrial Society*. London: Routledge.

Markel, Howard. 2011. *An Anatomy of Addiction: Sigmund Freud, William Halsted and the Miracle Drug, Cocaine*. New York: Pantheon.

Marx, Karl. 1976 [1887]. *Capital: A Critique of Political Economy*, vol. 1, trans. Ben Fowkes. London: Penguin.

—1978 [1852]. "The Eighteenth Brumaire of Louis Bonaparte". In *The Marx-Engels Reader*, 2nd edn, ed. Robert C. Tucker, 595–617. New York: W. W. Norton & Company.

—2008 [1848]. *The Communist Manifesto*. London: Pluto.

McGann, Jerome. 1983. *The Romantic Ideology: A Critical Investigation*. Chicago: University of Chicago Press.

Mießgang, Thomas. 2008. "Geschnitzt aus Bowies Rippe". *Zeit Online*. http://www.zeit.de/online/2008/06/falco-interview-markus-spiegel (accessed 26 May 2012).

Monroe, Alexei. 1999. "Thinking about Mutation: Genres in 1990s Electronica". In *Living Through Pop*, ed. Andrew Blake, 146–58. London: Routledge.

Murray, Charles Shaar. 2005 [1989]. *Crosstown Traffic: Jimi Hendrix and Post-War Pop*. London: Faber and Faber.

Oberhuber, Elfi. 2008. "Kunst oder Kommerz II, a: *Falco Symphonic* – Thomas Rabitsch & Peter Paul Skrepek arrangieren (sich /nicht)". http://intimacy-art-gossip.blogspot.co.uk/2008/02/kunst-oder-kommerz-iia-falco-symphonic.html?showComment=1218308340000 (accessed 23 August 2012).

Odier, Daniel. 2008 [1969]. *The Job: Interviews with William S. Burroughs*. London: Penguin.

"Österreich-Interview". 2012. "Falco-Ex Castaldi: 'Nur eine Ohrfeige'". Österreich. http://www.oe24.at/leute/oesterreich/Falco-Ex-Castaldi-Nur-eine-Ohrfeige/59811733 (accessed 12 July 2012).

Partridge, Christopher. 2012. "Introduction: Popular Music and Apocalyptic Discourse". In *Anthems of Apocalypse: Popular Music and Apocalyptic Thought*, ed. Christopher Partridge, ix–xxiii. Sheffield: Sheffield Phoenix Press.

Perkins, William Eric. 1996. "The Rap Attack: An Introduction". In *Droppin' Science*, ed. William Eric Perkins, 1–45. Philadelphia: Temple University Press.

Phelan, Peggy. 1993. *Unmarked: The Politics of Performance*. London: Routledge.

Potter, Russell A. 1995. *Spectacular Vernaculars: Hip-Hop and the Politics of Postmodernism*. Albany, NY: State University of New York Press.

—2001. "Soul into Hip-hop". In *The Cambridge Companion to Pop and Rock*, ed. Simon Frith, Will Straw and John Street, 143–57. Cambridge: Cambridge University Press.

Pratt, Vic. 2010. "Paul Jones (1942–)". Booklet to DVD edition of *Privilege*. London: BFI, 18–19.

Quantick, David. 1986. "Falco 3". *New Musical Express* 3/05: 18.

Rodway, Allan. 1963. *The Romantic Conflict*. London: Chatto and Windus.

Schieferdecker, Daniel. 2012. "Für alle war diese Zeit die intensivste in ihrem Leben". *Süuddeutsche Zeitung*, 22/04. http://jetzt.sueddeutsche.de/texte/anzeigen/5450 72 (accessed 18 December 2012).

Schorske, Carl E. 1979. *Fin-de-siècle Vienna: Politics and Culture*. London: Weidenfeld and Nicolson.

Serazio, Michael. 2008. "The Apolitical Irony of Generation Mash-Up: A Cultural Case Study in Popular Music". *Popular Music and Society* 31, no. 1: 79–94.

Shusterman, Richard. 1992. *Pragmatist Aesthetics: Living Beauty, Rethinking Art*. Oxford: Blackwell.

Sontag, Susan. 1994. "Notes on Camp". In *idem, Against Interpretation*, 275–92. London: Vintage.

Stam, Robert. 2000. "Beyond Fidelity: The Dialogics of Adaptation". In *Film Adaptation*, ed. James Naremore, 54–76. London: Athlone Press.

Stern, Anatol. 1959. *Wspomnienia z Atlantydy*. Warszawa: Wydawnictwa Artystyczne i Filmowe.

Stevenson, Nick. 2006. *David Bowie: Fame, Sound and Vision*. Cambridge: Polity.

Straw, Will. 1993. "Popular Music and Postmodernism in the 1980s". In *Sound and Vision: The Music Video Reader*, ed. Simon Frith, Andrew Goodwin and Lawrence Grossberg, 3–21. London: Routledge.

Street, John. 2001. "Rock, Pop and Politics". In *The Cambridge Companion to Pop and Rock*, ed. Simon Frith, Will Straw and John Street, 243–55. Cambridge: Cambridge University Press.

Stubbs, David, Erik Davis, Michel Faber, David Keenan and Ken Hollings. 2009. *Krautrock: Cosmic Rock and its Legacy*. Ed. Nikolaos Kotsopoulos. London: Black Dog Publishing.

Szemere, Anna. 2001. *Up From the Underground: The Culture of Rock Music in Postsocialist Hungary*. Pennsylvania: Pennsylvania State University Press.

Tinhof, Dietz. 2008. "*Falco Symphonic* Reanimated by Mr. Dietz!" *Nuendo 5 Archive*. http://www.nuendo.com/phpbb2/viewtopic.php?t=16978 (accessed 29 August 2012).

Truffaut, François. 1986. *Hitchcock*, revised edn. London: Paladin.

Trynka, Paul. 2011. *Starman: David Bowie, the Definitive Biography*. London: Sphere.

Urry, John, and Jonas Larsen. 2011. *The Tourist Gaze 3.0*. London: Sage.

Valéry, Paul. 1958. "On Speaking Verse". In *The Collected Works of Paul Valéry*, vol. 7, ed. Jackson Mathews. New York: Pantheon Books.

Vielmeister, Frank. n.d. "Mad verrat: *Jeanny III*". *Mad* 215: 18–19. http://www.falcoworld.net/falcoextrablatt/extra/?cat=30 (accessed 5 March 2012).

von Humboldt, Wilhelm. 1999. *On Language*, trans. Peter Heath. Cambridge: Cambridge University Press.

Wang, Ning. 2000. *Tourism and Modernity: A Sociological Analysis.* Amsterdam: Pergamom.

Wees, William C. 1993. *Recycled Images: The Art and Politics of Found Footage Films*. New York: Anthology Film Archives.

Weininger, Otto. 2005. *Sex and Character: An Investigation of Fundamental Principles*, trans. Ladislaus Lob. Bloomington: Indiana University Press.

Weissbrod, Uli. 1988. "Falco". *Musikexpress*, 10. http://www.falcoworld.net/falcoex-trablatt/extra/wp-content/uploads/2009/02/me10881te.jpg (accessed 23 February 2012).

Wollen, Peter. 1986. "Ways of Thinking about Music Video (and Post-modernism)". *Critical Quarterly* 1-2: 167–70.

Zimmermann, Günter. 2010. "Textautor Falco". In *Falco's Many Languages*, ed. Christian Ide Hintze, 15–35. Vienna: Residenz Verlag.

Žižek, Slavoj. 1997. *The Plague of Fantasies*. London and New York: Verso.

—2008. *Violence*. London: Profile Books.

—2009. *First as Tragedy, Then as Farce*. London: Verso.

Index

www.ingramcontent.com/pod-product-compliance
Lightning Source LLC
Chambersburg PA
CBHW070845300326

41935CB00039B/1450